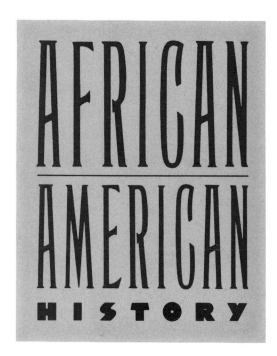

BY
LANGSTON HUGHES,
MILTON MELTZER, AND
C. ERIC LINCOLN

CONSULTANTS

PAT BROWNE, DIRECTOR
Black History/Multicultural Education,
Indianapolis Public Schools
Indianapolis, Indiana

ASA G. HILLIARD, III, ED.D.
Fuller E. Callaway Professor of Urban Education,
Georgia State University
Atlanta, Georgia

MARY McFARLAND, PH.D.
Instructional Coordinator of Social Studies,
Parkway School District
Chesterfield, Missouri

ISBN 0-590-35452-3

Publisher: Eleanor Angeles
Editorial Director: Carolyn Jackson
Project Director: Gerald Gladney
Production: Claudia Bruce, Al Somers Buist, Belén Negrón
Skills: Mollie Cohen

Art Direction: James Sarfati
Designer: Kathy Massaro
Photo Research: Rosalyn Sohnen
Maps: Moffitt Cecil, Frank Kubin, James McMahon
Charts: Nina Wallace

Historical Consultant: Steve Deyle
Contributors: Dallas L. Browne, Ph.D., Lisa Crawley, Tanya Bolden Davis, Steve Deyle, Warren Halliburton, Alan Hines, Norman Lunger and Clifford Thompson

For reprint permission, grateful acknowledgement is made to: Harper and Row Publishers, Inc. for "Heritage" by Countee Cullen from *On These I Stand*. Copyright © 1925 by Harper & Brothers, renewed 1953 by Ida M. Cullen. Joan Daves, agent for The Estate of Martin Luther King, Jr., for the excerpt from I HAVE A DREAM by Martin Luther King, Jr., copyright © 1963 by Martin Luther King, Jr.

Cover Art: "Hommage A Pinturicchio" (1969), a collage by Romare Bearden. Photograph by Manu Sassoonian.

TABLE OF CONTENTS

THE AUTHORS

Milton Meltzer (left) looks on as Langston Hughes

autographs a copy of *A Pictorial History of the Negro in America*

at New York City's Schomburg Center for Research in Black Culture in 1956.

Arna Bontemps (right) holds a copy of the book.

TO THE READER

At the center of this book are American people of African descent. Nearly 400 years of black American history are represented here. And because Africa is the ancestral birthplace of blacks, thousands of years of African history are also here.

Many of the names will be familiar to you, like Frederick Douglass, Harriet Tubman, Mary McLeod Bethune and Martin Luther King, Jr. But many more will be new discoveries. There's Imhotep, the multi-talented Egyptian who some call the father of medicine. There is Paul Cuffee, the black American captain who sponsored one of the first Back to Africa movements. There is Ella Baker, who with very little recognition, ran King's Southern Christian Leadership Conference and helped start the Student Non-violent Coordinating Committee. But this book is not just about individuals. It's also about events and movements as diverse as the invention of the cotton gin and the formation of Jesse Jackson's Rainbow Coalition, that have helped to shape life in America.

The book, *African American History,* has a history of its own. It is based on a book called *A Pictorial History of Black Americans* by Langston Hughes and Milton Meltzer. Hughes was a major writer, who produced poetry, novels, short stories, plays, as well as a variety of non-fiction work. Meltzer is a historian and biographer who has published nearly 70 books. Their book was first published in 1956 under the title *A Pictorial History of the Negro in America.*

Hughes and Meltzer met in New York City (at Hughes' Harlem apartment) on a Saturday morning in April 1955. They had been introduced by a mutual friend, writer and historian Arna Bontemps. Meltzer had spent several years assembling what Hughes called an "absolutely thrilling pictorial history" of blacks in America. Bontemps had agreed to collaborate on the text but was unable to meet the deadlines. He suggested his friend Hughes as a replacement. The Hughes-Meltzer team produced an important and popular history of black America.

The pictorial history has been revised four times for adult readers. Langston Hughes died in 1967. Writer and educator, C. Eric Lincoln helped revise the third, fourth and fifth editions.

This edition is designed especially for you. Two completely new parts have been added. Information has been updated. And introductions and summaries of each unit have also been added. They will guide you in studying the chapters and in practicing your skills.

The aim is to present many aspects of the experience of African Americans. Naturally, this is not the whole story, but it is a significant introduction. When you complete the eight parts, you will have an understanding of the experience of an important group of people.

Let's begin.

THE EDITORS

PART ONE

THE AFRICAN HERITAGE

PREHISTORY - 1890

Giraffe roam the plains of Amboseli in Kenya with Mount Kilimanjaro in the background.

LOOKING AHEAD - PART 1 - PREHISTORY – 1890

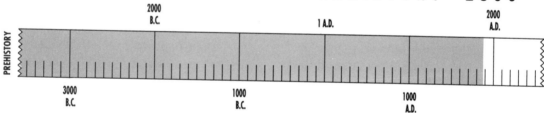

What is Africa to me:
Copper sun or scarlet sea,
Jungle star or jungle track,
Strong bronzed men, or regal black
Women from whose loins I sprang
When the birds of Eden sang?
One three centuries removed
From the scenes his fathers loved,
Spicy grove, cinnamon tree,
What is Africa to me?

—"Heritage" (1925)

Countee Cullen was imagining that vast continent from which his ancestors had come when he wrote this poem. Though many of us know of ancestors and fellow Americans who also came from Africa, we may not be certain where it is, what it actually looks like, or who lives there now.

If you were to travel east across the Atlantic Ocean from Charleston, South Carolina, you would reach northern Africa. Travel east from Buenos Aires, Argentina, and eventually you would sight the shores of southern

1

Africa. Africa covers 11,700,000 square miles, or one-fifth of the entire land area of the world. It is Earth's second largest continent. Only Asia is larger. The United States would fit into Africa more than three times.

Most of Africa is surrounded by water—the Atlantic Ocean, the Mediterranean Sea, the Red Sea and the Indian Ocean. The Equator almost cuts Africa in half. This places four-fifths of the continent between the Tropics of Cancer and Capricorn, and gives that area a tropical climate. Only about eight percent of Africa—all near the Equator— is covered by tropical rain forests. There the temperature averages 80 degrees. Enormous trees grow so close together that their tops prevent sunlight from reaching the ground. In forest areas where sunlight can penetrate the trees, there is jungle.

Grasslands called **savanna** cover half of Africa. Herds of antelope, zebra, giraffe and other wild animals roam here. Savanna is found in all of Africa's regions.

Desert covers another 40 percent of Africa. Some of it is barren with no vegetation. But most of Africa's desert has dry scrub and grass where livestock sometimes graze. Once, Africa's most forbidding desert, the Sahara, was a green and fertile home to ancient Africans. But about 18,000 B.C., it began to dry up. By about 5,000 B.C., it looked much the way it does today. The desert is expanding again. Modern Africans are concerned about giving up more of their farmable land. Each year soil erosion turns an area about twice the size of New Jersey into desert.

As everywhere on Earth, geography has played a large role in Africa's history. Its physical features have both protected it and isolated it from other civilizations. These same features, along with climate, have contributed to its uneven development. Sometimes African civilizations developed far ahead of those in other parts of the world. At other times, they lagged behind.

Africans, Ancient and Modern

Archaeologists have found evidence of human-like beings living in Africa about 4.5 million years ago. They believe Africa is the original home of humanity. Other scientists claim to have traced the actual person who was the mother of all modern races to Africa. The oldest remains of modern humans are thought to be of Africans who lived 110,000 to 250,000 years ago. Early Africans probably spread over the globe by walking across the Sinai Peninsula into the Middle East, and from there into Europe and Asia.

Today, Africa has about 600 million people. Some areas, however, may have no people at all. Others—like the Nile River Valley and parts of Nigeria—are very densely populated. Although more and more Africans are moving to cities to find work and food, about 70 percent remain in villages. Most of these villages have 40 or 50 people, although some number into the thousands. People who live in traditional villages spend most of their time working, telling stories and teaching their children various tasks essential for survival. Births, marriages and healing ceremonies are usually attended by all the people of a village, and these provide occasion for recreation.

Much of the culture, the folklore and the music of Africa has been passed along orally. Africans also have written poetry, novels and studies about their people and land and have the oldest literary tradition in the world. Legends, family histories and stories both age-old and contemporary, continue to be

A young boy in Niger, a modern country in Western Africa.

passed from one generation to the next.

Long ago Africans developed their own religious beliefs. Every event, they believed, was the work of unseen, but powerful, natural forces—in trees, streams, mountains and rivers, and even the souls of their ancestors. In traditional beliefs, every happening could be traced to this spirit world. In English, these beliefs are called **animism**. About half of the people in Africa today practice traditional African religions. Many others are Muslim or Chrisitian. Africans also have the world's oldest form of monotheism—belief in one god.

Modern Africans are a widely diverse and complex people. At least 800 African languages and dialects are spoken on the continent. Each language represents an ethnic group with its own traditions, culture and history. While different on the surface, these languages show a deep cultural unity. There have been Arabs in Africa since about 700 A.D., and Arabic is widely spoken. Many Africans also speak European languages—English, French, Portuguese, Spanish, Italian—because much of Africa was controlled by those countries in the nineteenth century.

In this part, you will learn more about the rich heritage some Africans left behind when they came to the Americas.

The Sahara covers more than 80% of the modern nation of Algeria in Northern Africa.

Africa: The Land and the People

It is hard to divide Africa into neat categories. As we have seen, deserts and savanna are common to much of the continent. Modern political boundaries tell us little about where its many ethnic groups live. In this chapter, Africa has been divided into five regions—Eastern, Southern, Central, Western and Northern Africa. You may not learn everything you want to know about them. But you can use these regions to form a broad picture of the continent.

Eastern Africa

Africa's interior is a series of broad areas of flatland called **plateaus.** They rise in elevation as they sweep eastward. In Eastern Africa, the plateaus reach their highest point. Then the land abruptly drops off to the coast on the Indian Ocean.

The highest mountains in Africa are located here. Volcanic eruptions produced massive mountains such as Kilimanjaro (kill-e-man-JAR-oh) in Tanzania (tan-sah-NEE-ah). The snow-covered cap of this volcano, which no longer erupts, can be seen over 100 miles away in Kenya's capital, Nairobi.

If you were to travel to the moon, you could look back at Earth, and see a large crack running through Eastern Africa. Millions of years ago, mountains formed and land sank nearby, creating the Great Rift Valley. This is the world's longest valley, several hundred feet deep in some places and plunging more than a mile in others. The valley begins at the mouth of the Zambezi (zam-BEE-zee) River in Mozambique (MOE-zam-

beak). Then it continues through Tanzania, Kenya and Ethiopia. It holds many breath-taking lakes, including Africa's deepest, Tanganyika (tan-gan-YEEK-a), and its largest, Victoria. Lake Victoria is the main source of the Nile, Africa's longest river. It winds 4,145 miles north through the Sudan and Egypt into the Mediterranean.

Savanna covers much of Eastern Africa. Kenya and Tanzania have set up wild game perserves where animals roam savanna and forest freely. Tourism in these game parks and along the beaches brings in millions of dollars each year and provides much needed jobs. Domesticated herds of cattle, sheep and camels also roam here. Nomadic tribes follow them across the savanna.

Most people in Eastern Africa are farmers. Cattle, cotton, rubber and coffee are major crops, though grains are the most important. As the desert expands, less land is available for farming. Not enough food is produced to feed everyone. **Famine,** food shortage that can lead to death, has been a problem in both the Sudan and Ethiopia. Many people are leaving their farms to settle near cities to escape starvation.

The eastern nation of Ethiopia (a Greek word meaning "burnt skin or black people") shows how complex African history often is. It was here that many of the first humans lived. The ancient Cushites farmed, herded and traded in Ethiopia up to the fifth century B.C. By the third century, an important kingdom called Axum had grown up. Its people became rich by trading gold, ivory

A villager of Lesotho in Southern Africa.

in what are today Somalia, Kenya, Tanzania and Mozambique. Out of a mix of African Bantu and Arabic came a new language, Swahili (swa-HEEL-e). In Tanzania, where over 100 languages are spoken, former President Julius Nyerere (ny-RARE-ee) adopted Swahili as the **lingua franca,** or common language.

Southern Africa

Southern Africa is one of the continent's richest and most industrialized areas. Because of its poor race relations, however, it is one of the most troubled.

This region of desert, savanna and tropical forest spans the lower quarter of the continent. At the southern point, around the Cape of Good Hope, a warm current from the Indian Ocean collides with a colder one from the Atlantic Ocean on the west, sometimes creating furious storms. The large island of Madagascar lies off the Southeastern African coast.

Fifteenth-century Portuguese sailors returned home with stories of an exotic land rich in gold and ivory. Portuguese voyages of trade and exploration were followed by those of other countries. In 1652, the Dutch set up a settlement at the Cape of Good Hope.

By the late nineteenth century, the British, German and Portuguese had staked claims to parts of Southern Africa. Europeans controlled the region for most of the century. Today, these countries are independent. Most, however, are dictatorships.

In the country of South Africa, the ruling Afrikaners—descendents of the early Dutch settlers—have established a system of **apartheid** (ah-PAR-tied), or strict separation of the races. (American response to apartheid is the subject of Chapter 43 in Part 8.)

and spices with Arabia, Egypt, Greece, India, Persia and Rome. Axum became a Christian nation in the fourth century. Iron-fisted Christian kings ruled for 700 years. In the twelfth century, they carved 11 magnificent churches out of solid rock at Roha that are still standing. In the nineteenth century, Emperor Menelik II of Ethiopia built the first modern schools and hospitals. The last king in this line was Haile Selassie, who ruled from 1931 until 1974. He was overthrown by the military. In between, Ethiopia was invaded twice by Italians. However, it was earlier able to resist Arab invasion.

Arabs played an important role elsewhere in Eastern Africa. By the eighth century, they had mingled with the people along the coast

FIVE REGIONS OF AFRICA

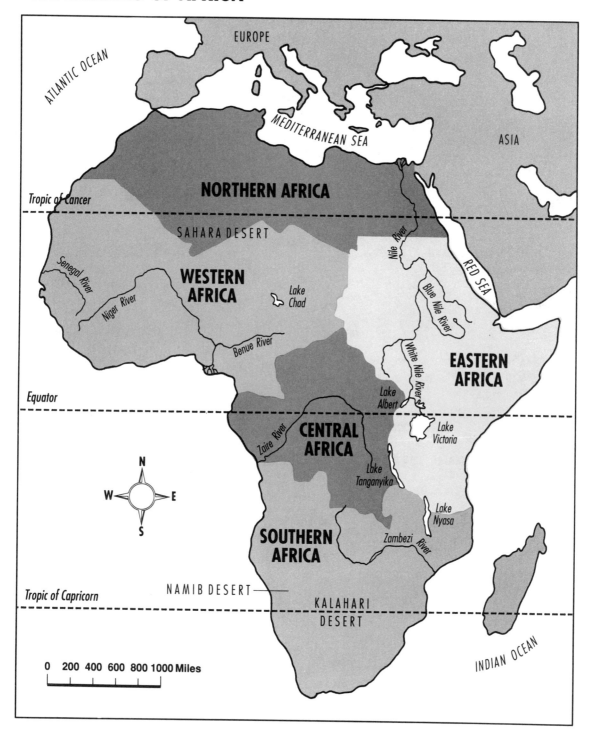

AFRICA TODAY

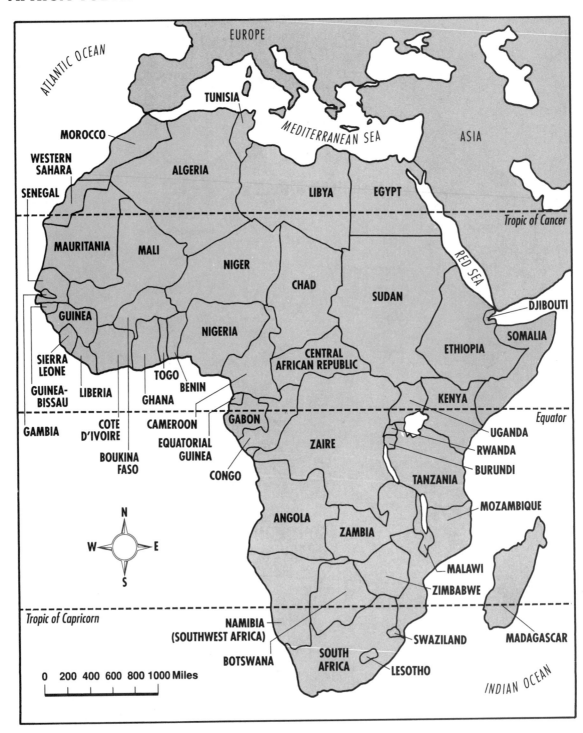

EUROPE

ATLANTIC OCEAN

TUNISIA

MOROCCO

WESTERN
SAHARA

SENEGAL

ALGERIA

LIBYA

EGYPT

MEDITERRANEAN SEA

ASIA

Tropic of Cancer

MAURITANIA

MALI

NIGER

CHAD

SUDAN

RED SEA

DJIBOUTI

SOMALIA

GUINEA

NIGERIA

CENTRAL
AFRICAN REPUBLIC

ETHIOPIA

SIERRA
LEONE

TOGO

GUINEA-
BISSAU

LIBERIA

BENIN

GHANA

KENYA

Equator

GAMBIA

COTE
D'IVOIRE

CAMEROON

GABON

UGANDA

RWANDA

BOUKINA
FASO

EQUATORIAL
GUINEA

ZAIRE

BURUNDI

CONGO

TANZANIA

MOZAMBIQUE

N

ANGOLA

ZAMBIA

W   E

MALAWI

S

ZIMBABWE

Tropic of Capricorn

NAMIBIA
(SOUTHWEST AFRICA)

SWAZILAND

MADAGASCAR

BOTSWANA

SOUTH
AFRICA

LESOTHO

INDIAN OCEAN

0   200 400 600 800 1000 Miles

South Africa is the most industrialized country on the continent. Automobiles, chemicals, clothing, processed foods, iron and steel are among the goods produced here. It is also the world's largest producer of gem diamonds and gold.

Mining and agriculture play vital roles in the economies of this region. Rich deposits of copper are mined in Zambia and Zimbabwe. Manganese, iron ore, coal, uranium, zinc and tin are also valuable resources. Most farmland is used to grow grains, citrus fruits, tobacco, coffee, rubber and palm oil.

South of the roaring Victoria Falls on the Zambezi River in the center of Southern Africa is the Kalahari (kal-lah-HA-ree) Desert. This vast desert extends 225,000 square miles, and covers most of Botswana (BOT-swan-ah) to Namibia (na-MIB-ee-ah). It is not as dry and barren as the Sahara, so wild melons, tough grass, some cattle, gazelles and wild dogs can live there.

The San, or Bushmen hunters and gatherers since prehistoric times, roam this area freely. **Click languages** are spoken primarily in Southern Africa. When speaking these languages people often make clicking sounds, more or less like a rider urging a horse to move.

Central Africa

This region is bound on the west by the Atlantic Ocean. Tropical forests and small areas of savanna span eastward to Lake Tanganyika and the Great Rift Valley.

Today, about 40 percent of the world's diamonds come from Zaire (ZI-ear). Rich copper deposits are also mined here. The

Two San children at the entrance to their grass home.

economies of the small countries of Gabon and the Congo rely on petroleum exports.

The Zaire River (formerly called the Congo) is the fourth longest river in the world. It provides 7,200 miles of navigable waterways through the heart of the region. Lands drained by this river form the Zaire Basin. Hardwoods and other timber are a major source of revenue for countries with tropical rain forests such as the Central African Republic and Zaire. Today, lumberjacks and miners threaten to destroy these forests. Increasingly, it becomes necessary to protect these forests from destruction. On the sa-

vanna, poachers collecting ivory tusks are causing the elephants to become extinct. In many places, elephants are already endangered and hunting them is illegal.

Central Africa was a destination of one of history's greatest migrations. About the time of Christ, Bantu-speaking people moved south and east out of Western Africa. This movement was probably prompted by a need for more land for a growing population. It continued for 1,000 years. As a result, skills in farming and ironwork were spread through Africa. And Bantu languages spread as well.

A waterfall in Angola in southwestern Africa.

In the fifteenth century, several powerful nations arose in Central Africa. They had elaborate governments and cultures. Sculpture, music and oral poetry were a part of these cultures. One kingdom, the Kongo, developed around the mouth of the Zaire River and lasted until the early eighteenth century.

Western Africa

On the western Atlantic coast between Angola and the Senegal River, early European merchants traded for gold, ivory and pepper. But by the sixteenth century, the value of these resources had been surpassed by that of enslaved Africans. Many Africans brought to the United States came from this region.

Narrow strips of lowlands are found along the coast of Western Africa, but savanna and tropical rain forest cover most of the region. The dry area between the savanna and the Sahara Desert in northern Chad, Nigeria and Mali is called the Sahel (SAH-hil), from the Arab word for "changing". Desert often overruns the Sahel during times of drought.

The settlement of this region's people varies from one extreme to the other. While coastal southern Nigeria is congested, other areas of Nigeria, Mali and Chad are either uninhabited or have less than 25 people per square mile.

Bantu-speaking people dominate Western Africa. They can also be found to the south, below the Equator, and as far east as Kenya. The Hausa (HOUSE-ah) language serves as a lingua franca in Western Africa much as Swahili does in the east.

Lake Volta, one of the few lakes found here, was made by building the Akosombo Dam across the Volta River. Lake Chad, in the northern part of the region, is the center of a large area called the Chad Basin. The Ni-

A young man in Zimbabwe in Southern Africa.

ger River, a 5,300-mile system of inland waterways, drains into the Atlantic Ocean. In the Niger Delta, the soil is fertile enough for large-scale farming.

Though small deposits of diamonds are also found here, tin, iron ore and chromite mines contribute most to the economies of the western region. Vast oil reserves are also located along the coast. Nigeria retains three percent of the world's reserves.

Some of Africa's most remarkable cultures developed in Western Africa. You will read about three of them—Ghana, Mali and Songhay—in Chapter 3.

Northern Africa

Nearly 40 percent of Northern Africa is desert covered with sand, rocks and gravel. Since rainfall is usually less than 10 inches per year, moisture is scarce, except at small green watering holes called **oases**.

The Sahara Desert is the world's second largest wasteland (next to Antarctica). Sahara, in fact, is an Arabic word for "wasteland." This area covers 3.2 million square miles and is larger than the continental United States. Camel caravans maintained fragile trade links across this desolate region for centuries. Its barrenness discouraged large groups of people from moving across it.

When the Sahara was being formed, many of the animals and people who once thrived in its interior moved to its edges. Large populations settled along the Nile Valley. Nomadic tribes remained in the Sahara and made its oases their base.

One of the most remarkable civilizations of all time developed along the Nile River in Northern Africa. Ancient Kemet's (Egypt) accomplishments are the topic of Chapter 2. When its influence declined, Egypt was overthrown by Persians, Greeks and Romans.

For centuries, Arabs, Indians and Chinese, as well as Europeans, traded with Africa. Millions of Arabs live in Northern Africa today. Their ancestors came to Africa about 700 A.D. and slowly converted many Africans to Islam. Culturally, the modern nations of Morocco, Algeria, Libya and Egypt have much in common with Middle Eastern nations like Saudi Arabia and Syria. At the same time, Arab culture has influenced much of Africa, south of the Sahara. The Arabs brought their religion and their language. They also brought their knowledge of science, philosophy, geography and history.

A small number of people of Northern Africa still herd sheep, camels and goats across the desert. Most of the people, though, live near water. Today, the flooding of the Nile is controlled by a modern dam at Aswan. Along the Nile and the Mediterranean, people grow crops and raise animals where there is ready water for drinking and irrigation.

Some day you may want to visit Africa. But for now, you may want to take a long imaginary journey in time and distance to the Egypt of the pharaohs.

CHAPTER CHECK

1. Describe the deserts, savanna, and tropical rain forests of Africa. Approximately how much of the continent is covered by each? (You may refer to Looking Ahead.)
2. In what region of Africa are the following located? (a) the Sahel, (b) Lake Victoria, (c) the continent's largest desert, (d) the Cape of Good Hope, (e) the Zaire River.
3. Imagine . . . you are planning a trip to Africa. Which region would you want to visit most? What would you want to see?

An Enad woman in Niger.

This alabaster sphinx at Memphis dates to ancient Egypt's Old Kingdom.

CHAPTER 2

Ancient Egypt

Of all the kingdoms and empires of early Africa, ancient Egypt made the greatest impression on the world at large. One key reason was Egypt's location. It lay at the crossroads between Africa, Asia and Europe and carried on trade and warfare not only with other Africans but with people from other continents. Thus, its reputation spread far and wide. But there were other reasons for Egypt's fame. The Egyptians were among the first people to develop writing, and they left records that later generations could decipher. Moreover, the ancient Egyptians built monuments that survived down the centuries and can still be admired. Egyptian temples, statues and pyramids are among the glories of the ancient world.

Today, Egyptians speak Arabic and are often thought of as Middle Eastern. This is due to the heavy migration of Arabic people in the seventh century. But Egypt's glorious past is part of Africa's heritage.

"A Gift of the River"

"Hail to thee, O Nile, that issues from the earth and comes to keep Egypt alive."

Ancient Egyptians sang those words of praise to a mighty river that gave them life. Flowing northward out of the heart of Africa, the Nile made Egypt a long green oasis in a dry and forbidding desert. It also provided a link to Egypt's African roots—even as Egypt turned its face to the outside world.

Since prehistoric times the Nile has served as a highway for transportation, but it is not a smooth one. At intervals, steep cliffs pinch the river into raging rapids called **cataracts**. Boats from the Mediterranean can sail up the Nile (that is, south) for about 600 miles. However, they can go no farther than the city of Aswan. There, in the present century, two massive dams were built near the first of six cataracts. Despite such barriers to travel, Egypt has had continuous contacts with African people who live farther south.

Today, as in the distant past, almost all of Egypt's people live in a narrow valley that extends about 20 miles on either side of the Nile. Within the valley, canals and ditches carry the Nile's water to fields planted in crops like wheat, onions and cotton. Until completion of the second Aswan dam in 1971, the Nile flooded the valley almost every fall, depositing thick layers of valuable silt that enriched the soil and nurtured the next year's crops. Even deeper layers of silt built up in a broad, marshy triangle called a **delta**, where the Nile empties into the Mediterranean. Because Egypt's fortunes were so closely tied to the Nile's ebb and flow, the Greek historian Herodotus dubbed Egypt "a gift of the river."

The Sands of Time

Egypt was not always an oasis in a dry and barren desert. As you have read, up to about 20,000 years ago much of the Sahara was green and fertile. In those early times, people probably roamed a much wider area of Northern Africa than they do today, and contacts between Egypt and the rest of Africa were relatively easy. During this period, many of Egypt's inhabitants appear to have come from deeper within the African continent. Then desert sands spread, travel became more difficult, and contacts with inner Africa became fewer.

Changing environmental conditions

ANCIENT EGYPT

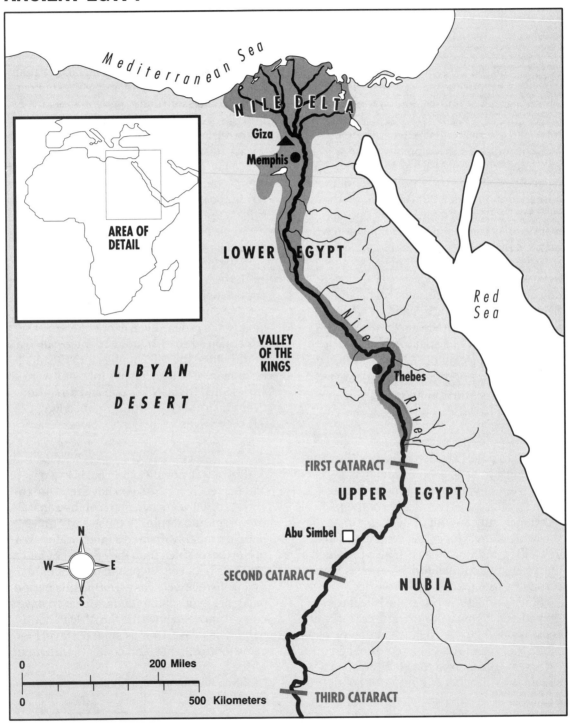

Mediterranean Sea

NILE DELTA

Giza

Memphis

LOWER EGYPT

VALLEY OF THE KINGS

LIBYAN DESERT

Nile

Thebes

River

Red Sea

FIRST CATARACT

UPPER EGYPT

Abu Simbel

SECOND CATARACT

NUBIA

THIRD CATARACT

AREA OF DETAIL

N
W   E
S

0   200 Miles
0   500 Kilometers

drove people and the herds they hunted closer to the Nile. Sahara rock art shows that by 5500 B.C. people were tending cattle and farming the fertile Nile valley. Eventually, they settled into villages, called **nomes**.

Egypt became a center for cultural exchange between inner Africa and the early civilizations of Mesopotamia (present day Iran and Iraq). Egyptians were the first Africans to develop an urban way of life, beginning sometime before 4000 B.C. People wore sandals, kilts, cloaks of skins and woven materials. They carved jewelry and ornaments from wood, ivory and bone. Highly refined pottery decorated their sun-dried brick homes.

A key advance was the development of **irrigation**—the supplying of water to crops through ditches or other means. Irrigation helped to create diversity. Since not everyone was needed to produce food, some people could take other jobs. Egypt became a complex society of administrators, priests, artisans, soldiers and artists.

Egyptians were monotheistic but worshiped many forms of one god. Osiris (oh-SYE-ris) was one of the most important. He was the god of the Nile. Legend said he was murdered by his brother Set, who caused the crops to wither. However, Osiris had a beautiful black wife, Isis (EYE-sis), who brought him back to life. Every year, Egyptians celebrated Osiris's death and rebirth, which coincided with the rise and fall of the Nile. They came to believe he judged the souls of the dead.

While the Nile brought life to Egypt, the deserts protected it from invaders. As time passed, Egypt developed its own distinct way of life. Nomes joined together to form larger and larger territories. Eventually, two large kingdoms emerged. The one in the south (up the Nile) was called Upper Egypt.

About 3100 B.C., a ruler from the south united the two kingdoms into one Egypt. This ruler is sometimes called Narmer, sometimes Menes. Over the next 2,800 years, a succession of 330 monarchs in 31 ruling families, or **dynasties**, would reign over Egypt. This brought a continuity and a unity rare in human history.

Boats sail the Nile today as they have for thousands of years.

Ramses II, ancient Egypt's last great pharaoh, ruled from 1279–1212 B.C.

The Rise and Fall of Dynasties

Most of what we know about ancient Egypt has to do with its rulers, known as pharaohs (FAY-rohz). We know less about the life of the common people, except that they toiled on from year to year to supply the luxuries enjoyed by the ruling classes.

The succession of rulers was not always easy. At times, foreign armies invaded or internal rivalries temporarily weakened the kingdom. Egypt's history may be divided into several distinct periods—

Archaic Period	(3100–2664 B.C.)
Old Kingdom	(2664–2155 B.C.)
Middle Kingdom	(2052–1786 B.C.)
New Kingdom	(1570–1075 B.C.)
Late Period	(1075–332 B.C.)

Egyptian Achievements

Even before the Archaic Period, Egyptians had developed **hieroglyphics**, a form of writing that used pictures. Pharaohs and their courts encouraged scribes to record and glorify their deeds. Egyptians made the world's first paper from reeds called **papyrus**, and they wrote on the paper using pen and ink. As time went on, Egyptians wrote down technical and scientific knowledge on papyrus scrolls and collected them in huge libraries. A famous library at Alexandria, Egypt, is said to have contained more than 400,000 scrolls dealing with astronomy, geometry, geography and many other subjects.

It was during the Old Kingdom that Egyptians began constructing the massive pyramids, some 35 in all. Later observers would marvel at the Egyptians' architectural skills. Using levers and ropes, armies of workers and cattle pulled huge stone blocks, weighing more than two tons each. They dragged the blocks up brick ramps and then maneuvered them into place.

The pyramids served as tombs for pharaohs. The Egyptians believed their rulers to be gods who served as a link between ordinary people and other gods. To preserve a dead person's body, Egyptians used a process known as **mummification**. The body was first embalmed, then wrapped in linen cloth. The resulting mummy was then placed in a casket. According to Egyptian belief, mummification preserved the body as a home for the immortal soul. Tombs were stocked with supplies that Egyptians thought the dead would need. These included wigs, musical instruments, food, clothing, cosmetics, jewelry and weapons.

In addition to the tremendous wealth and labor required in building the pyramids, complex mathematical skills were needed. Egyptians had already developed geometry to a fine art. They could draw accurate boundaries between neighboring farms and lay out plans for large temples and buildings. By observing the flooding of the Nile, they had also developed a calendar with 365 days a year.

Ramses II ordered this temple at Abu Simbel built into cliffs along the Nile.

The first of the great pyramids was built for a pharaoh named Zoser, who died about 2645 B.C. Its designer is believed to have been the pharaoh's prime minister, Imhotep (em-HOH-tehp), a man of many talents. Besides serving as administrator, scribe and architect, Imhotep was a doctor who gained insight into human anatomy through knowledge of embalming. He was the first to write about the circulation of blood in the body.

Imhotep was also a skilled creator of proverbs. He wrote: "Eat, drink and be merry, for tomorrow we die." For 3,000 years after his death he was revered as the semi-divine patron of the scribes and as the father of medicine.

Egypt's Empire

During the New Kingdom, Egypt built a great empire. Its armies swept east to the Euphrates River in Mesopotamia, west into the Libyan desert and south into a land called Nubia.

Also in this period, Egypt put together a comprehensive code of laws. This system, called **maat**, or justice, drew upon age-old practices as well as new laws decreed by the pharaoh. The laws were held to apply even to the pharaoh himself.

Although custom decreed that the pharaoh be male, a woman named Hatshepsut (hat-SHEP-soot) declared herself ruler around 1478 B.C. Her stepson Thutmose (thoot-MOH-suh) was heir to the throne but he was too young to assume responsibility. On special occasions, Hatshepsut wore a man's kilt and attached the pharaoh's long, braided ceremonial beard to her chin. Under her 22-year rule, Egypt prospered. She was better known for encouraging trade than for waging war.

Her successor, Thutmose III, conducted 15 victorious invasions into Palestine and Syria. He was so fearless that he once single-handedly attacked a bull elephant in battle. Thutmose III was an art patron, a collector of natural history specimens and a noted temple builder.

The Spread of Egypt's Influence

As an imperial power, Egypt ruled over a variety of different people. Many of them gradually assumed Egyptian practices and adopted Egypt's civilization. Some of Egypt's late rulers were descended from neighboring African people such as the light-skinned Libyans and the dark-skinned Nubians. For example, a line of Nubian kings ruled Egypt from about 736 to 657 B.C.

Some of the glory of Egypt's civilization passed to African kingdoms to the south that had been influenced by Egypt. The Nubian Kingdom of Kush held sway over large areas along the upper Nile for several centuries, and its rulers even built small pyramids in the Egyptian style. Another African kingdom, Axum, conquered Kush in A.D. 350. It was the forerunner of modern Ethiopia.

But Egypt's golden age came to an end with the fall of the New Kingdom in 1075 B.C. For centuries to come, foreign conquerors would rule the land of the pharaohs. After a brief period of Persian rule, Alexander the Great seized Egypt in 332 B.C. He founded the great city of Alexandria, and for the next three centuries Egypt was Greek. Then came a period of Roman rule, until Arab armies swept out of the Arabian peninsula in about A.D. 640 to conquer Egypt and spread the new religion of Islam across Northern Africa. Arab conquest proved the most durable of all. It endowed Egypt not only with a new religion but also a new language, Arabic.

Through all its long history—which also included periods of Turkish and British control—Egypt never lost sight of its African heritage. Although the Egyptian people speak Arabic today and generally consider

Ruins at Luxor on the site of ancient Thebes.

themselves to be Arabs, their government plays an active part in African affairs.

The early Egyptians built a powerful African civilization that endured for almost 3,000 years, and many of their achievements were world firsts. Scientists today recognize that Egypt's social structure and culture evolved from patterns that appear in various forms in other African cultures. At a time when the ancestors of most modern people were living primitively, the Egyptians maintained a grand civilization. They left a glorious heritage for Africa and the world.

CHAPTER CHECK

1. Why might Egypt be called a "gift of the Nile"?
2. Describe at least three important developments in ancient Egypt.
3. Imagine . . . you could ask three questions of Imhotep. What would they be?

Three West African Kingdoms

In the year 1324, there was an amazing spectacle in the Middle East. The king, or mansa, of Mali in Western Africa was on his way to Mecca in Arabia. Like all devout Muslims, it was his duty to make a pilgrimage to Muhammed's birthplace. But Mansa Musa was no ordinary pilgrim. He brought with him about 60,000 people. Before him traveled 500 slaves, each carrying a staff of gold. Eighty camels carried 12 more tons of gold. So much gold was spent in Egypt that it almost destroyed the economy. Who was this man, and where had he come from?

Europeans knew little or nothing about him. But in the Arab world, his capital of Timbuktu was well known. Mali, in fact, was the second of three great West African king-doms that dominated the savanna south of the Sahara from about 1000 to 1600. Together, they created a Golden Age.

The first of these wealthy kingdoms was not Muslim but traditional African. It lasted the longest—about 1,000 years. The ancient kingdom of Ghana was located in the areas covered today by southeastern Mauritania and western Mali. Its wealth was built on a mysterious ritual.

The Silent Trade

Imagine for a moment that you are living in the year 800. You are hiding behind some scrub along the Niger River. Arab traders ride their camels to the river's edge. They dismount and unload something very heavy

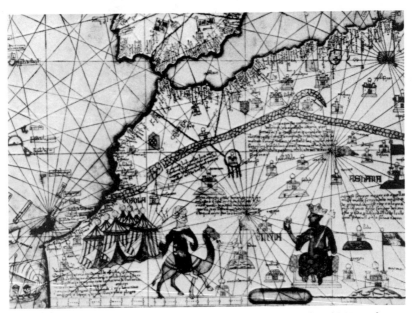

This 14th century map shows Mansa Musa and the Kingdom of Mali. Note the gold nugget in his hand.

from the camels' backs. Then each man puts a mark on his pile of goods. Drums are beaten. Then the camel riders retreat.

A little while later, other traders approach the spot by boat. They inspect the cargo left by the camel riders. Then they take something from their boat, place it on the ground and leave. Soon, you see that the camels are returning. Their riders dismount again and look to see what is on the ground beside their cargo. They talk to each other in very serious voices. Then they get on their camels and ride away.

Before you can get any closer, the boat returns. Its occupants take something else from their boats. They leave it on the ground and row away. This time, the returning camel riders look more satisfied. They load the cargo from the boat onto their camels and ride away. Before long, the other traders have put the heavy cargo from the camels

Timbuktu was an important trading city in Western Africa for centuries. Today (above), it is a tiny trading post and (below) as it appeared in the nineteenth century.

THE KINGDOM OF GHANA 11th Century A.D.

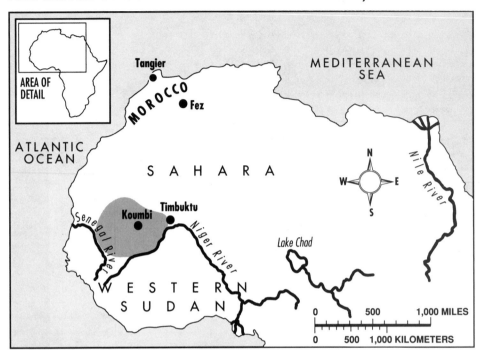

into their boat. Not a word has been spoken between the two groups. But everyone seems satisfied.

If you could have gotten closer, you would have seen that the cargo brought by the camels was salt in 200-pound slabs. The boat people had exchanged it for gold.

The salt probably came from Taghaza (tog-AHZ-a), a village in the Sahara. The gold came from a place called Wangara (wong-AR-a) somewhere to the south along the Niger and Senegal rivers. The exact location of the gold mines was a closely guarded secret.

Ghana's Middlemen

The first written references to the ancient kingdom of Ghana call it "the land of gold." It was in Ghana that the famous silent trade occurred. Ghana's kings had a reputation for splendor. It was said that one hitched his horse to a 30-pound gold nugget.

But in truth, the Soninke (so-NINK-ah) people who lived in this kingdom were not miners but farmers and traders. Their wealth came from taxes they collected, going and coming, from those who traded there.

Salt was a necessity for people who lived in Africa's hot central regions. In the heat, it was needed to preserve food and to replace the body salts lost in the hot sun. But what Wangara lacked in salt, it made up for in gold. And gold was a precious metal in short supply in the Middle East and Europe. It could be traded for grain, leather and cloth, as well as salt.

Why did the trading take place in Ghana? Historians suggest a couple of reasons. First, it offered security to both Arabs and Wangara. The Soninke knew how to smelt iron. Iron could be used for strong weapons to control their neighbors, who had wooden weapons. The king of Ghana could field a tremendous army. Such a land was unlikely to attract bandits.

Secondly, Ghana's ruler controlled the supply of gold. He claimed all nuggets for himself, although common people had access to gold dust. While the king was without a doubt Ghana's richest man, many others shared the wealth. Even ordinary people seemed to have lived comfortably. With all its remarkable achievements, Ghana never had a written language. What we know about the ancient kingdoms of Western Africa comes from a variety of sources. Written reports of Arab scholars and traders who visited the region are one source. The people of the region, however, relied on a group of oral historians called **griots** (GREE-os). These were professional historians assigned to important people to mentally record and pass down events both past and present. Griots were poets and musicians as well. Much of what has been reported by all these sources has been confirmed by scientific investigation.

The Dogon have lived in this village near Timbuktu since the 12th century.

While Ghana was not a Muslim kingdom, it maintained friendly relations with Muslims. In fact, the king set up a separate city for Muslims six miles away from the city where he and his people lived. In the end, however, a group of Muslim Berbers from Northern Africa waged war against Ghana. They attacked Ghana for more than a decade in the eleventh century.

The Rise of Mali

As Ghana tired of resisting its attackers, new life sprang up in the nearby kingdom of Mali. Mali had occupied a small area since the seventh century, but it was not until the thirteenth century that it became great. Its first important ruler was Sundiata Keita (sun-

The market of Gao today.

DIA-ta KEY-ta), who ruled from 1230 to 1255. Sundiata captured Ghana's old capital. Then, he took over the Wangara gold mines. With this rich base, Mali expanded into the Sahara and south and west into modern Guinea and Senegal.

Sundiata was the grand uncle of Mansa Musa, who ruled Ghana 60 years later. Under Mansa Musa, Mali took over the trading centers of Timbuktu and Gao (gah-O). Mali's rule eventually spread about 1,000 miles eastward from the Atlantic Ocean. And thanks to the publicity brought by Mansa Musa's pilgrimage, Europeans drew in Mali on their maps.

Although Mali's leaders were Muslim, most of its people were not. Traditional African religions were followed by the common people. Visiting Arabs were often surprised to see Africans lie on the ground in front of the mansa and sprinkle dust on their heads. These were signs of respect. Strict Muslims were also shocked at the amount of freedom and responsibility given to women south of the Sahara.

But they were impressed by the high level of civilization. The Arab scholar Ibn Batutta (IB-n ba-TOO-ta) visited Mali. In his book *Travels in Asia and Africa: 1325 and 1354*, he remarked on the "complete and general safety" of travel in the kingdom. He also reported that if a rich white man died in Mali, his treasures would be returned home.

Most importantly, Ibn Battuta noticed "the small number of acts of injustice that one finds there; for the Negroes are of all peoples those who most abhor (hate) injustice."

Ancient Mali was the richest kingdom Africa had ever known. But, over the years, its gold mines began to run out. Newer mines

THE KINGDOM OF MALI   14th Century A.D.

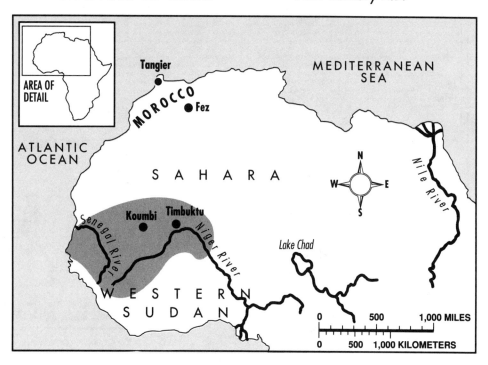

were opened east of Mali. Trade routes followed. By the late 1300s, Mali was weak. Control of the gold trade passed to others.

Songhay, Center of Learning

Like Mali, Songhay had a long history. The roots of its civilization went back to the eighth century. But for hundreds of years, it was not developed. Songhay was, for a time, a part of Mali's empire. But, as Mali declined, Songhay began to grow. By the time Columbus sailed for the Americas in 1492, Songhay was the most important power in Western Africa.

In 1493, a powerful general, Askia Mohammed, took power from the king. He had big plans for Songhay. First, he built a profes-

sional army of slaves and prisoners of war. The army was successful too. Soon, Songhay had built the largest empire in the history of Western Africa.

Like Mansa Musa, Askia Mohammed made a pilgrimage to Mecca. But he was not interested in impressing those he met with Songhay's wealth. Instead, he wanted to learn how to govern better. He took scholars and government officials with him. They talked with many educated people along the way. They asked how to organize a government, how to write a legal code, and how to educate Songhay's people.

Upon their return, they divided the empire into smaller territories. Chiefs were appointed to govern these territories. Muslim

THE KINGDOM OF SONGHAY   16th Century A.D.

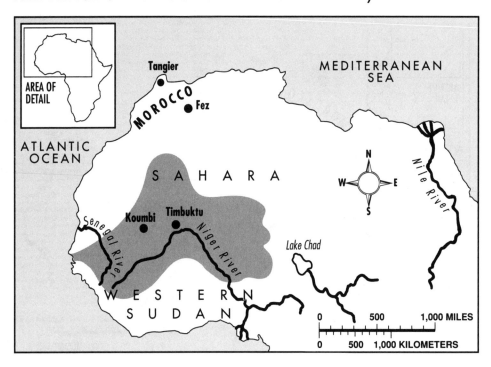

law was made a basis for governing. Banks and credit were improved.

The most important thing Askia Mohammed did was to promote education. Many scholars of Western Africa and of Europe and Asia came to Songhay to learn and teach. Timbuktu, Jenne (jen-neh) and Gao became centers of learning. At the University of Sankore (sang-or-AY), black and white students studied law, grammar, literature and medicine. By the sixteenth century, the region was developing a literature of its own.

Songhay was now an important civilization. It was so successful, in fact, that other peoples envied it. Askia's son pushed him from the throne. His reign was followed by periods of decline and rebuilding. In 1591, a Moroccan army crossed the Sahara to attack Songhay. Although most of its men died, their cannons quickly overpowered Songhay's 27,000 warriors. They were armed only with swords and spears. The Golden Age of West Africa was over.

CHAPTER CHECK

1. How and where did the "silent trade" take place? What three groups benefited from it?
2. What two purposes did Mansa Musa's pilgrimage to Mecca serve?
3. Imagine . . . you lived on the route to Mecca during the pilgrimages of Mansa Musa and Askia Mohammed. Which ruler would impress you the most? Why?

Slaves being taken from Africa.

CHAPTER 4

New World Slave Trade

I n his book *Roots,* American writer Alex Haley writes about an African ancestor named Kunta Kinte. Haley imagines the fright and rage this man must have felt when slave hunters captured him and spirited him off to the New World. Kunta Kinte was one of an estimated 50 million black Africans who became victims of the slave trade from the 1500s to the 1800s. This trade caused one of the greatest forced migrations in history.

The New World slave trade began innocently enough. Trading contacts developed between Portuguese sailors and coastal people of Africa. The ships of Portugal's Prince Henry the Navigator first reached the coast of Western Africa in 1441.

For a time, the Portuguese bought few Africans. Mainly they bought gold, ivory and peppers. In return, they sold the Africans horses, liquor, cloth and guns.

Trade between Africa and Europe might have continued in this way had Columbus not discovered the Americas in 1492. Suddenly, Europeans saw a New World to colonize and put to commercial use. Settlers from Spain, Portugal, England and other countries wanted a large labor force to toil in American gold and silver mines. They also set up plantations in the Caribbean and North and South America. They wanted strong workers to grow crops like sugar on these plantations.

At first, the Europeans tried to use the Native Americans. But they would not do.

SAHARAN TRADE ROUTES

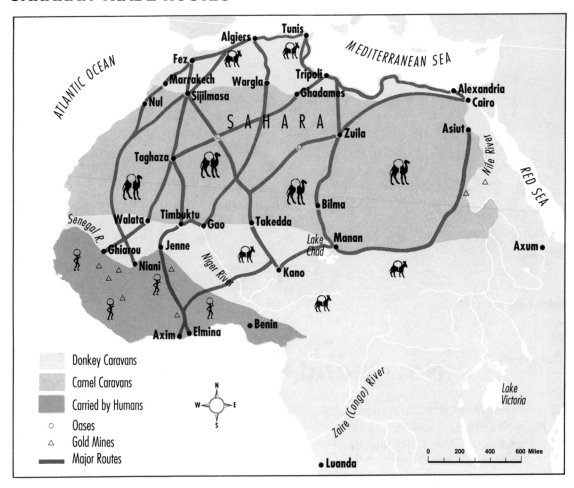

Smallpox and other diseases brought from Europe often killed them. Also Native Americans easily escaped to rejoin their people. So the colonizers turned to Africa for the workers they needed.

African Slavery

Africa could provide a ready source of workers in the form of slaves. In the 1400s and 1500s, slavery was known throughout the world. Many people considered slavery to be morally permissible.

Africans often held other Africans as slaves. But not all served as slaves for life. Some were treated like the serfs of Europe. Slaves in Africa were usually captives of war, or people being punished for a crime. In either case, many slaves in Africa had some rights. Some could marry. Occasionally they were set free.

Being a slave is hard even under the best masters. But most slaves in Africa were better treated than those in the Americas. Africans who were carried off to the Americas had no rights and little hope of ever regaining their freedom. Many suffered harsh physical abuse.

Slave Wars

The Europeans quickly found ways to obtain African slaves. The most common method was to turn one group of Africans against another. They offered guns and liquor to an African ruler in exchange for slaves. Then they made the same offer to a rival ruler. Guns gave a military advantage to whoever had them. Therefore, a race began to see which African group could capture the most slaves and thus get the most guns. Africans who hated slavery could not escape this race once it started without falling victim to slave hunters themselves.

The rising demand for slaves caused continual wars among slave-trading African states. As time passed, African armies and their European allies struck deeper and deeper into the interior, seeking captives to enslave.

For those who were captured, the horror had just begun. Organized into closely-guarded slave caravans, the captives began the long, slow march to the sea. Guards showed no mercy toward weak or injured captives. They would cruelly murder any child or other captive who could not keep up the pace.

At the coast, survivors of the slave caravans were crowded into prison camps called **bulking stations**. Here they awaited the arrival of a slave ship. An African ruler would arrange to supply a certain number of slaves on a particular date. But, slave ships did not always show up on time. Conditions in the bulking stations were unhealthy, and food sometimes ran out. Captives often died there. Many more lost their lives during the torturous crossing of the Atlantic.

Some ships carried slaves directly to North America. But most headed for South America and the islands of the Caribbean. European sugar growers in Brazil and on Caribbean islands like Jamaica and Barbados bought many slaves. Conditions on the sugar plantations were harsh and a slave's working life was short.

Most slaves who came to the Americas were from Western Africa. Some came from the continent's western hump. This area is occupied by the modern countries of Senegal, Gambia and Sierra Leone. Others were obtained from the "gold coast," where the nation of Ghana now stands. Many came from the nearby "slave coast." Today the countries of Togo, Benin, and Nigeria are located there. Other parts of Africa also supplied slaves for the New World. Many came from Eastern Africa. But the numbers were never

A SLAVE-SHED.

Captured Balolo in what is today the Congo.

as large as from the western part of the continent.

The slave trade had a devastating effect on African people—both enslavers and enslaved. Cruelty and suspicion took the place of traditional values like kindness, generosity and trust. Africans who had once banded together to build mighty empires now turned against one another in the competition for guns and safety.

It was a hostile world. Africans were either trying to enslave their neighbors or struggling desperately to remain free. The slave trade had made unity impossible. Yet unity had become essential, for the outside world threatened Africa as never before.

Until the slave trade began, Africans had enjoyed a standard of living roughly similar to that of Europeans. But conditions soon changed. Africans spent much time fighting or hiding to evade capture. Little time was spent growing food, so famines became common. People had less time or energy for

building, inventing and creating. Thus, cultural and economic activity dwindled.

Perhaps the greatest blow to Africa was a sharp drop in population. The slave trade killed or removed millions of the continent's youngest, strongest and most productive women and men. In many areas of Africa, only the old, the sick or the blind remained. Most of the others were either dead or were tilling the plantations of the Americas.

It has been estimated that Africa lost 50 million people to the slave trade. Some 15 million survived the slave wars, caravans, bulking stations and ocean travel to reach the New World.

Death of the Slave Trade

Ever so slowly, opinions about slavery began to change. During the period known as the Enlightenment, which came in the eighteenth century, European thinkers began to stress the use of reason as the basis for human society. Enlightenment thinkers ar-

Slave hunters and a group of captives.

gued that all humans possessed certain natural rights, including the right to freedom. Demands for political freedom led to independence for the 13 American colonies, and to a violent revolution in France beginning in 1789. Ideas about freedom nagged at the consciences of many people. Didn't slaves have the same right to freedom as everyone else? Wasn't the slave trade an evil business?

Guilty consciences were only one of the forces working against slavery. Slaves tried to help themselves by staging revolts. Most of these were short-lived and unsuccessful. But on the island of Santo Domingo, slaves managed to carry out a full-scale revolution. In 1804, they created the independent republic of Haiti. This was the second free nation (after the United States) in the western hemisphere. The Haitian leader, Toussaint L'Ouverture (TU-sahnt LEW-veh-tur), was an intelligent and resourceful black man. His accomplishments frightened slaveholders everywhere.

Within the British Empire, the profits from the slave trade were declining, and opposition to slavery was on the rise. As a result, Britain outlawed the slave trade in 1807. Britain outlawed slavery itself in 1833, although the practice continued for ten more years in parts of the empire. The British government spent millions of dollars to compensate slaveowners for their losses.

In the New World, slavery persisted for many more years. The United States abolished slavery in 1865. Brazil did not do so until 1890.

In the end, the slave trade caused lasting harm to both the African and the European. The loss of Africa's youth to slavery slowed its economic and cultural progress. It affects

Toussaint L'Ouverture.

development in many African states even today. For white North Americans, slavery was a betrayal of the ideals for which they had fought a revolution. It would contribute to a bloody civil war over the rights of all people, and years of racial tensions that are only now slowly eroding.

CHAPTER CHECK

1. What historic event triggered the demand for African slaves? What work did they do?
2. How was the slave trade destructive of African society?
3. Imagine . . . you are an Enlightenment thinker. What would you say about slavery to European heads of state?

A Dogon village in Western Africa.

Main Events

1. Before 3100 B.C., Egyptians develop hieroglyphic writing.
2. Around 3100 B.C., King Menes unites Upper and Lower Egypt.
3. Around 2645 B.C., Imhotep designs and builds the first of the great pyramids for the pharaoh.
4. Alexander the Great conquers Egypt in 3323 B.C.
5. First Arab traders cross the Sahara to trade salt for gold around A.D. 100.
6. Ghana is one of the world's most important kingdoms by 1070.
7. In 1324, Mansa Musa of Mali leads a 60,000-person caravan on a pilgrimage to Mecca.
8. The ships of Portugal's Prince Henry reach the coast of Western Africa in 1441.
9. Askia Mohammed becomes the king of Songhay in 1493 and builds the largest empire in Western Africa's history.
10. In the fifteenth century, several powerful kingdoms arise in Central Africa. One of them, Kongo, lasts until the eighteenth century.
11. European slave traders begin bringing African slaves to the New World in the sixteenth century.
12. In 1652, the Dutch settle at the Cape of Good Hope in South Africa.
13. In 1804, the independent republic of Haiti is established under the leader-

ship of Toussaint L'Ouverture.

14. In the nineteenth century, Emperor Menelik II of Ethiopia builds modern schools and hospitals.
15. British outlaw slavery in 1833.
16. The United States outlaws slavery in 1865.
17. Brazil outlaws slavery in 1890.

Words to Know

Match the following with their correct definitions. Number your paper from 1 to 12, and write the correct words beside each number.

animism	irrigation
bulking stations	maat
cataracts	oases
famine	papyrus
griot	plateaus
hieroglyphic	savanna

1. grasslands where herds of wild animals roam
2. broad areas of flatland
3. food shortage that can lead to death
4. belief that every event is the work of unseen but powerful natural forces
5. small, green watering holes
6. raging rapids
7. artificial supplying water to crops
8. form of writing that uses pictures
9. substance used to make the world's first paper
10. comprehensive Egyptian code of laws
11. oral historian
12. prison camps used to hold slaves

Thinking and Writing

A. Understanding the region.

Unit 1 mentions several important natural phenomena of Africa. Three of them are the Great Rift Valley, the Nile River and the Sahara Desert. Write three paragraphs explaining the impact of these natural phenomena.

B. Explaining some events.

Review Chapter Three. Choose one of the three Western African kingdoms discussed and explain how it rose to prominence and how it fell.

A Dogon ritual object.

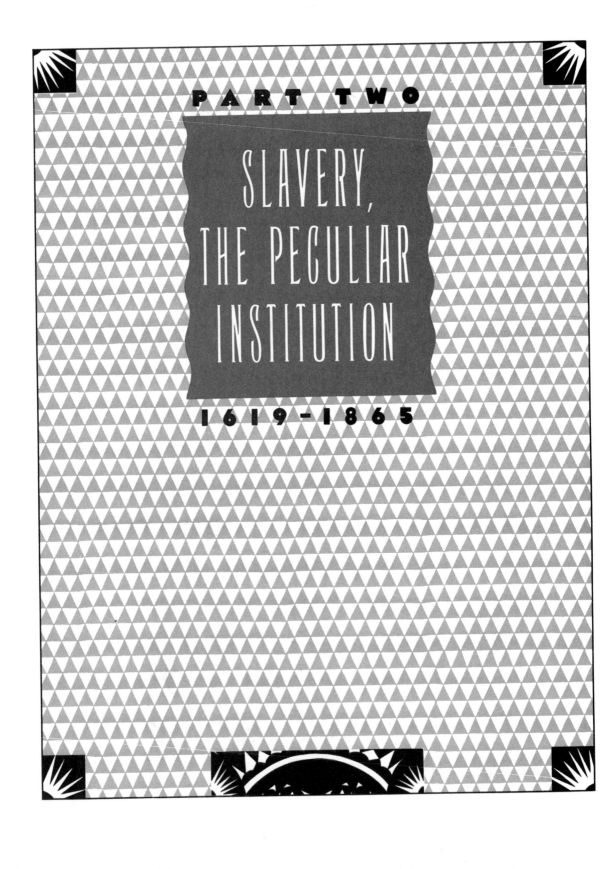

PART TWO

SLAVERY, THE PECULIAR INSTITUTION

1619 – 1865

Advertisement for slaves in a ship anchored off Charleston.

LOOKING AHEAD - PART TWO - 1619-1865

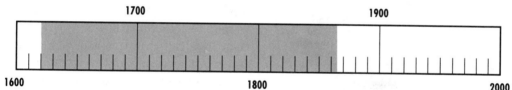

The institution of slavery defines the period in African American history from 1619 to 1865. It was in 1619 that 20-odd captured Africans were sold from a Dutch warship to a merchant of the Virginia Company in Jamestown, Virginia. In 1865, the Thirteenth Amendment to the Constitution ended slavery throughout the United States. Not every African who came to the New World was a slave. And not every white colonist was a slaveholder, but everyone in the New World was affected by this institution.

Slavery has existed all over the world, including Africa. Africans had been slaves in Portugal, Spain, the Canaries, the Madeiras and the Caribbean for more than a hundred years before the first Africans were sold in

Virginia. What set slavery apart in North America was that it was so philosophically at odds with the growing spirit of freedom among the colonists. Slaves were treated more brutally in the Caribbean and Brazil. But the system in North America was torturous, both psychologically and physically. In the next five chapters we'll take a closer look at American slavery. Here's a summary of what we'll see.

How it started. Slavery existed throughout colonial America but developed mainly in the South. The Dutch traders captured slaves from the Spanish and brought them to Virginia to be sold. Laws defining slavery appeared only after the institution itself was established. In Part Two you will see how slavery influenced the drafting of the Decla-

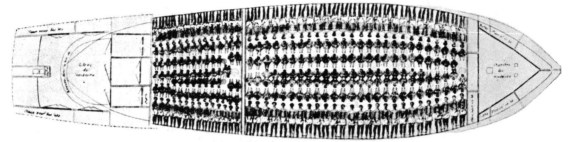

Loading plan of a slave ship whose passengers are shackled with irons.

Cross-section of a loaded slave ship.

ration of Independence and the Constitution.

How it grew. Slavery grew because the demand for a labor force grew. Large tracks of land had to be tended. Staple crops like rice, indigo and tobacco had to be harvested. Eli Whitney's invention of the cotton gin drastically reduced the time it took to prepare cotton for sale. Even more slaves were then needed to plant and pick cotton.

Slavery became an important part of the colonial economy. It was profitable for traders and owners. Slave labor was less important in the North where the colonial economy was based on shipping and small farms.

In the nineteenth century, the growth of industry made slavery even less workable in the North. Partly because the North's economic stake in slavery was not the same as the South's, resistance to it took hold there.

How it crumbled. It would take nearly 250 years for slavery to end. For it had become a very important part of America's economic and emotional life. Slavery's champions drilled into the American mind that it was both necessary and even beneficial.

The existence of slavery in a nation that proclaimed freedom created tension and controversy. In fact, it became so controversial that it threatened the unity of the country. Blacks—both slave and free—did what they could to end slavery. In Part Two you will study the slave revolts of Gabriel Prosser, Denmark Vesey and Nat Turner.

Prominent Northerners—both black and white—also fought for an end to slavery. But for years the official thrust was in the direction of compromise. Laws limited the extension of slavery into new territories. But the outright abolition of slavery was slow in coming. Southerners wanted more territory to produce their crops. And they wanted to take their slaves with them. In the end, it was the fight over the extension of slavery into new territories that led to the Civil War.

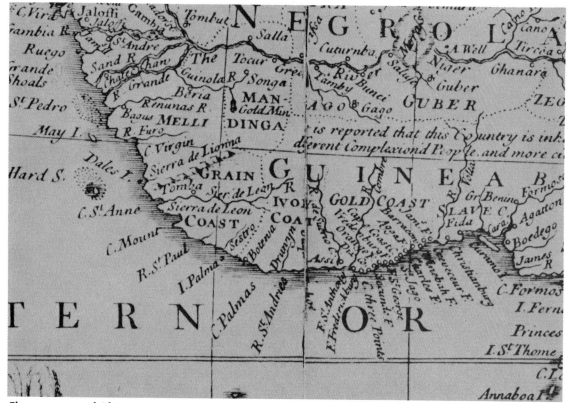

The west coast of Africa.

CHAPTER 5

How Africans Came to America

Out of Africa, from ancient times through the Middle Ages, almost to yesterday, to the rest of the known world came gold and silver, ivory, and human beings exported as slaves. At first, African slaves were prizes of war. The more beautiful women were carried off by armed conquerors. Both men and women became servants. Triumphant armies made slaves of conquered peoples, regardless of color.

Slavery is as old as civilization. In ancient Greece and Rome there were thousands of slaves, black as well as white. Slavery was a feature of European civilization. In fact, the word "slave" is a literal reminder of the time when the Slavs of Eastern Europe were sold by the Germans for what they would bring in the slave markets of the rest of Europe.

A French slave galley in the 1600s.

Working slaves and their overseers.

Tacitus, the historian, recounting the Roman occupation of England during the first century, wrote that the Britons were "too stupid" to make efficient slaves. Nevertheless, the use of Englishmen as slaves continued until the Norman Conquest of 1066, after which William the Conqueror decided that slavery could be continued locally, but that no more Britons could be sold on the international markets.

Ironically, the English were later to become major slavers, plundering Africa for its peoples. By the mid-eighteenth century, more than 300 slave ships sailed out of Liverpool alone.

Slavery was customary throughout Asia. When the Moslems came to Africa, they sold Africans by the thousands to traders in Arabia and Persia. During the fourteenth and fifteenth centuries, fashionable Venetians, Spaniards, and Portuguese kept black page boys and slave girls in attendance. But it was not until commercial expansion led to the exploration and colonization of the New World that African slavery became a highly profitable institution.

Eventually it was to develop into a monstrous enterprise, regulated by international agreement among the "civilized" nations of the world. This enterprise depopulated the towns and villages of West Africa as effectively as some dreadful plague. Torn from their homes and their families, bound to each other in chains, men and women of Africa were brought to America.

But that all began a hundred years after America was discovered. The first Africans, according to historian Ivan Van Sertima, came to America as explorers. They mixed with the Olmec tribes as early as the eighth century, B.C.

When Balboa discovered the Pacific Ocean in 1513, there were 30 black men in his party who helped clear the first road across the isthmus between the two oceans. (An **isthmus** is a narrow strip of land that joins two larger bodies of land.) Balboa reported seeing Africans in the Isthmus of Panama. Narvaez's expedition to Florida in 1528 lost all but a handful of men in attacks by the Native Americans. Two soldiers, Cabeza de Vaca and his black companion, Esteban, escaped and wandered on the North American continent for six and a half years.

In 1539, another black, Esteban Dorantes, or "Little Steven," set out from Mexico City in the party of Friar Marcos de Niza, in search of the fabled Seven Cities of Cibola. When the others wearied, Esteban went on ahead with his Native American guides. They opened up the rich area that is now Arizona and New Mexico to European settlers.

Even then, however, the Portuguese were engaged in selling Africans in South America. A century later the English were involved in slave trading in Spanish-controlled American waters. The practice, although illegal, was widely engaged in by some ship captains. One captain, the famous British buccaneer Sir John Hawkins, shipped slaves aboard their vessel called the *Jesus of Lubeck*. So did Sir Francis Drake, another British pirate.

In 1619, a Dutch ship dropped anchor at Jamestown, Virginia, with a cargo of 20 Africans, which they bartered for fresh provisions. These Africans were destined to become the first black slaves in English America.

"Black Gold"

By the middle of the sixteenth century more than 1,000 Africans a year were being sold to the European colonists in the Caribbean. Portuguese ships were the first to engage in the slave traffic. It was not long before Spanish, French and Dutch slavers took it up.

The English colonists in the New World imported white indentured workers at first, but found there weren't enough of them. (An **indentured worker** was someone who served an employer for a specified amount of time.)

The Native Americans refused to work for white colonists or, in the main, proved to be poorly fitted for long hours of hard labor. In the long run, the Europeans found it easier and cheaper to import Africans as slaves. Thus, by the seventeenth century, the African slave trade was thriving in the Americas. To compete with the Dutch and French, the King of England in 1672 chartered the Royal

African Company. The slave dealers made so much money from their human cargoes that soon Africans came to be known as "black gold."

The sea lane across the Atlantic which the slave ships followed from Africa to the New World was known as the **Middle Passage**.

Sailing vessels took many weeks to cross the Atlantic Ocean. During the long voyages many slaves died. They were stacked like logwood in dank holds. They were chained together and allowed on deck only a few minutes per day for fresh air and exercise. In bad weather they got neither. The food was often spoiled, the water stagnant, their quarters filthy. For each seven slaves delivered safely to the Americas, historians estimate that one perished on the way. Some slaves committed suicide by jumping into the water, or by swallowing their own tongues. Those who rebelled were often shot down or beaten to death on shipboard.

Arab traders of the late nineteenth century on a slaving expedition in East Africa.

Many of the Africans imported to the Americas came from Gambia, the Gold Coast, Guinea or Senegal. Historian Claudia Vass notes that after the United States became involved in the slave trade, some slaves came from ports in Angola and Mozambique. The natives of Senegal, who were often skilled **artisans** (craftspeople), brought the highest prices. On the other hand, the Ibos from Calabar were rated as undesirable merchandise, as they frequently preferred suicide to bondage. Those from the Congo were considered weaklings.

By the seventeenth century slaves could be secured in Africa for about $25 a head, or an equal amount in merchandise, and sold in the Americas for about $150. But later, when the slave trade was declared illegal, Africans brought much higher prices. Many slave-ship captains could not resist cramming their black cargo into every foot of space, even though they might lose from 15 to 20 percent of them on the way across the ocean. It is estimated that 6 million Africans were imported to the New World during the eighteenth century alone, when the slave trade became one of the world's greatest businesses.

CHAPTER CHECK

1. Why did the English colonists begin importing Africans as slaves?
2. What were some of the hardships encountered on the Middle Passage?
3. Why were Africans referred to as "black gold"?
4. Imagine . . . you are a member of an African tribe during the seventeenth century. How would the European settlement of America effect your life?

CHAPTER 6

Slaves in the New World

Slaves extract and boil the juice of sugar cane.

Whenever a slave ship sailed into an American port, its arrival was usually announced by an advertisement in the local newspaper. Homeowners and planters, as well as professional slave dealers, came down to the docks to select house servants and field hands.

To the slaves, Norfolk or New York or Charleston were unfriendly cities in an unfriendly new world. It was a world that was occupied by mysterious white people who spoke a language they could not understand. But at least the seasickness and cramped quarters on shipboard were over. What lay ahead, the Africans did not know. Soon enough they learned what their lot might include. It often included a lifetime of hard work without pay, meager food and the lash of the whip.

Families might be sold away from each other, never to meet again. In their new homes their fellow slaves might be from diverse parts of Africa, with no common language. Indeed, as a safeguard against rebellion, it was customary to separate Africans of the same tribe and to disperse relatives.

In the New England colonies there was no demand for large numbers of slave workers. But from Maryland to the Carolinas, and later as far west as Louisiana, manpower was sorely needed. Vast stretches of fertile land had to be cleared and tended for ever-increasing plantations of tobacco, rice and sugar cane. So it was the colonies in the South that became the greatest buyers of slaves.

In the early days many of these slaves were brought from the Caribbean, rather than directly from Africa. But by the late 1600s an increasing number of slave ships were sailing directly into North American ports. Busy slave markets had been established at Philadelphia, Norfolk, Charleston and New York. In Maryland and Virginia a

Tobacco is housed, aired and sold in Virginia.

thriving business in the selling of slaves for Southern plantations developed during the colonial period.

The American settlers soon found tobacco to be a profitable export crop. Many slaves were put to work in the tobacco fields. Columbus had found the Caribs on Hispaniola using tobacco. The white explorers took to it with enjoyment. Early in the sixteenth century they carried it back to Europe, where tobacco-smoking and snuff-taking soon became fashionable.

As the export business increased, more and more slaves were imported to cultivate tobacco. In Maryland, the Piedmont section of Virginia and in North Carolina, vast acreages were given over to tobacco. But by the mid-1600s so much tobacco had been grown that the European market was glutted and prices fell.

The colonial planters then turned their attention to the cultivation of rice and indigo. These, too, required many hard-working laborers to clear the land, to plant and harvest the crops. There was no let-up in the importation of Africans.

Gradually, in the Caribbean, sugar cane became an important source of income. The cane fields were tended almost entirely by slaves. They did everything from planting and cutting to crushing of the stalks for juice. The crushed cane was used for fuel and molasses and as a base for rum. Molasses and rum, in turn, were often used as barter in the **triangular trade** linking Africa, the Caribbean and North America.

Invention of the Cotton Gin

In early colonial days cotton was not a major crop. Converting the white bolls into clean lint for the making of thread was slow and tedious. Human hands were then the only means of separating the lint from the seeds. (The process of separating cotton from seeds is called **ginning**). To clean enough cotton for a few yards of cloth by hand was a long drawn-out process. A whole family, with the help of the house servants, might gather before the fireplace in the evening to remove the white fluff from the seeds, fiber by fiber, to acquire by bedtime only a few pounds of lint.

Yet, since cotton cloth was highly valued, the colonies grew a little cotton for their own use and colonial housewives mixed it with wool for their spinning wheels. King George III accepted cotton in payment of rent on crown lands. Some American cotton was grown for export to English mills. But not until Eli Whitney invented his famous gin did cotton become a major crop.

Eli Whitney received his diploma from Yale in 1792. He then journeyed South to fill a position as tutor in a Carolina planter's home. He was invited by the widow of a leading Revolutionary War general, Mrs. Nathanael Greene, to break his journey by spending a few days on her plantation near Savannah. "During this time," Whitney later wrote his father, "I heard much said of the extreme difficulty of ginning cotton. There were a number of very respectable gentlemen at Mrs. Greene's, who all agreed that if a machine could be invented which would clean the cotton with expedition, it would be a great thing both for the country and for the inventor."

In a few days the young Yankee worked out a plan for such a machine. Ten days later, he made a successful model. Within six months he had built a contraption that enabled a man to seed 10 times as much cotton

Eli Whitney at 55 and his cotton gin (below). Whitney was never able to patent his gin or make much money from it. Later, he became wealthy making firearms.

as before, and to clean it more efficiently. With the aid of a horse to turn the gin, a man could clean 50 times as much cotton as before. Whitney's cotton gin was a major contribution to the Industrial Revolution which was then taking place. Within a few years it had changed the economy of the entire South. Cotton quickly became a leading crop and one of the chief products to sell abroad.

To grow cotton and to pick, gin and bale it took a great deal of hard work. For example, if one man alone were to bring one acre of cotton to fruition, that man would have to walk almost a thousand miles. From spring to fall, up and down the rows of his single acre, he would be plowing, planting, chopping and picking, then piling his bags into a wagon to haul them to the gin.

In the South, this labor was done by the slaves. Thus, in 1803 alone, less than 10 years after the invention of the cotton gin, more than 20,000 blacks, many of them supplied by New England slave traders, were brought into Georgia and South Carolina to work the cotton fields. Whitney's gin made cotton big business. It fastened the chains of slavery tighter than ever about the ankles of black men and women.

Slaves as Skilled Workers

Not all slaves, however, were assigned to the fields. There were houses and docks to be built, bridges to be constructed, gates and fences to be made and mended. For these and similar purposes, skilled artisans were developed among the slaves, especially in urban communities. The custom of hiring out **bondsmen**, or slaves, to others became a pattern. Some masters encouraged their slaves to learn a trade, since their wages went to their masters and skilled slaves com-

Sea trade made docksides busy places in the eighteenth century.

manded a better rate of hire. Some slaves became expert brickmasons, carpenters and workers in iron. They built many stately Southern mansions. They molded the beautiful iron grillwork of the gates and balconies of old New Orleans and Charleston. Owners of foundries and tobacco factories, as well as contractors, employed slaves in skilled and semi-skilled work.

As railroads were developed, thousands of blacks were employed in the laying of roadbeds. The first fireman on the first locomotive built in America (1830) was a slave. In the construction of the Muscle Shoals Canal

Car driven by a horse, whipped by a slave. It could carry a dozen passengers at 12 mph.

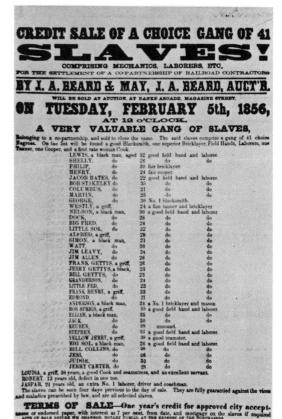

in South Carolina, the contractors gave special compensation to the masters of any slaves who were injured or killed by explosions or cave-ins. Similar arrangements were made in the case of slaves employed in coal, copper and gold mines.

In some parts of the South more slaves than whites were engaged in skilled trades. The competition between slave labor and free white labor developed to such an extent that bitterness sometimes flared into violence against blacks. White workers protested the custom of hiring out slaves as artisans. This practice forced white labor to compete with bondsmen for a low wage scale.

Picking cotton on a Georgia plantation.

In Virginia, a law was passed as early as 1784, limiting the number of slaves in each ship's crew. This law was a result of protest from white seaman who were out of work.

Slave Domestics

House servants were generally much better off than field hands. Being nearer the master's kitchen, they often ate better. And the white family's cast-off clothing usually became theirs. The living quarters for favored black servants were sometimes far more comfortable than the housing poor whites could afford. In New England, a slave might be taught to read and write. But in the South, it was illegal. Slave companions often learned to read from white children.

The privileges enjoyed by house slaves

created a gulf of suspicion and envy between domestic servants and field hands. The latter, whose lives were barren of delicacies, cast-off finery or creature comforts, did not trust the slaves in the Big House. It is important to note that the lives of house servants were not always rosy. They rarely escaped the attention of their master. And unlike field servants, they were on call 24 hours a day.

However, between black domestics and the white families whom they served, close bonds of affection and friendship often developed. There are many examples of affection between bondservants and their masters. Pierre Toussaint and his family, slaves of Jean Berard in Santo Domingo, were brought by their owner to New York during the turmoil of the Haitian Revolution. Poverty overtook the master there, but at his death Pierre Toussaint assumed the family burden and, earning a living as a hairdresser, supported his master's widow in luxury until she married again. She later freed Toussaint.

Famous Bondsmen

Through a combination of personal talent and luck, a few slaves were able to become outstanding. Such a slave was Phillis Wheatley. She was brought from Senegal as a child and was sold on the docks at Boston in 1761 to John Wheatley, a tailor. He gave the girl the family name. His wife taught her to read and write. Before she was 20, Phillis achieved some renown as a poet. She was eventually given her freedom. She became one of the best known poets of New England.

As early as 1746, Lucy Terry, a slave of Deerfield, Massachusetts had published poetry. Later, the writer-preacher Jupiter Hammon circulated his poems on single sheets of paper. In 1787 he published *An Address to*

Phillis Wheatley, a slave commended by General George Washington for her poetry.

Negroes in the State of New York. That book was reprinted three times. Hammon hoped to buy his freedom from the book's profits, but was not successful.

In 1789, there appeared in England an autobiography, *The Interesting Narrative of the Life of Oloudah Equiano, or Gustavus Vassa.* Vassa was a former slave from Virginia. He had purchased his freedom and made his home in England. A half-century later at Chapel Hill, North Carolina, a slave poet, George Moses Horton, published his first book. It was called *The Hope of Liberty*.

CHAPTER CHECK

1. What type of work did most slaves do in the Southern colonies?
2. How did the invention of the cotton gin change the Southern economy and the institution of slavery in the South?
3. What were some differences between field slaves and domestic servants? Which do you think had the most difficult life? Why?
4. Imagine . . . you are a skilled slave in the South. How would your life be different from most other slaves? What special problems would you face?

SALE OF
VALUABLE
SLAVES,
(On account of departure)

The Owner of the following named and valuable Slaves, being on the eve of departure for Europe, will cause the same to be offered for sale, at the NEW EXCHANGE, corner of St. Louis and Chartres streets, on *Saturday,* May 16, at Twelve o'Clock, *viz.*

1. SARAH, a mulatress, aged 45 years, a good cook and accustomed to house work in general, is an excellent and faithful nurse for sick persons, and in every respect a first rate character.

2. DENNIS, her son, a mulatto, aged 24 years, a first rate cook and steward for a vessel, having been in that capacity for many years on board one of the Mobile packets; is strictly honest, temperate, and a first rate subject.

3. CHOLE, a mulatress, aged 36 years, she is, without exception, one of the most competent servants in the country, a first rate washer and ironer, does up lace, a good cook, and for a bachelor who wishes a house-keeper she would be invaluable; she is also a good ladies' maid, having travelled to the North in that capacity.

4. FANNY, her daughter, a mulatress, aged 16 years, speaks French and English, is a superior hair-dresser, (pupil of Guilliac,) a good seamstress and ladies' maid, is smart, intelligent, and a first rate character.

5. DANDRIDGE, a mulatoo, aged 26 years, a first rate dining-room servant, a good painter and rough carpenter, and has but few equals for honesty and sobriety.

6. NANCY, his wife, aged about 24 years, a confidential house servant, good seamstress, mantuamaker and tailoress, a good cook, washer and ironer, etc.

7. MARY ANN, her child, a creole, aged 7 years, speaks French and English, is smart, active and intelligent.

8. FANNY or FRANCES, a mulatress, aged 22 years, is a first rate washer and ironer, good cook and house servant, and has an excellent character.

9. EMMA, an orphan, aged 10 or 11 years, speaks French and English, has been in the country 7 years, has been accustomed to waiting on table, sewing etc.; is intelligent and active.

10. FRANK, a mulatto, aged about 32 years speaks French and English, is a first rate hostler and coachman, understands perfectly well the management of horses, and is, in every respect, a first rate character, with the exception that he will occasionally drink, though not an habitual drunkard.

All the above named Slaves are acclimated and excellent subjects; they were purchased by their present vendor many years ago, and will, therefore, be severally warranted against all vices and maladies prescribed by law, save and except FRANK, who is fully guaranteed in every other respect but the one above mentioned.

A Richmond slave auction in 1856.

CHAPTER 7

Slavery and the Law

In 1801, Thomas Jefferson, became the third president of the United States. He was born in Virginia of a slave-holding family. He himself owned slaves. But he was a man whose political convictions were influenced by his study of liberal European philosophers like Rousseau, Locke and Montesquieu.

Jefferson was chairman of the committee which drafted the Declaration of Independence in 1776. In his first draft he wrote a paragraph condemning human bondage. He also denounced King George III for his role in spreading slavery to the colonies and other English territories.

But slavery was too profitable a business in some colonies. Those words of Jefferson were not acceptable to the Southern delegation. They were omitted from the final version of the Declaration as adopted by the Continental Congress on July 4, 1776. So, from the beginnings of the new nation's history, the voteless bondsman influenced the policies and documents of the new republic.

In the Constitution

The question of slavery came up again when the Constitutional Convention met in Philadelphia in 1787. It was the dominant issue between the Northern and Southern states. A compromise was worked out to prevent the two regions from splitting apart. Slavery was permitted to remain legal for the sake of the South, where it was important for the production of major crops. An agreement was reached that allowed the South to count three-fifths of its slaves as a basis for representation in Congress. The African slave trade was allowed to go on another 20 years. The states were required to return fugitive slaves to their owners.

The United States bought Louisiana from France in 1803. The institution of slavery was still further entrenched by the establishment of many great sugar cane and cotton plantations there. In 1807, Congress passed a law prohibiting the importation of African slaves. The law went into effect January 1, 1808. Its enforcement was lax and violations were many. The soaring price of blacks and the demand for slave labor led to the spread of slave smuggling. As late as 1859, the yacht *Wanderer* landed more than 400 blacks on a Georgia dock. But no one was punished. Over 50,000 slaves were smuggled into the United States in this way.

The Entrenchment of Bondage

As pioneer settlers streamed westward, those who had slaves took them along into the new lands. The new freedom of the frontier did not mean freedom for black people. In the West, both the natural resources of the

A slave family in front of their cabin.

frontier and the human resources of slavery were ruthlessly exploited. Men were desperately needed to clear the land and grow the crops. The price of slaves went up. The trading in slaves in the newly settled regions became a major enterprise.

In 1821, Missouri entered the Union as a slave state, as did Texas in 1845. Interstate slave-trading firms developed and soon offered thousands of slaves for sale. Some companies which sold dry goods, furniture and agricultural tools, also handled slaves. Blacks were looked upon as just another piece of merchandise, not as human beings.

Newly imported Africans were believed to be heathens. In 1670, the colony of Virginia passed a law declaring that all persons not believing in Christ —that is, Africans— might be held as slaves. Ministers of Southern churches defended human bondage on the grounds that Africans were barbarians.

Planters claimed that the prosperity of the South depended on slave labor. Southern politicians running for office championed the system. In 1835, Governor McDuffie of South Carolina declared that domestic slavery "was the cornerstone of our political edifice."

In 1858, the *Southern Literary Messenger* said: "We assert that in all countries and at all times there must be a class of hewers of wood and drawers of water who must always of necessity be the substratum of society. We affirm that it is best for all that this class should be formed of a race upon whom God himself has placed a mark of physical and mental inferiority."

From defending and apologizing for it, the South had turned to asserting that slavery was a positive good and liberty a threat to humankind.

The Montgomery House in New Orleans.

Corn Shucks, Fat Back and Malaria

As plantations grew larger, the condition of slaves generally worsened. The quarters provided for field hands usually consisted of crudely-built shacks with dirt floors. Slaves slept on beds made of corn shucks. Their standard food was cornmeal, fat back and molasses. This was also the diet of many poor whites.

About 88 percent of the country's slaveholders owned 20 slaves or less. Most plantations were owner-operated and managed. The planters themselves often worked in the fields. They usually were reasonably decent to their slaves, though there was some harshness and cruelty.

Half of all slaves, however, lived on plantations with more than 30 slaves. Cruelty was more often the case where an **overseer** managed the plantation for an absentee owner.

Profit-sharing overseers too often were interested only in getting as many hours of work and as large a crop out of the slaves as they could. To this end they used the whip and occasionally various forms of torture. Even minor infractions might be punished by nailing a slave to the side of the barn by his ear or by stringing him up by his wrists and flogging him. Severe discipline was generally thought necessary to keep the slaves in check and prevent rebellion.

CHAPTER CHECK

1. Why was Thomas Jefferson's paragraph against slavery omitted from the Declaration of Independence?
2. In the Constitution of 1787, how were slaves to be counted for determining representation in Congress? Why?
3. Imagine . . . you are the slave of a Southern cotton planter. Would you rather be on a small farm with only a few other slaves or on a large plantation with many slaves? Explain.

CHAPTER 8

Slave Revolts

Nat Turner arrested.

The earliest slave rebellions go back to the seventeenth century. There were several instances of rebellion aboard ship before the slave cargoes reached America. On the *Kentucky*, more than 40 slaves were put to death for staging an uprising in mid-ocean. Such slave revolts occurred so often during the Middle Passage that they were rated an occupational hazard by the traders. Once ashore, the danger did not cease.

In Gloucester County, Virginia, as early as 1663—less than 50 years after Africans reached Jamestown—slaves had joined with white indentured servants to plan a rebellion. The plot was nipped and the heads of the black ringleaders were cut off and displayed in the public square. In New York, in 1712, rebel slaves killed nine whites in a fire. In the same city, in 1741, a rumor spread that some one hundred slaves were to join with white indentured servants to strike back at their masters. Sixteen of these blacks were hanged and 71 were deported. Four white persons, including two women, were hanged.

The Stono Uprising

The Stono Uprising of 1739 is considered an important rebellion in the history of South Carolina. This slave revolt marked the

INSURRECTION IN VIRGINIA!

Extract of a letter from a gentleman to his friend in Baltimore, dated

'RICHMOND,' August 23d.

An express reached the governor this morning, informing him that an insurrection had broken out in Southampton, and that, by the last accounts, there were seventy whites massacred, and the militia retreating. Another express to Petersburg says that the blacks were continuing their destruction; that three hundred militia were retreating in a body, before six or eight hundred blacks. A shower of rain coming up as the militia were making an attack, wet the powder so much that they were compelled to retreat, being armed only with shot-guns. The negroes are armed with muskets, scythes, axes, &c. &c. Our volunteers are marching to the scene of action. A troop of cavalry left at four o'clock, P. M. The artillery, with four field pieces, start in the steam boat Norfolk, at 6 o'clock, to land at Smithfield. Southampton county lies 80 miles south of us, below Petersburg.'

From the Richmond Whig, of Tuesday.

Disagreeable rumors have reached this city of an insurrection of the slaves in Southampton County, with loss of life. In order to correct exaggeration, and at the same time to induce all salutary caution, we state the following particulars:

An express from the Hon. James Trezvant states that an insurrection had broken out, that several families had been murdered, and that the negroes were embodied, requiring a considerable military force to reduce them.

The names and precise numbers of the families are not mentioned. A letter to the Post Master corroborates the intelligence. Prompt and efficient measures are being taken by the Governor, to call out a sufficient force to put down the insurrection, and place lower Virginia on its guard.

Serious danger of course there is none. The deluded wretches have rushed on assured destruction.

The Fayette Artillery and the Light Dragoons will leave here this evening for Southampton; the artillery go in a steamboat, and the troop by land.

We are indebted to the kindness of our friend Lyford for the following extract of a letter from the Editors of the Norfolk Herald, containing the particulars of a most murderous insurrection among the blacks of Southampton County, Virginia.—*Gaz.*

NORFOLK, 24th Aug. 1831.

I have a horrible, a heart rending tale to relate, and lest even its worst feature might be distorted by rumor and exaggeration, I have thought it proper to give you all and the worst information, that has as yet reached us through the best sources of intelligence which the nature of the case will admit.

A gentleman arrived here yesterday express from Suffolk, with intelligence from the upper part of Southampton county, stating that a band of insurgent slaves (some of them believed to be runaways from the neighboring Swamps,) had turned out on Sunday night last, and murdered several whole families, amounting to 40 or 50 individuals. Some of the families were named, and among them was that of Mrs. Catharine Whitehead, sister of our worthy townsman, Dr. N. C. Whitehead,—who, with her

climax of a series of smaller rebellions in the surrounding areas. News items in the northern and southern colonies reported what appeared to be isolated incidents of rebellion. These reports told of deaths of slave owners from arson and poisonings usually attributed to a slave. Colonists were more fearful, however, of organized resistance like the Stono Uprising.

Like many rebellions, the Stono Uprising occured during the leisure hours of an early Sunday morning. The planters were away at church. Twenty slaves gathered at the Stono River. Recent conflicts between the Spanish and English colonists were widely reported. It was believed slaves would be given refuge in St. Augustine, Florida, among the Spanish colonists. Led by a slave named Jemmy, a group of slaves headed for St. Augustine. At a nearby store, firearms and gunpowder were stolen and used against the storeowners. As the group trailed the fields of the low country, their ranks swelled as other slaves joined them. Most volunteered, but some were forced. Most planters, overseers and their families were murdered by the crowd. A few fortunate souls, who were kind to their slaves, were spared.

After a 10-mile trek, the group came to an abrupt halt in an open field. Word of the slave revolt had quickly spread in the vicinity. At 4 p.m., a group of armed planters captured a substantial number of the rebel slaves. However, six days passed before the largest group of rebel slaves were caught by a white militia company. A few rebels remained at large. It is believed nearly 25 whites lost their lives in the melee. The number of slaves who died remains unknown.

The most damaging effect of the insurrection were the fears and tensions it stirred up

Turner's uprising as told by the *Liberator*.

in the slave-holding community.

The aftermath of the rebellion marked the creation of a number of laws to limit the activities of slaves and free blacks. The Negro Act of 1740 subjected free blacks to a second-rate judicial process. A year later a duty was imposed on the purchase of new slaves to discourage their growing population. Another statute imposed a fine on planters whose slaves were caught gathering in groups.

Gabriel Prosser

Throughout the colonies a master's control over his slaves went unquestioned, even to the meting out of torture or death. Restlessness among the slaves was intensified by the Revolutionary War and its proclaimed ideals of liberty and independence. Some slaves took the Christian version of the Bible literally. They believed that God meant *all* men and women to be free. Such a slave was

Osman, who escaped slavery to live in Dismal Swamp.

Gabriel Prosser of Virginia. He felt he was divinely called to deliver his people to freedom. Carefully, Gabriel made plans for over a period of months. He swore his black followers to secrecy. They were thought to include as many as 10,000 slaves.

Gathering his followers in Old Brook Swamp, Gabriel planned to attack Richmond on August 30, 1800. But he was betrayed by two slaves he had confided in. On the very evening set for the outbreak, a great storm came up, with torrential floods and gales. The doomed rebellion was washed away. Richmond, by then, was under martial law. Scores of slaves were imprisoned or hanged on the spot. Several weeks later their leader was captured. On October 7, after refusing to talk, Gabriel Prosser was publicly hanged.

Denmark Vesey and Nat Turner

In 1822, in Charleston, South Carolina, the carpenter, Denmark Vesey, planned one of the most extensive revolts against slavery ever recorded. Vesey used his knowledge of the French and Haitian Revolutions, and the Congressional debates on the Missouri Compromise, to promote the principle of equality among the slaves, and the realization of their common power. But he was betrayed by a frightened house slave and, with 34 others, was put to death.

In Virginia, in 1831, the greatest revolt of all occurred. It was led by Nat Turner, a plowman and a preacher, whose father had escaped to freedom. Deeply religious, like many of the other black rebels, Turner felt that he was called by God to lead "the children of Egypt" out of bondage. With five others, Turner swore to massacre all the whites on the nearest plantations and then gather followers as he advanced. Fifty-five whites

Osceola,
a Seminole chief.

Abraham,
a black who spoke Seminole.

Caocoochee (Wild Cat),
a friend to slaves.

were killed in Southampton County and the whole South was thrown into panic. In retaliation, more than 100 blacks, innocent and guilty, were struck down before the rebellion was quelled.

Frederick Law Olmsted, a special correspondent for the New York *Times*, made a tour of the slave states a few years before the Civil War. He reported that he found "no part of the South where the slave population is felt to be quite safe from a contagion of insurrectionary excitement." The South had become a powder keg. Slavery was the powder.

Refuge Among Native Americans

Many slaves seeking freedom simply ran away. Sometimes they joined the Native Americans. The Native Americans, who had been conquered or harassed by the early settlers, were not averse to aiding discontented slaves to strike back. In Connecticut, in 1658, Native Americans together with blacks burned the homes of a number of slave masters. Runaway blacks often found shelter

among the Native Americans and frequently intermarried with them. In 1690, in Massachusetts, a similar group planned a revolt. In 1786, an "idle set of free Negroes" was said to be inhabiting an Indian reservation in Virginia.

During the War of 1812, one of the charges against the British was that they encouraged slaves to escape to Native American territory. There they fought with the British and the Native American against the United States. When a British commander abandoned a fort in western Florida, just south of the Georgia border, about a thousand runaway slaves living among the Creeks and Seminoles took it over.

In 1816, General Andrew Jackson ordered troops to "destroy the fort and return the stolen Negroes and property to their rightful owners." The fort was blown up by a cannon which exploded the powder magazine. It killed 344 men, women and children within the fort, among them some Native Americans. Three survivors were executed. In December 1817, Jackson was ordered to remove the Seminoles from Florida. United States troops invaded Florida. Thus began the first of the Seminole Wars. The war consisted mainly of burning Native American villages.

After these incidents, the Southern leaders continued to accuse the Seminoles of harboring fugitive slaves and urged the government to remove the Native Americans forcibly to the West. This led to the Second Seminole War in 1835. In this war, Osceola, whose parents were a Seminole chief's daughter and a white trader, played a prominent part. Osceola married a girl whose father was a Native American and whose mother was a fugitive slave. A government agent kidnapped Osceola's wife and took her into slavery. Osceola was imprisoned. But he escaped and, with his Seminole troops, ambushed and killed the government agent in revenge. More than 500 black exiles were seized and enslaved in the course of the Second Seminole War. It lasted eight years. The two Seminole Wars, which resulted in the re-enslavement of these blacks, cost the United States $40 to $50 million.

The Roots of Jim Crow

On a Cincinnati street in 1830, Dan Rice, a famous white "blackface" minstrel, saw a ragged little black boy singing "Jump, Jim Crow." Rice copied the boy's lively song-and-dance and for years performed the act to great applause. Gradually, the words **Jim Crow** came to be applied to the legal segregation of blacks from whites in everyday life. The blackface minstrels, by their stage portrayal, helped to establish the stereotype of black inferiority and the desirability of segregation.

Slave music and dance entertained many Americans.

WALNUT STREET THEATRE,

Box 50 cents—Pit 25 cents—Gallery 18 3-4 cents.
Doors will be opened at half after 6, and the Curtain rise at a quarter after 7 o'clock, precisely.

On this occasion

Mr. J. R. SCOTT
AND
MR. HOWARD,
WILL APPEAR

Mr. RICE
As the Far Famed

Jim Crow

Will also appear, and discuss
10 New Subjects,
In his Fashionable Lyric Style.

Monday Evening,
JUNE 3, 1833.

Will be presented, (1st time these 5 year) Macklin's admirable Comedy of the

Man
OF THE
WORLD.

Sir Pertinax M'Sycophant,	Mr. Maywood.
Egerton,	Mr. Wood.
Lord Lumbercourt,	Mr. Faulkner.
Sidney,	Mr. Murdoch.
Melville,	Mr. Walstein.
Plausible,	Mr. Hadaway.
Eitherside,	Mr. Durley.
Sam,	Mr. Eberle.
John,	Mr. Crater.
Tomline,	Mr. Watson.
Lady M'Sycophant,	Mrs. Turner.
Lady Rodolpha,	Mr. Maywood.
Constantia,	Mrs. Roper.
Betty Hint,	Mrs. Thayer.
Nancy,	Mrs. Walstein.

AFTER WHICH,
Mr. RICE
Will appear and discuss in Lyric Style, the following
10 NEW SUBJECTS.

1—Important News from Washington,
2—Interview with the President,
3—Benefit of Temperence Societies,
4—Reformation of Jim Crow.
5—Trip from Baltimore,
6—Description of the various passengers; and
7—Every one for himself.
8—News of Massa Randolph.
9—De general turn out in de Department, and
10—De Wonder of JIM CROW.

To conclude with the Nautical Drama of

Black Eyed
SUSAN.

WILLIAM,	Mr. J. R. SCOTT.
Captain Crosstree,	Mr. Murdoch.
Gnatbrain,	Mr. Hadaway.
Dogvrass,	Mr. Walstein.
Raker,	Mr. Jervis.
Hatchet,	Mr. Drummond.
Jacob Twig,	Mr. Whiting.
Quid,	Mr. Eberle.
Seaweed,	Mr. Watson.
BLUE PETER,	Mr. HOWARD.

in which he will sing THREE STANZAS of
Black Eyed Susan.
AND
"TELL HER I LOVE HER."

Slavery's defenders, J.D.B. DeBow and George Fitzhugh.

Jim Crow, the character invented by "Daddy" Dan Rice, a white entertainer who mimicked blacks.

That blacks were biologically and mentally inferior to whites, was a basic argument employed in every way to bolster the slave system. Senator John C. Calhoun of South Carolina, contended that blacks could never absorb education. He claimed that bondage was good for the slaves.

The Southern press was nearly unanimous in its support of slavery. The New Orleans journal, *DeBow's Review*, published an essay by sociologist George Fitzhugh. In it, Fitzhugh declared that "slavery, black or white," was necessary and was the proper condition of the working man. He called for the ousting of Northern teachers in the South. He also urged that Southerners write all textbooks used in the schools.

The rift between the North and the South over the issue of slavery began to widen rapidly. This rift was expressed in bitterly opposing opinions in both politics and literature. The United States was split into two camps. One camp was for the continuation of slavery. The other camp called for slavery's abolition.

CHAPTER CHECK
1. In what way was the South a "powder keg" shortly before the Civil War?
2. What dangers did rebellious and fugitive slaves face?
3. Why did the United States wage two wars in Florida against the Seminoles?
4. What was the origin of the term Jim Crow? What meaning did it take on? What role did the blackface minstrals play in continuing slavery?
5. Imagine . . . you are (a) a Southern slave owner, and (b) a Southern slave. How would you react in either case to the news of Nat Turner's Revolt?

CHAPTER 9

Firebell in the Night

News of the Mexican War reaches a small town.

The long and stormy debate in Congress over the extension of slavery into the territories and new states was stilled for a time by the passage of the Missouri Compromise in 1820. Missouri was admitted into the Union as a slave state. Maine was admitted as a free state. The sectional balance was now 12 states each. The informal line barring slavery from all new states north of the Ohio River—which had been recognized and respected from the founding of the Republic—had now been advanced to the lands west of the Mississippi River. By law, slavery was now to be prohibited "forever" in any new United States territories north of Missouri's southern border.

To old Thomas Jefferson, news of the bitterness and fiery passion of the debate came "like a firebell in the night," tolling the "knell of the Union."

In the North, immigrants were pouring into the industrialized towns and cities. In the South, cotton's rising value and the search for new lands on which to grow it, pushed the frontiers ever westward. John C. Calhoun feared that the Northern states might dominate the new territories. So he tried to cement a political alliance between the South and the West. The cotton growers of the South and the farmers of the West were both hungry for more land. Their eyes turned toward Texas, a vast empire that might be conquered for slavery.

The North protested against the annexation movement as well as any movement designed to extend slavery. (**Annexation** involves adding a territory to a nation). In reply, the Southerners used the gag rule which put aside all anti-slavery petitions. Soon, the entire country became a debating society with a single question on everyone's lips.

Should slavery be extended or abolished? On John Quincy Adams' motion, the gag rule was finally dropped in the House of Representatives in 1844. But the problem of slavery continued to plague the nation. It reached a new climax in the war with Mexico over the annexation of Texas.

The prospect of adding more territories as a result of this war led to another heated debate in Congress. The Democrats defended the war as a just one. The Whigs denounced it as a drive for new slave lands. The House passed the Wilmot Proviso to bar slavery from any of the domains taken in the Mexican War. But the bill was defeated in the Senate, where Calhoun attacked it as a threat to Southern rights and power.

To Calhoun, the writing on the wall was clear: the industrial North was outstripping the agrarian South. He warned that if Southern domination of the Supreme Court, the

ANTI·SLAVERY PEACE PLEDGE.

WE, the undersigned,

hereby solemnly pledge ourselves not to countenance or aid the United States Government in any war which may be occasioned by the annexation of Texas, or in any other war, foreign or domestic, designed to strengthen or perpetuate slavery.

Name.	Residence.

A peace pledge circulated by abolitionists.

foreign service, the armed forces and the administrative offices—a power that South held since the turn of the century—should be broken, it would mean civil war and widespread disaster.

Compromise and Crisis

With the decade of the 1850s about to begin, the political pot came to a boil. At the door of the Union stood California, seeking admission as a free state. The western lands were filling rapidly with Southern highlanders, settlers from the middle Atlantic seaboard, New Englanders and immigrants from foreign shores. Which way would the new territories go? What would be done about the outright refusal of many free-staters to return fugitive slaves to their masters? What about the renewed insistence upon the adoption of the Wilmot Proviso in the new lands of the Southwest?

Congress met in December 1849, with both Democrats and Whigs divided over slavery. It took 59 ballots to elect a Speaker of the House. Disunion talk erupted from Northern abolitionists and Southern secessionists alike. (An **abolitionist** was a person who called for the legal end of slavery. A **secessionist** was someone who called for withdrawal from the union).

The great debate opened with Kentucky Senator Henry Clay's attempt to find a middle ground that would unite the nation. He proposed that 1. territories carved from lands taken from Mexico decide the slavery question for themselves; 2. Allow California to enter the Union as a free state; 3. Kill the slave trade, but not slavery in the District of Columbia; and 4. Write a new law that would force the North to return runaways to their owners.

The admission of the Nebraska and Kansas territories into the Union made slavery an issue once more.

THE BLACK LIST.

Total vote from free States in favor of the Fugitive Slave bill.

DEMOCRATS.—*Maine*--Messrs. Fuller, Gerry, Littlefield—3.
New Hampshire.—Messrs. HIBBARD and PEASLEE—2.
New York—Mr Walden—1.
New Jersey—Mr Wildrick—1.
Pennsylvania—Messr.s Dimmick, Job Mann, McLanahan, Robbins, Ross and James Thompson—6.
Ohio—Messrs. Hayland and Miller—2.
Indiana—Messrs, Alberston, William J. Brown, Dunham, Gorman, McDonald—5.
Illinois—Messrs. Bissel, T. L. Harris, McClernand, Richardson, Young—5.
Michigan—Mr A. W. Buel—1.
Iowa—Mr Leffier—1.
California—Mr Gilbert—1. Total 27.
WHIGS.—Messrs. Elliot, of *Mass.*; McGaughey, of *Ind.*; John L. Taylor, of *Ohio*—Total, 3.
Total Ayes from free states, 30.

A circular published by abolitionists against those who voted for the Fugitive Slave Act.

Southern slave-catchers recapture a fleeing black.

Senator Calhoun opposed Clay's compromise and again threatened secession. On March 7, 1850, Daniel Webster of Massachusetts rose in the Senate and supported Clay's compromise. He urged the North to carry out the fugitive slave clause "with all its provisions, to the furthest extent."

Representative Thaddeus Stevens of Pennsylvania voted against the bill. He predicted the compromise would be "the fruitful mother of future rebellions, disunion and civil war." But Daniel Webster's voice was to carry the measure. By September it was law —to the liking of neither the North nor the South. An uneasy truce prevailed.

The Fugitive Slave Law of 1850

The New Fugitive Slave Law was signed by President Millard Fillmore on September 18, 1850. It provided that any federal marshal who did not arrest on demand an alleged runaway might be fined $1,000. Fugitive slaves or suspects could be arrested on request without a warrant and turned over to a claimant on nothing more than the claimant's sworn testimony of ownership. (A **warrant** is a written order giving the holder authority to take action. A **claimant** is a person who claims the rights to a person or a thing).

A black fugitive, or captured free man, could not ask for a jury trial nor testify in his own behalf. Any person aiding a runaway slave by giving him shelter, food or any sort of assistance, was liable to six months imprisonment and a $2,000 fine. Officers capturing a fugitive slave were entitled to a fee. This last provision caused unscrupulous (crooked) officers to become kidnappers of even free blacks. It was easy to find greedy claimants who would falsely swear to ownership and gladly pay the bribe for a new slave.

At the passage of this bill, despair and

Dred Scott, a slave returned to his master by a Supreme Court decision.

panic swept over the black population of the North. It was estimated that more than 50,000 fugitives had found shelter above the Mason-Dixon Line—the line that divided the North from the South. Many had married free blacks. Now no black person felt safe. Frederick Douglass said, "Under this law the oaths of any two villains (the capturer and the claimant) are sufficient to confine a free man to slavery for life."

Thousands of blacks in the North fled overnight to Canada. Some of the more active black abolitionists went to England. For free blacks, a reign of terror had come. Armed clashes frequently developed between the zealous slave-catchers and black and white abolitionists. In deliberate defiance of the law, abolitionists made many attempts to rescue fugitives. Some attempts succceeded, some failed.

Northern writers such as Wendell Phillips, James Lowell, John Greenleaf Whittier, Ralph Waldo Emerson and Henry David

Thoreau thundered denunciations of the Fugitive Slave Law. Meanwhile Southerners continually complained that it was not being adequately enforced. The South threatened secession and a boycott of Northern industries and trade. (A **boycott** is an organized refusal by one group to do business with another group). The South demanded that both the federal and state officers enforce the Fugitive Slave Law to the fullest. But it could not get full cooperation from the citizenry.

The Kansas-Nebraska Bill

Four years after the great debate, which many believed had settled the question of slavery's extension, Stephen A. Douglas of Illinois introduced his Kansas-Nebraska bill to the Senate. The Senator proposed, in effect, to repeal the Missouri Compromise and, under the principle of "squatter," or "popular sovereignty," to permit the new territories to come into the Union with or without slavery. Again, protests flooded Congress from the North. This time the protestors included conservatives who had supported the 1850 Compromise in the hope that it would bring peace and halt the spread of slavery.

In Ripon, Wisconsin, angry men met to resolve that if the Douglas bill went through, they would organize a new party dedicated to opposing the extension of slavery. This coalition of Northerners and Westerners who bolted from the Whig, Free Soil and Democratic parties wrote the name "Republican" on their new political banners.

In May 1854, the Kansas-Nebraska bill became law. Frederick Douglass called it "an open invitation to a fierce and bitter strife." The race to settle Kansas began. Southerners took their slaves along, and Northerners,

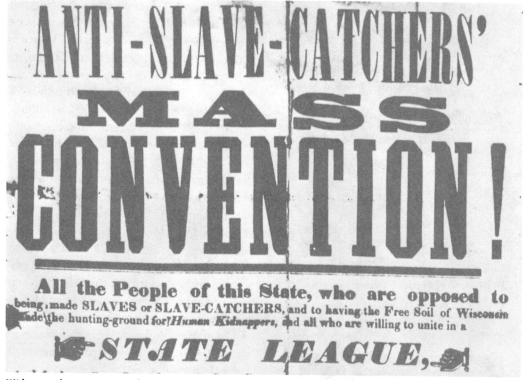

ANTI-SLAVE-CATCHERS' MASS CONVENTION!

All the People of this State, who are opposed to being made SLAVES or SLAVE-CATCHERS, and to having the Free Soil of Wisconsin made the hunting-ground for Human Kidnappers, and all who are willing to unite in a

STATE LEAGUE,

Widespread resistance to the Fugitive Slave Act developed in the West and North.

their militant opposition to slavery. From his pulpit in Brooklyn, Henry Ward Beecher hurled harsh words at all slaveholders, shouting that a gun was a greater moral agency in Kansas than a Bible. The rifles supplied by sympathizers in the East to the Free Soilers in Kansas were soon called "Beecher's Bibles."

When Kansas elected its first territorial legislature in March 1855, armed Missouri slaveowners poured over the borders to vote. They were fearful that their slaves might escape into Kansas if it remained free soil. Although less than 3,000 qualified voters were enrolled, the number of votes cast that day exceeded 6,000, most of them on the side of slavery. The new legislature, illegally elected, set up a code of laws providing prison sentences for those who contended slavery was not legal in Kansas. It imposed the death penalty for anyone helping a slave to escape. It also imposed two years in jail for possessing abolitionist literature. This so angered the anti-slavery party that it called a new convention in Topeka, Kansas, drafted a new constitution and set up a separate government.

The Dred Scott Decision

In the 1856 presidential election, the battle over slavery shifted to the ballot boxes. The Democrats nominated James

A caricature of President James Buchanan.

Roger B. Taney,
Chief Justice who ruled against Scott.

Buchanan of Pennsylvania. The Republicans chose John C. Fremont, the California explorer-hero. The disintegrating Whigs endorsed the ticket of the Know-Nothings, who had picked former President Millard Fillmore. Buchanan won, with 1,800,000 votes to Fremont's 1,300,000 and Fillmore's 875,000. The Republicans had not won the election, but they had gained great strength.

On March 6, 1857, two days after Buchanan's inauguration, the Supreme Court handed down a decision that made Dred Scott the best-known black man in America.

Dred Scott was a Virginia-born slave who had been carried by his master, an Army doctor, from Missouri into the free state of Illinois, and then into the the free territory of Minnesota. He stayed away from Missouri for four years before being returned.

On the grounds that he had become a free man by virtue of residence on free soil, Dred Scott, in 1846, sued for his liberty. A St. Louis court upheld his contention but was overruled by the Missouri Supreme Court. Meanwhile, Scott was sold to another master. With the help of various sources, he carried his fight for freedom to a still higher court. In 1856, the final dispositon of his case came before the highest court of the land.

Of the nine justices composing the Supreme Court, five, including 70- year-old Chief Justice Roger B. Taney, were Southerners. At first, the judges tried to avoid the crucial issue. But eventually Taney announced that the questions of "peace and harmony" of the country required a settlement by judicial decision.

When Taney read his opinion, only one justice concurred with him. Five others read separate and varied concurring opinions, and two dissented. The Chief Justice ruled

Five free staters were massacred in Marais des Cygnes, Kansas, May 19, 1858, in an attempt to stop the spread of slavery.

that from the founding of the country blacks had been "considered as a subordinate and inferior class of beings." They therefore "had no rights which the white man was bound to respect."

Taney further declared that blacks could not rightfully become citizens of the United States, since the words of the Declaration of Independence and the Constitution were never meant to include blacks. Dred Scott therefore had no right even to bring the suit. Furthermore, Congress could not legally deprive slaveholders of their right to take human "articles of merchandise" into any part of the Union, North or South. In effect, the Supreme Court declared the Missouri Compromise and all other anti-slavery laws to be unconstitutional.

Taney's decree made the slaveholders and slave-catchers jubilant. But in the North and the West, great mass meetings were held in furious protest against this decision. White voters in ever greater numbers were driven toward the anti-slavery movement.

While some friends of freedom lost hope Frederick Douglass declared, "My hopes were never brighter than now. . . The Supreme Court is not the only power in this world . . . Judge Taney cannot bail out the ocean, annihilate the firm old earth or pluck the silvery star of liberty from our Northern sky."

CHAPTER CHECK

1. What were the terms of the Missouri Compromise of 1820? Why would Thomas Jefferson refer to the compromise as a "firebell in the night"?

2. What were the provisions of the Compromise of 1850? Why did neither side like it?

3. Why was there a rush to settle Kansas after the Kansas-Nebraska bill became law?

4. What was Chief Justice Taney's decision in the Dred Scott case?

5. Imagine . . . you are a free black living in a Northern state in 1851. What would be your reaction to the new Fugitive Slave Law of 1850?

Cleaning cotton with an early gin.

Main Events

1. In 1619, the first known African slaves landed in English America at Jamestown. Europeans enslaved millions of Africans to work in their New World colonies in the seventeenth and eighteenth centuries.

2. Southern colonies became dependent on African slaves to work on large plantations growing tobacco, rice, indigo and sugar cane.

3. The Declaration of Independence in 1776 failed to include freedom for slaves. In 1787, the Constitutional Convention decided to count slaves as "three-fifths of other persons."

4. Eli Whitney invented the cotton gin in 1792, which increased the South's need for slaves.

5. The Louisiana Purchase of 1803 opened up new territory for settlement by slave owners. The African slave trade was forbidden after 1807.

6. The Missouri Compromise of 1820 prohibited slavery in the western territory, north of the southern boundary of Missouri.

7. In 1831, the greatest slave revolt was led in Virginia by plowman and preacher Nat Turner.

8. In 1850, California came into the Union as a free state, but a harsh fugitive slave law was passed.

9. The Kansas-Nebraska Act of 1854 allowed new states to decide whether they would permit slavery.

10. The Dred Scott decision of 1857 made slavery "legal" throughout the Union.

Words to Know

Match the following words with their correct definitions. Number your paper from 1 to 16, and write the correct word beside each number.

abolitionist
annexation
artisan
bondsman
boycott
ginning
indentured worker
isthmus

Jim Crow
Mason-Dixon
Middle Passage
overseer
petition
secessionist
triangular trade
warrant

1. The process of separating cotton from seeds.
2. A written order giving the holder authority to take action.
3. The part of the Atlantic Ocean between Africa and the New World.
4. The traffic in goods between Africa, the Caribbean and North America.
5. Term applied to the legal separation of blacks from whites in everyday life.
6. The line that divided the slave-free North and the slave-holding South.
7. A person hired to manage property that the actual owner could not attend to.
8. Another word for slave.
9. Making a smaller territory a part of a nation.
10. A formal request from an organized group of people.
11. A person who called for the legal end of slavery.
12. A person who called for withdrawal from the Union.
13. Someone who served an employer for a specific amount of time.
14. An organized refusal by one group to deal with another group.
15. A narrow strip of land that joins two larger bodies of land.
16. A person trained in a skilled trade.

Thinking and Writing

A. Making Comparisons

Gabriel Prosser, Denmark Vesey and Nat Turner were different from most slaves because they openly revolted against slavery. They also lost their lives because of their actions.

Read through Chapter 9 quickly to find the following information: (a) the qualities that made these men different from most other slaves; (b) the reasons why they did what they did; and (c) what happened to their movements after they failed? Then, write several paragraphs explaining what type of person led a slave revolt and why? Explain why you think more slaves did not revolt. Give a title to your essay.

B. Seeing Both Sides

By the 1850s, it was becoming harder for the North and the South to reach a compromise over slavery. Both sections had developed sharp differences in their views. One major source of conflict was the issue of fugitive slaves.

Make a list giving all the reasons why Northerners opposed the Fugitive Slave Law of 1850. Make another list giving all the reasons why Southerners thought it was important. (Review Chapter 10 if you need to.) Then discuss how each section viewed this law and why you think compromise was difficult.

PART THREE

FREE MEN OF COLOR

1770 - 1850

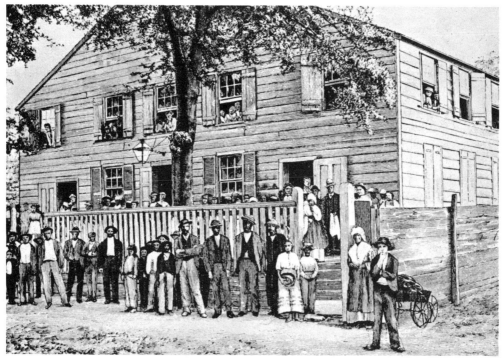

The First Baptist Church for black worshipers in Savannah, Georgia, built in 1776.

LOOKING AHEAD - PART THREE - 1770–1850

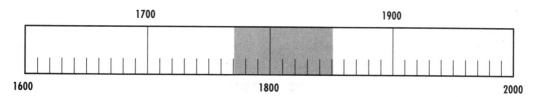

The majority of whites were determined to enforce slavery in America. Whether in the North or South, they fought to deny blacks their freedom. This included the freedom to worship. But colonial blacks were not to be denied. Repeatedly turned away from the white church, they started churches of their own.

The church became the only salvation for colonial blacks. This was despite the spirit and promise of the Revolutionary War. Denied the opportunity to fight for their country, blacks served in whatever ways they could. They helped build army installa-

tions and worked at menial jobs. They were accepted into the army only when they posed the danger of joining British troops. Participating in the Revolutionary War from beginning to end, few were to gain the freedom won by their white comrades. Black participation in the War of 1812 didn't gain freedom for blacks, either.

Black Americans had caught the spirit of freedom along with white Americans. But, while one enjoyed their independence, the other could not. Most free blacks dedicated themselves to freeing those still enslaved in the South. Many spoke and wrote about freedom. Meeting together with white abolitionists , they planned strategies for political action. These meetings resulted in the first Convention of Color. Held at Philadelphia in 1830, it was the first of many protests against slavery. Many blacks emerged as leaders.

Also stressed was the importance of education, and the value of training in literature, the sciences and the mechanical arts. These goals were not so easily achieved. Whether in the North or South, white resistance to education for blacks remained strong. The fate of Sarah Harris was a living example. When she was accepted as a non-resident student at Miss Prudence Crandall's boarding school in Connecticut, white parents promptly withdrew their daughters. Left without students, a determined Miss Crandall opened the school expressly for colored girls. Local villagers went wild, setting the building afire and polluting the school well. Seeing the school open despite their efforts, local officials made up new laws designed to close

down the school. That failing, a mob set out to destroy the property. Fearful for her students, Miss Crandall finally closed the school.

Paul Cuffee, a black sea captain, showing the first signs of nationalism, proposed a most daring idea. It was escape to Africa. Taking aboard 38 freed men and women, he sailed for Sierra Leone. Cuffee's successful return to Africa was to inspire the very controversial American Colonization Society. Led by rich slaveholders, the colonization society persuaded Congress to purchase territory in Africa. This territory was called Liberia. A decade later only 15,000 black Americans had signed on.

The American Colonization Society ended about 10 years before the Civil War. Many black and white abolitionists were happy about this. From the very beginning, they had opposed the idea of black Americans returning to Africa. For better or worse, America was their home, too, and black Americans were determined to make the most of its opportunities.

A shield with a likeness of Captain Paul Cuffee and his ship the *Traveller*.

Peter Salem, (left, with rifle) a hero at the Battle of Bunker Hill in 1775.

CHAPTER 10

Black Fighters for Freedom

In the North American colonies there was much chafing and muttering and talk of freedom from English tyranny. Since Britain's colonies existed chiefly for the purpose of enriching the mother country, they were taxed. Their products could seldom be sold to other countries except by way of England. And they could be shipped only in English or American ships. The British stamp had to be affixed to most items sold in the colonies. Imports were taxed and British officials were sent to enforce these regulations. And the colonists were required to support the royal troops.

"Taxation without representation" and the presence of British Redcoats in the streets of Boston angered the citizens. On March 5, 1770, a group of them threatened the British soldiers with snowballs and stones. The troops, in turn, fired upon the rebellious colonists. The first to be shot down was a former slave, Crispus Attucks, who had long ago run away from his master to become a seaman. Two other men fell dead that night, and two more lay mortally wounded. Several were less seriously injured. The people of Boston were so incensed at this attack that the British troops thought it best to withdraw to Castle Island. The body of Crispus Attucks was laid in state in Fanueil Hall. He was entombed in a common sepulchre, along with three of the other victims of the Boston Massacre, as thousands bared their heads at the cemetery.

Blacks in the American Revolution

From the earliest battles at Lexington and Concord, in the spring of 1775, to the proclamation of victory at Yorktown, Virginia, eight years later, blacks fought for American independence. Some 5,000, both slave and free, served under Washington's command.

When the Continental armies were formed, blacks were not welcomed and soon were officially barred. But when it was learned that the British had declared all slaves free who joined their side, the colonies became concerned about possible wholesale desertion of slaves to the enemy. They adopted various policies regarding the use of blacks. Some masters sent their slaves to war instead of going themselves.

Washington revoked an order prohibiting blacks from serving in the ranks. At Valley Forge, he agreed to the formation of an all-black unit in Rhode Island. Alexander Hamilton and James Madison not only urged enlistment of slaves, but argued for their freedom in return for service under arms. New York State passed a bill granting freedom to all slaves who served until honorably discharged.

In 1776, New York had passed a law allowing white men who had been drafted to send free blacks to enlist. By 1778, Massachusetts and Rhode Island allowed slaves to enroll in the services. Most blacks were integrated into the fighting groups with whites, in both the North and the South.

The Marquis de Lafayette, a French noble who praised the valor of black soldiers.

Bravery Under Fire

At the battle of Bunker Hill in 1775, Peter Salem became a hero when he shot a British officer. Another black, Salem Poor, won commendation as a "brave and gallant soldier." At the battle of Brandywine, Pennsylvania, in 1777, Edward Hector, "a giant Negro armed with a scythe," performed "great deeds of valor." That same year at Newport, Rhode Island, Jack Sisson, a black soldier, aided in the capture of a General Prescott.

In 1778, at the Battle of Rhode Island, the black regiment commissioned by Washington, thrice drove back Hessian troops who charged against them. In 1779, a black spy named Pompey supplied information leading to the victory of Stony Point. That year, too, during the siege of Savannah, several hundred Haitian blacks fought with American-allied French troops against the British. In 1781, a unit of black soldiers fought valiantly in defense of Colonel Greene at Points Bridge, New York. This was one of the war's bloodiest battles. Many soldiers were killed.

The Marquis de Lafayette, who came from France to aid the colonists, praised the valor of black soldiers. He also credited a black spy, James Armistead, with having helped to save his forces from defeat by British General Cornwallis.

In the Continental Navy, many black sailors served on gunboats. A black, "Captain" Mark Starlin of the Virginia navy, was commander of the *Patriot*. At war's end, despite his battle record, Starlin was re-enslaved by his old master.

The South Resists

Maryland was the only Southern state to take slaves openly into its army. In Virginia, it was illegal for slaves to serve. Yet some did, because in 1783, Virginia granted freedom to all slaves who had fought in the Continental Army.

Only Georgia and South Carolina resisted the enlistment of black soldiers to the end of the war. (Even they used slaves to build forts, tend horses, and as body servants to

Francis Marion, "the old swamp fox," and his brigade crossing the Pedee River in South Carolina, 1778.

Colonists protest the Stamp Act of 1765 by publicly burning stamps in Boston.

Colonists protest British tax by throwing 342 chests of tea into Boston Harbor.

officers.) But these states paid dearly. Between 1775 and 1783, some 25,000 black slaves in South Carolina escaped to British lines. And an equally large number ran away from Georgia to join the enemy. At the siege of Augusta, about a third of the troops manning Fort Cornwallis for the British were runaway slaves.

For several years after the war, a group of escaped slaves raided white settlements along the Savannah River. They called themselves "the King of England's soldiers."

Gallantry under fire notwithstanding, many masters sought to retain their slaves after the war. Many a British ship had left America with fleeing blacks aboard. Washington thought that some of his own slaves, still missing at the end of the war, might have sought refuge abroad.

At the close of the Revolution, freedom from Britain had not bought freedom for most black Americans.

CHAPTER CHECK

1. Why would the British offer freedom to any slave who joined their side?
2. Why do you think the colonists were so hesitant to use blacks at the beginning of the war? Why do you think Southern states never did officially enlist them in their armies?
3. How was the American Revolution important in the struggle for freedom of many black Americans?
4. Imagine . . . you are a slave in one of the Southern states. How would you react to the British offer of freedom to any slave who joined their side? Would you try to escape and join them, or would you attempt to get into the American army? Why?

Bethel African Methodist Episcopal Church, founded in Philadelphia in 1794.

CHAPTER 11

Separate Churches

Lemuel Haynes fought in the Continental Army at Ticonderoga, New York. He later became one of the first blacks in the United States to serve as a pastor for a white congregation. He headed various churches in Connecticut, Vermont and New York for many years. In the early days of slavery, some blacks, particularly in New England, were permitted to belong to otherwise white churches. But few preached in them. If blacks attended church services with whites, they were duly segregated.

It might be said that blacks in the colonies became Christians almost in spite of Christianity as it was practiced by their owners. Other than the Quakers, all sects sanctioned slavery. "Servant, obey your masters" was a familiar text in many pulpits.

In some communities serious attempts were made to Christianize slaves. Balconies were set aside for them in white churches.

But in many communities, slaves were forbidden to assemble for worship, because of the threat posed by large groups.

African religious rituals were forbidden. Drums were banned, since in Africa drums had been employed, not only for religious ceremonies, but also to send messages. Colonial planters feared the drums might be used on American plantations to signal a revolt. Slave rebellions that might flare up beyond control were a constant threat.

The planters feared, too, that the Bible might be interpreted by slaves as proving the brotherhood, and therefore the equality of all men, not excluding blacks. Besides, the Bible was a book. If slaves learned to read the Bible, they might come to read books with really dangerous thoughts in them. Religion had hard going in the Southern states. After the great slave revolts of the early nineteenth century, blacks almost everywhere in the South were prohibited

Peter Williams standing in the doorway of the John Street Methodist Church in New York.

A.M.E. Church founder, Richard Allen.

from preaching or gathering for any purpose whatsoever.

Among the free blacks of the North, conditions were different but they were not always welcome. Blacks seldom formed separate churches until they had been forced to withdraw from, or were denied access to, existing churches. A favorite text among them was: "Upon this rock I will build my church and the gates of hell shall not prevail against it." One of their favorite songs became "Go down, Moses, 'way down in Egypt land, and tell old Pharaoh to let my people go."

Pulled from his knees by a white usher, one Sunday while at prayer in the St. George Methodist Episcopal Church in Philadelphia, Richard Allen made a firm resolution to form a church where blacks could be sure of a welcome. A few years later, he founded the African Methodist Episcopal denomination. In Philadelphia, Allen established its first meeting house—Bethel—dedicated in 1794. He became its first bishop.

In New York, Peter Williams, sexton of the John Street Methodist Church, found his own people unwelcome there. In 1796, he led in the founding of what would become the A.M.E. Zion Church. From his earnings as a tobacco merchant, he financed the building of its first temple.

Black Baptists

Prior to the great slave rebellions which caused Southern whites to prohibit black churches, several large black Baptist congregations came into being in the South. In Virginia, churches were organized for black Baptists in Petersburg in 1776, in Richmond in 1780 and in Williamsburg in 1785. In Savannah, Georgia, George Liele founded a Baptist congregation for blacks in 1779. Under the pastorship there of Andrew Bryan, a slave, the first Baptist Church for black worshippers was built in 1796. Though white men sought to abolish this church by whipping its members and jailing Bryan, it continued to function. And in 1799, a second black Baptist Church was erected in Savannah.

In setting up their own houses of worship, blacks developed initiative, and encouraged capacities for leadership. Unable to take part in politics or to attend schools, and possessing no social centers, the blacks made their churches focal points for community activities.

From the churches emerged many distinguished leaders. One such leader was the Reverend Absalom Jones who, with Richard Allen, founded the **Free African Society** in Philadelphia. A civic and religious organization, it was of great help to the city during the devastating yellow fever epidemic of 1793.

Free African Society founder Absalom Jones.

Early in the nineteenth century, an increasing number of separate Baptist churches began to spring up. In 1805, a free black, Joseph Willis, founded such a church at Mound Bayou, Mississippi. The Reverend Thomas Paul, in 1809, established the first African Baptist Church in Boston. He later aided in the organization of the Abyssinian Baptist Church in New York. Abyssinian was to become the largest Baptist church in the world.

Methodists, Presbyterians and Episcopalians

Meanwhile, the separate Methodist, Presbyterians and Episcopalians sects continued to spread. In 1818, the African Methodist Church, under the leadership of the Reverend Morris Brown, listed more than a thousand members in Charleston. But, after the Denmark Vesey rebellion of 1822, this church was forced to suspend services. Morris Brown fled to the North, where he later became a bishop.

When white Methodists refused to ordain black elders, the black Zionites, under the leadership of Charles Anderson, George Collins, Christopher Rush and James Varick, themselves elected and ordained a number of black elders. In 1822, Varick became their first bishop. Rush later became a bishop of the A.M.E. Zion Church.

Separatism first appeared among Presbyterians in 1807, when John Gloucester organized the First African Presbyterian Church in Philadelphia. In 1819, St. Philip's Episcopal Church was opened for blacks in New York City, with Peter Williams, Jr. as its first rector. And in 1829, the black Dixwell Avenue Congregational Church was established in New Haven, Connecticut.

Traveling black evangelists of various faiths, preached to large groups of both blacks and whites, South as well as North. One, known as Uncle Jack, preached to both masters and slaves from plantation to plantation in Virginia. In the early 1800s, Black Harry, sometimes alone and at other times accompanying the white Bishop Asbury, attracted large audiences. Harry Evans so stirred up the people of both races in Fayetteville, North Carolina, that the city officials tried to stop him from preaching. At Upper Sandusky, Ohio, John Stewart, a free black, became the first Methodist Episcopal missionary working among the Wyandots.

CHAPTER CHECK

1. Why were African religious practices banned in the states?
2. Why did most planters refuse to let their slaves read the Bible? Why did many communities refuse to allow slaves to assemble for worship?
3. Why did blacks in the North establish their own churches?
4. What important functions did black churches provide free blacks?
5. Imagine . . . you are a free black minister in the North. Would you establish your own black church or try to work within an existing church? Why?

A black sailor at the Battle of Lake Champlain.

CHAPTER 12

At War with Britain Again

When the City of Washington was captured by the British in the War of 1812, Philadelphia requested help to defend it from a similar fate. Among the leading citizens asked to help were Bishop Richard Allen and the Reverend Absalom Jones. They recruited more than 2,500 black men, who worked almost two days at Gray's Ferry. The **battalion** was on the verge of marching, but saw no action because peace was declared.

A number of blacks served in the Navy on the Great Lakes. After the Battle of Lake Erie, Captain Oliver H. Perry praised them highly. Concerning a black man named John Johnson who was killed in a naval battle, Commander Nathaniel Shaler said, "When America has such tars (sailors), she has little to fear from the tyrants of the ocean."

New York State passed a bill providing for the formation of two regiments of color for the Army. General Andrew Jackson, in preparing for the battle of New Orleans, called all free blacks to the ranks. He stated,

John Randolf's will set his slaves free upon his death.

"Through a mistaken policy, you have heretofore been deprived of participation in the glorious struggle for national rights in which our country is engaged. This no longer shall exist."

On January 8, 1815, two battalions of men of color took such a valiant part in the battle of New Orleans that Andrew Jackson declared, "I expected much from you . . . but you surpassed my hopes . . . Soldiers, the President of the United States shall be informed of your conduct on the present occasion; and the voice of the Representatives of the American nation shall applaud your valor, as your General now praises your ardor."

Many slaves took part in the War of 1812, hoping to become free afterward. It did bring freedom to some, but others were returned to their masters at the end of hostilities. As in the Revolution, slaves were encouraged by the British to escape to their ranks on the promise of freedom. Some earned their liberty this way. Others were sold into new **bondage** in the Caribbean. At the end of the war, the United States demanded payment guaranteed by the Treaty of Ghent for all confiscated property, including slaves. Eventually the British paid more than a million dollars.

The gallantry shown by black soldiers was forgotten, however, not long after the smoke of the battle cleared.

Back to Africa?

Shortly after the close of the war, a black sea captain, Paul Cuffee of Massachusetts, took 38 black people aboard one of his own vessels. They set sail for Sierra Leone in Africa. Cuffee paid all of their expenses out of his own pocket. His purpose was to settle the blacks so that they might instruct the Africans in agriculture and mechanics and find a better life for themselves.

It was not the first time someone had proposed taking blacks back to Africa. Fifty years earlier, men like Thomas Jefferson had thought it feasible to combine gradual emancipation with deportation.

To many Southerners, the presence of free blacks was a threat to the institution of slavery. "A free African population," said a South Carolina judge, "is a curse to any country . . . and corrupters of the slaves."

In the North, with its **immigration** of Irish and German workers, the competition of black labor made free blacks unwelcome. Colonization, dramatized by Cuffee's voyage, was a way to diminish the number of free blacks.

Within a few years of Cuffee's experiment, the American Colonization Society was formed. It was led by such prominent slaveholders as John C. Calhoun, Henry Clay, John Randolph and Bushrod Washington. They persuaded Congress to purchase territory in Africa. They named it Liberia after the word "Liberty" and its capital Monrovia after President Monroe.

At the very outset, the society was attacked by free blacks and white abolitionists alike. In 1817, an audience of 3,000 Philadelphians heard black leaders Richard Allen, Absalom Jones and James Forten brand the society as an "outrage" formed for the benefit of slave-holding interests.

The first group of black colonists set sail for Liberia in 1820. Ten years later, some 1,400 blacks had been settled in the colony. But it was a slow trickle. Hartford blacks asked, "Why should we leave this land so dearly bought by the blood, groans and

Joseph Roberts, first President of Liberia.

tears of our fathers? This is our home; here let us live and here let us die."

Under heavy assault, colonization died. Hardly 15,000 blacks left American shores.

Work and Freedom

Like Crispus Attucks and Paul Cuffee, many free blacks were seamen. Few free blacks were farmers. Most of them lived in urban centers. Those in Southern towns who had a knowledge of certain skilled trades were usually able to work at them. More than 50 trades, however, were closed to blacks. In the North, they often encountered opposition from competing white workers. German and Irish immigrants at times resorted to violence against them.

The greater number of free blacks, however, had no special skills. To earn a living they worked at common tasks from street-cleaning to ditch-digging. Most of the women were domestic servants, some were seamstresses. A few became teachers. Some people went into business as street

Black and white oarsmen worked side by side in the whaling industry. Below: Occupations held by free blacks in colonial America.

Chimney sweep

Servant

vendors, barbers, sailmakers, carpenters, brickmasons, tailors and shopkeepers.

In Baltimore, in 1860, there were several black grocers and druggists. In Atlanta, there was a black dentist, Roderick Badger. In Creole New Orleans, where color lines were less harsh, there were even architects and lithographers of color. A young slave doctor, James Derham, worked out his freedom as an assistant to a white Dr. Dove, then set up his own office. By 1861, free people of color in New Orleans owned more than $15 million worth of property.

A few free blacks achieved considerable wealth. Paul Cuffee owned several sailing ships. In Louisiana, Cyprian Ricard owned almost a hundred slaves who worked his large acreage. In North Carolina, a successful black cabinetmaker, Thomas Day, employed a white helper. Solomon Humphries, a black grocer in Macon, Georgia, left at his death an estate valued at $20,000, including a number of slaves.

But these men were unusual, for most free blacks existed on meager earnings. Many had escaped to freedom with no possessions, no skills and no education. Fortunately, as more and more white people headed West during the nineteenth century, Northern urban communities began to experience a labor shortage. So blacks could usually find some sort of work to do. Certainly only a very, very few free blacks ever voluntarily went back into slavery.

Hardships Endured

The fear of re-enslavement shadowed free blacks everywhere. Generally not allowed to testify in their own behalf, or to bear witness against whites in court, a black, once taken in tow by the slave-catchers, had small chance to escape. With practically no political power, people of color exercised no control over laws or lawmakers. In the South, blacks were allowed no firearms, watch-dogs, poisons or alcoholic beverages.

For even the petty crimes, courts dealt them harsh sentences. In North Carolina, a free black boy was hanged for allegedly taking five dollars' worth of candy from the home of a white "lady of great respectability." Legally, the lash might be used on free blacks as well as slaves in the South. And some courts even sentenced free blacks into slavery for misdemeanors.

Free people of color in most Southern communities were required to carry passes. Their freedom of movement was severely restricted. In some Southern states it was

Fruit vendor

Watercartman

Illustration from an anti-slavery journal showing a freeman being enslaved by Northerners.

against the law for free blacks who left the state to return, no matter how many relatives they left behind.

Lacking most of the rights of citizenship, free blacks in most localities were nevertheless taxed equally. In Baltimore, blacks paid school taxes, although black children were not allowed to attend the city schools. Outside of some areas in New England, free blacks could not vote.

Ohio excluded black people from the **franchise** (right to vote) in 1803. Other states followed, and by 1846, 93 percent of Northern black men were excluded. Only in Massachusetts, New Hampshire, Vermont and Maine did black men vote on an equal basis with whites. Three times between 1827 and 1841, the free blacks of Cincinnati were run out of town by mobs. In 1839, whites burned the black section of Pittsburgh. During the 1830s there were anti-black riots in a number of cities in New York State. In 1834, a three-day reign of terror gripped Philadelphia.

None of these things kept blacks from their striving to be free. One ex-slave known as Uncle Sandy had purchased his freedom for $1,500. When the slave-catcher tried to take him, he plunged a knife into his own hip, cut the muscles of his ankle, then chopped off the fingers of one hand with a hatchet to render himself useless for work. With knife in hand, he dared the slavers to touch him. With all its hardships, freedom was ever preferable to slavery.

CHAPTER CHECK

1. How did blacks participate in the War of 1812?
2. What was the American Colonization Society? Why was it not successful?
3. What was life like for most free blacks in America before the Civil War?
4. Imagine . . . you are a free black. How would you feel about the American Colonization Society?

Charles Sumner,
Radical Republican Senator.

Robert Morris, who fought
against school segregation in Boston.

CHAPTER 13

The Drive for Education

To acquire an education was the burning desire of most free blacks, especially those who had been slaves. Only a few Northern communities, and no Southern ones, had free public schools open to blacks. Ohio, from 1829 to 1849, excluded blacks from the public schools. Most of the other Western states made little or no provision for them.

In 1834, the City of New York took over the support of its seven African Free Schools. The first of these schools had been founded by the Manumission Society in 1787, with a white teacher, Cornelia Davis. Thus black children had free education available to them in New York years before there were public schools for white children.

The African Free School became the forerunner of the New York free public school system. Later, Manhattan's African schools had black men and women teachers.

Many distinguished persons were graduated from them, including artist Patrick Reason, statesman Henry Highland Garnet and actor Ira Aldridge.

In 1849, Benjamin F. Roberts sued the city of Boston, Massachusetts, on behalf of his daughter Sarah. He accused them of discrimination for refusing to admit Sarah to a white school. (**Discrimination** is the act of treating people differently, usually because they belong to a different group.) Her lawyer was Charles Sumner, who was to become a noted abolitionist Senator. Sumner's legal assistant was Robert Morris, a young black attorney. Their case was lost. But in 1855, the Massachusetts legislature addressed the same issue. It stated that "no person shall be excluded from a Public School on account of race, color or religious opinions."

In the South, of course, the few educational facilities which existed for free blacks were illegal. Often the teaching of blacks had to be concealed. For 30 years, a black preacher, John Chavis, conducted a school in Raleigh, North Carolina. He taught black students by night and white students by day. He had to dismiss his black students after Nat Turner's rebellion in 1831.

The first black student to graduate from an American college was John Russwurm. Russwurm received a degree from Maine's Bowdoin College in 1826. Oberlin College in Ohio, in 1834, put to its white students a questionnaire "as to the practicability of admitting persons of color." Oberlin was one of the first colleges in the West to enroll not only blacks, but women. It had been established by abolitionists who had withdrawn from Lane Theological Seminary in Cincinnati after the school ended free discussion of the evils of slavery.

Berea College in Kentucky freely admitted blacks as well as whites. It was set up by an anti-slavery editor and an abolitionist minister in 1855. Its **charter** began with the phrase: "God hath made of one blood all nations that dwell upon the face of the earth."

Cover of Benjamin Banneker's *Almanac.*

A drawing of New York's African Free School by black artist Patrick Reason.

But most institutions of higher learning still had no place for free blacks. Colleges especially for the education of black youth had to be established. Wilberforce in Ohio (1856) and Ashmun Institute (later renamed Lincoln University) in Pennsylvania (1854) were among the first colleges for black youth. Wilberforce was supported by the Methodist Episcopal Church and Lincoln by the Presbyterian Church.

Arts and Sciences

Benjamin Banneker was a black man of many interests. He studied mathematics, the stars and the cycle of the four seasons. He also believed in the advantages of peace over war, as well as the abolition of slavery. After the age of 60, Banneker had achieved such distinction that Thomas Jefferson presented his name to President George Washington for membership on the commission to survey and plan the city of Washing-

ton. For two years, Banneker carried out his work. Then he returned to his farm in Maryland. There he continued writing and publishing an annual **almanac** which was popular in American households until 1802.

Banneker was born near Baltimore in 1731, and learned to read from his grandmother. She was an English woman who had been an indentured servant. Eventually, she herself owned slaves and married one of them. Little Benjamin went to a private school and displayed a talent for mechanical sciences. While still a young man, he made the first wooden clock in America. But it was not until he was in his 50s that Banneker became absorbed in astronomy. (**Astronomy** is the science about the motion, size and makeup of the stars, planets and comets.) In 1789, Banneker predicted a solar eclipse with astonishing accuracy.

In 1793, he published an article in his almanac by Philadelphian Benjamin Rush. It

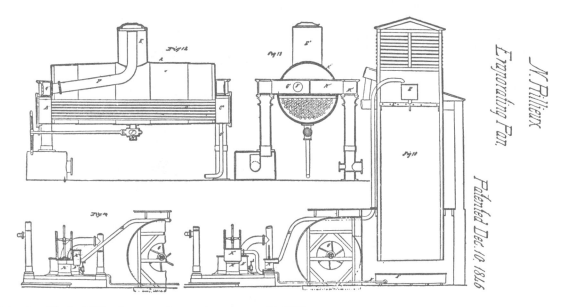

A drawing of Norbert Rillieux's evaporating pan. It was patented in 1846.

was called *A Plan of Peace-Office for the United States.* It recommended that a Secretary of Peace be appointed to the Cabinet. It also suggested that militia laws, military titles, parades and uniforms, which fascinate the minds of young men, be done away with. He concluded that "were there no uniforms, there would probably be no armies."

Another free black with a creative mind was Norbert Rillieux. He was born in New Orleans in 1806 and educated in France. Rillieux made a most important contribution to the advance of the sugar industry. In the 1840s he invented an evaporating pan that revolutionized the refining of raw sugar. Rillieux established the scientific principles that form the basis of most modern industrial evaporation.

During the same period, Charles L. Reason achieved distinction as an educator. He headed the Institute for Colored Youth in Philadelphia. He was also appointed professor of literature at a white institution, Central College, in McGrawville, New York.

Elizabeth Taylor Greenfield, the "Black Swan," achieved considerable fame as a singer. Frances E. W. Harper was a poet and speaker. Edmonia Lewis was a sculptor. Patrick Reason fashioned the massive coffin plate for Daniel Webster's funeral.

The Written Word

All of the black writers of the period before the Civil War had a cause to plead: freedom for the slaves. Free black intellectuals devoted the major portion of their talents to that cause, often neglecting the profession for which they had trained. The physician, James McCune Smith, was a graduate of the University of Glasgow, Scotland. He devoted as much time to the

The Reverend Dr. J.W.C. Pennington, historian.

Dr. James McCune Smith, physician, scientist, and abolitionist.

William Wells Brown

anti-slavery struggle, if not more, than he did to medicine. The Reverend J. W. C. Pennington, held the degree of Doctor of Divinity from the University of Heidelberg, Germany. He preached against slavery from New England to Europe and frequently wrote about the condition of his people.

The titles of many of Frances E. W. Harper's poems, such as "The Slave Auction" and "Bury Me in a Free Land," indicate clearly where her chief interest lay. William Wells Brown, one of the first black novelists in America, had trained as an apprentice printer with the abolitionist editor Elijah P. Lovejoy. Brown became an agent of the Western Massachusetts Anti-Slavery Society. His popular novel, *Clotel, or The President's Daughter,* was published in London in 1853, and in the United States in 1864.

Only the free Creole black writers of Louisiana, many of them educated in Paris, expressed little interest in the problems of bondage and of race. In their collection of poems, *Les Cenelles,* edited by Armand Lanusse and published in New Orleans in 1845, there is much about lovely ladies, sunsets and love, but nothing about slavery.

The Convention Movement

Almost all free blacks were outspoken against slavery. Some became outstanding abolitionists, speakers and organizers of meetings and conventions.

At Philadelphia, in the autumn of 1830, blacks from seven states met to discuss their problems. They also published an *Address to Free People of Color of These United States.* Out of this meeting grew the first National Convention of Colored People, which convened for six days the following June. They passed a number of resolutions, among them, one favoring the continued settlement of blacks in Canada. They also passed another resolution opposing any plans for repatriation to Africa.

From this time on, large groups of blacks continued to hold meetings in various Northern cities to protest against slavery, to petition state legislatures and Congress for freedom for their brothers in bondage, and to bolster, with oratory and resolutions, the continuing struggle for the achievement of full citizenship.

As a means to that end, the conventions stressed the importance of education for blacks, and the value of training in literature, the sciences and the mechanical arts.

Among the outstanding organizers and speakers in the convention movements were William Wells Brown, Samuel Cornish, John B. Vashon, Robert Purvis and the Presbyterian minister Henry Highland Garnet. At the Buffalo Convention of Colored Citizens, held in 1843, the Reverend Garnet urged blacks to "Arise! Strike for your lives and liberties . . . Rather die free men than live to be slaves . . . Let your motto be resistance . . . No oppressed people have secured their liberty without resistance."

People's Independent Ticket.

Members to State Council.

PHILADELPHIA:
Rev. J. CLINTON,
R. PURVIS,
BENJAMIN B. MOORE,
ALPHONSO M. SUMNER,
DAVID B. BOWSER,
JAMES MAC. CRUMMILL,
ROBERT COLLINS,
J. J. G. BIAS,
SAMUEL WILLIAMS,
Rev. ADAM S. DRIVER,
JAMES H. WILSON, M. D.
FRANCIS A. DUTERTE.
S. VAN BRAKLE.
WEST PHILADELPHIA:
Rev. WILLIAM JACKSON.
HARRISBURG:
Rev. E. BENNET,
GEORGE W. CARR.
PITTSBURG:
H. WALTERS,
Rev. LEWIS WOODSON.
P. JACKSON,
Rev. A. R. GREEN.

An election leaflet
listing free black candidates in Philadelphia.

An 1854 convention of free blacks ended its resolution: "We advise all oppressed to adopt the motto, Liberty or Death." This clause was considered so revolutionary that the convention voted it down. But everywhere it was clear that no black wanted slavery. And few wanted colonization in Africa.

These conventions had the aid and some participation of prominent white abolitionists. Among them were Benjamin Lundy, Arthur Tappan and William Lloyd Garrison.

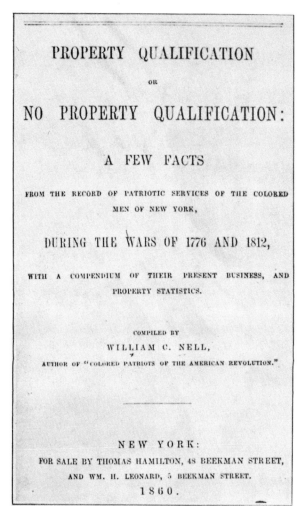

Title page of William C. Nell's book on the service of black soldiers during the Revolutionary War and the War of 1812.

Henry Highland Garnet, minister, editor and orator.

They made the entire country aware of their sentiments and did much to disprove the charge of black inferiority. Though methods differed as to how their goals should be achieved, there was great unity among blacks on the goals themselves: freedom and citizenship.

CHAPTER CHECK

1. Why was it important for most free blacks to acquire an education?
2. Why was education forbidden to most free blacks in the South?
3. How did Benjamin Banneker contribute to the early history of the United States?
4. How did black intellectuals help in the anti-slavery movement?
5. What was the Convention Movement? Why do you think it came into being? Why do you think it grew more radical over time?
6. Imagine . . . you are a Northern black student in the early nineteenth century. What is your education like? How does it compare with education today?

Black riflemen help the American colonists to win the battle of New Orleans.

Main Events

1. On March 5, 1770, the first person to be shot in the Boston Massacre was a former slave named Crispus Attucks.

2. During the American Revolution, both the English and the Americans sought the aid of blacks. Many slaves fought on each side and won their freedom.

3. Following the war, most free blacks in the North, and some in the South, formed their own churches.

4. Unable to take part in politics and lacking social centers, blacks made their churches focal points for community activities.

5. Most free blacks lived in urban centers and existed on meager earnings, although some did work in skilled trades.

6. By 1840, blacks had been denied the right to vote on the same basis as whites in all states except Maine, New Hampshire, Vermont, and Massachusetts.

7. The first of the African Free Schools in New York City was started in 1787. This became the forerunner of the New York free public school system.

8. Free black intellectuals, such as Frances E. W. Harper and William Wells Brown, devoted most of their talents to obtaining freedom for the slaves.

9. In 1830, blacks met in Philadelphia, for the first of many conventions addressing the many problems which black Americans faced.

Black children being denied entrance to a school.

Words to Know

Match the following words with their correct definitions. Number your paper from 1 to 9, and write the correct word beside each number.

almanac   discrimination
astronomy franchise
battalion   Free African Society
bondage   immigration
charter

1. right to vote
2. the act of treating people differently, usually because they belong to a different group
3. an official document establishing an organization or college
4. a publication that contains information about the skies and the weather
5. the science about the motion and makeup of the stars and planets
6. a civic and religious organization, set up by Richard Allen, to help the citizens of Philadelphia
7. the state of being held in captivity
8. a company of soldiers
9. the act of residing in a country of which one is not a native

Thinking and Writing

A. Making a Chart

It is often useful to organize information in chart form. All the important facts can be put on one page and grouped with the same kind of information. Copy the chart below onto a piece of paper. Fill in your chart using information from Chapter 13. **Hint:** Look through the chapter quickly to find the names of the artists and scientists. Then read about the contributions that they made to American society. Pick out the dates of their major works.

ARTISTS OR SCIENTISTS	MAJOR WORKS OR CONTRIBUTIONS	DATE

B. Writing a Letter

Many of the soldiers fighting in the American Revolution were slaves. Imagine that you are a black soldier in either the American or English army. Write a letter to a friend describing your experiences. Give some facts about your life. Tell how you got into the army and what you do there. Then discuss your feelings. Why did you join the army? Why did you choose to fight for that side?

PART FOUR

THE NORTH STAR

1660-1865

A Union soldier reading the Emancipation Proclamation to a group of blacks in the South.

LOOKING AHEAD · PART FOUR · 1660–1865

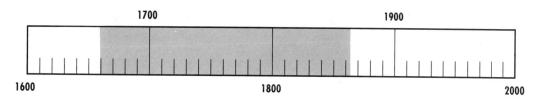

The campaign to end slavery was a partnership between blacks and whites. The most prominent blacks were former slaves, and the most prominent whites came from the northeastern United States.

As early as 1773, slaves petitioned for their freedom in Massachusetts. In 1775, Philadelphia Quakers organized an anti-slavery society. During the Revolutionary War, slaves and free blacks presented petitions to the Massachusetts legislature. There would be another war before they attained their goal.

The American struggle against slavery began in earnest in the 1820s. It was fought largely with words—both on the lecture stage and in a large number of publications. Speakers like the former slave Frederick Douglass, Bostonian Wendell Phillips, and Quaker Lucretia Mott were skilled at appealing to the consciences of white Americans.

Anti-slavery journals kept the fight going, but they also aroused the anger of white bigots. No publication had a more powerful influence than William Lloyd Garrison's *Liberator*. It was neither the first nor alone in its crusade for black equality. By 1840, the American Anti-Slavery Society had published more than two dozen journals. But their effectiveness was confined to the North.

The most powerful black voice was that of Frederick Douglass. Born a slave, he escaped the shackles of bondage to become a spokesmen against slavery and against oppression throughout the world. Douglass became a living example of his conviction that "he who has endured the cruel pangs of Slavery is the man to advocate Liberty."

The spirit of Douglass' words were carried in the antislavery politics of free blacks and their belief in the vote. But the power of the ballot was a painfully slow process. While the struggle went on, millions of blacks remained in bondage.

Slavery's foes began to rescue slaves who

Members of the House of Representatives and spectators cheer when the Thirteenth Amendment is passed.

Presentation of colors to the 20th Colored Infantry New York, March 1864.

would escape. They built an "underground railroad" which provided escapees a secret route North. Leading the way as a "conductor" on the **Underground Railroad**, Harriet Tubman, herself a former slave, engaged the help of white friends. They oriented themselves by the North Star, which became a symbol of their movement. Together they hid hundreds of fugitive slaves in their escape into the North. By the beginning of the Civil War, 50,000 others are estimated to have escaped to freedom. During these escapes, the risks were high. There were many failed attempts in which "conductors" were jailed, and some paid with their lives.

Slaveholders were influential in the federal government, and they were alarmed about the loss of slaves. In 1850, Congress passed a **Fugitive Slave Law**, making it a crime to harbor escaped slaves and offering a fee for capturing them. Now the anti-slavery forces had two problems: helping slaves escape and protecting them from recapture.

In 1852, a New England minister's wife with six children wrote a novel that dramatized the crime of slavery. In *Uncle Tom's Cabin*, Harriet Beecher Stowe made the plight of slaves come to life. Banned in the

Black volunteers line up outside recruiting office.

South, the book was a runaway best-seller in the North. It galvinized Northern opposition to slavery among an even broader group.

Another white, John Brown, was even more determined to end slavery. In 1859, he led 21 men in a raid of the arsenal at Harper's Ferry. By distributing arms to local slaves, he hoped to arouse a revolt across the South. The plot failed, and Brown was hung. But the spirit of his rebellion was to survive in the the tune of "John Brown's Body," which Union troops sang in the Civil War.

Pressure to end slavery became even more intense during the mid-nineteenth cen-

A black soldier standing guard at a Union storehouse.

Cavalrymen bringing in Confederate prisoners.

tury. And so did the resolve of Southern planters that they would rather leave the Union than loose their way of doing business. In general, the Democratic party supported them.

In a Senate campaign speech in 1858, Republican Abraham Lincoln declared, "A house divided against itself cannot stand. I believe this government cannot endure permanently half-slave and half-free." Three years later, as President, he would see his words come true. The South had left the Union, and the Union would not let it go without a fight.

But even the federal government held an odd attitude about black Americans. The War Department said it had "no intention to call into the service of the Government any colored soldiers." It did not matter that much of the war was over the issue of slavery. While Douglass and others urged the government to enlist black troops, tens of thousands of slaves escaped from slavery. Countless others helped to build the hospitals and barracks needed for war. Many slaves supplied invaluable information about enemy forces and delivered materials for Union troops. Eventually, Washington changed its mind. Blacks were accepted into the Union army. By the end of the War, 186,000 black Americans had enlisted in the Union Army, and some 38,000 had died to save the nation.

On January 1, 1863, President Lincoln issued the Emancipation Proclamation. This freed black Americans from slavery in the rebellious states. Not until the Thirteenth Amendment was passed in 1865 was slavery finally outlawed in all the United States.

WALKER'S

APPEAL,

IN FOUR ARTICLES,

TOGETHER WITH

A PREAMBLE,

TO THE

COLORED CITIZENS OF THE WORLD,

BUT IN PARTICULAR, AND VERY EXPRESSLY TO THOSE OF THE

UNITED STATES OF AMERICA.

Written in B ston, in the State of Massachusetts, Sept. 28, 1829.

SECOND EDITION, WITH CORRECTIONS, &c.

BY DAVID WALKER.

1830.

Frontispiece and title page for David Walker's *Appeal.*

CHAPTER 14

Petitions for Liberty

When the eminent New England minister Cotton Mather drafted his rules for slave behavior in 1693, he permitted blacks to sing, preach and pray. He also required them to inform on runaways and to promise not to seek freedom for themselves.

Seven years later, another citizen of Massachusetts, Samuel Sewall, published one of the first anti-slavery tracts printed in the colonies. *The Selling of Joseph* began with these words: "Forasmuch as Liberty is in real value next unto Life: None ought to part with it themselves, or deprive others of it, but upon most mature Consideration." For his tract Sewall received only "frowns and hard words." But so strongly did he believe, that he boldly reprinted the tract for many years.

Few American blacks could read, but they had ears. A few knew that some white citizens were on the side of freedom for the blacks. There are records as early as 1661 of individual slaves petitioning for their own **manumission** (freedom). During the American Revolution, the number of people supporting **abolition** (an end) of slavery increased.

In 1773, "The humble Petition of many slaves, living in the Town of Boston," praying "for such Relief as is consistent with your Wisdom, Justice and Goodness" was presented to the governor of Massachusetts and the colonial legislature.

Quakers like John Woolman, Benjamin Franklin, Dr. Benjamin Rush and Anthony Benezet openly encouraged blacks to seek the abolition of slavery.

Thomas Paine's first article, "African Slavery in America," appeared in a Pennsylvania paper in 1775. Paine was co-author of a law adopted in Pennsylvania in 1780 which gradually abolished slavery in that state.

Many colonists realized the inconsistency of fighting for national freedom while upholding slavery. In 1775, a group of Philadelphia Quakers organized the first American anti-slavery society.

As early as 1777, blacks petitioned the Massachusetts legislature to end the slave trade. In 1788, a group of free blacks tried again to get the legislature to end slave trading and the sale of free blacks into slavery. This group was lead by Prince Hall, who had fought in the Revolutionary War. In 1797, the first petition to the Congress of the United States by blacks was presented by a group of free men from the South living in Philadelphia. They asked that their freedom be protected. Congress declined even to receive the petition.

Prince Saunders,
Northern abolitionist.

Lunsford Lane,
anti-slavery agent from
Raleigh, North Carolina.

Charles B. Ray,
a leader of the American and
Foreign Anti-Slavery Society.

Robert Purvis,
an organizer of the first
convention of free black

Black Abolitionists

After the Revolution, free blacks became increasingly active in the anti-slavery movement. Some of them had fought in the war. Others had escaped to freedom during the war or had gained freedom through military service. All of them had heard the words "liberty" and "freedom" over and over. They sought freedom for the millions still in bondage.

Pulpit, platform and press were turned over to their use, and the demand grew for political action. Petitions were drawn up and presented to embarrassed, more often enraged, state legislatures. "Life" the free blacks had, but "liberty" was precarious. And "the pursuit of happiness" still a far-distant goal.

Techniques for achieving freedom for all blacks varied from preaching and praying, speaking and organizing, to outright demands for violence. David Walker, free-born but the son of a slave father, hated slavery so intensely that he moved from North Carolina to Massachusetts. There he became a leader in the Massachusetts General Colored Association. In 1829, Walker published the first edition of his famous *Appeal*. Within a year it went into three printings, greatly stirring all blacks who could read and infuriating the slave forces. It asked, in part:

> Can our condition be any worse? Can it be more mean and abject? If there are any changes, will they not be for the better, though they may appear for the worst at first? Can they get us any lower? Where can they get us?... How would they like for us to make slaves of, and hold them in cruel slavery, and murder them as they do us?

Freedom's Journals

A journal with six subscribers was one of the first anti-slavery newspapers. Benjamin Lundy was the white editor who began publishing his *Genius of Universal Emancipation*

Jermain Loguen, escaped slavery in Tennessee.

Charles Lenox Ramond, a delegate to the London Anti-Slavery Conference.

Charles L. Reason, professor of literature at New York Central College.

Samuel Ringgold Ward, pastor of a New York Presbyterian church.

in 1821—first from Mt. Pleasant, Ohio, then Greenville, Tennessee, and finally from Baltimore—in his long effort to secure freedom for the black man. Within 20 years, there were dozens of energetic editors, white and black, knitting together the abolitionist movement in thousands of towns and villages across America. Readers were urged to vote, to petition, to debate, to refute, to protest!

These journals were a power, although many of them were cut down almost overnight. Others maintained a continuing influence, such as the *National Anti-Slavery Standard*, the *National Era* and the *Anti-Slavery Bugle*. One white editor, Elijah Parish Lovejoy, lost his life in defense of abolition. Lovejoy, who was also a clergyman, first attacked slavery in a religious paper, the St. Louis *Observer*. When that paper was attacked, he moved across the Mississippi River to Alton, Illinois, where he published the Alton *Observer*. After three of his presses were wrecked, Lovejoy came to the defense of a

new press in November 1837. "Before God and you all, I here pledge myself to continue it, if need be till death." With five bullets in his body, Lovejoy died, defending his press.

Three times mobs wrecked the Cincinnati office of the *Philanthropist*. The life of its editor, James Birney, was often threatened. A Philadelphia mob destroyed the office of John Greenleaf Whittier's *Pennsylvania Freeman* in 1838. Cassius Clay's *True American*, launched in Lexington in 1845, had been published only three months when 60 townsmen deported the press to Cincinnati.

Black Journalists

Black newspapers had an even harder time getting born. Few survived the rigors of publishing without funds or advertising. *Freedom's Journal* was the earliest to appear, in 1827. It was edited by Samuel E. Cornish, pastor of the African Presbyterian Church in New York, and John Russwurm. When Russwurm left for Liberia, Reverend Cornish continued the paper until 1830 under the

Masthead of *The Philanthropist,* an abolitionist journal published by the Ohio State Anti-Slavery Society.

William Lloyd Garrison, abolitionist editor.

Wendell Phillips, abolitionist orator.

name of *Rights of All*. In 1837 he put out with Phillip Bell, the *Colored American*.

In another year, New York saw David Ruggles' *The Mirror of Liberty*. In the 1840s came Stephen Myer's *Elevator in Albany*, and William Allen's and Henry Highland Garnet's *National Watchman* in Troy. Westward, in Pittsburgh, Martin R. Delany issued the *Mystery* in 1843.

The most influential black journalist of his time was Frederick Douglass. He published his first paper, the *North Star*, from 1847 to 1851 in Rochester, New York. He later served as editor and publisher of three other papers—*Frederick Douglass' Paper*, *Douglass' Monthly*, and the *New National Era* until 1873.

Garrison and Phillips

The most important abolitionist newspaper—William Lloyd Garrison's *Liberator*—had its roots in Baltimore. In 1829, when Gar-

rison was 24 years-old, he joined Lundy's *Genius*. The young editor served seven weeks in jail for denouncing a ship-owner who was busily profiting from the coastal slave trade. Released when Arthur Tappan paid the fine, Garrison made his way to Boston. He announced "I have a system to destroy, and I have no time to waste."

When the first issue of the *Liberator* appeared on New Year's Day, 1831, its rhymed Salutation informed the world:

To date my being from the opening year,
I come, a stranger in this busy sphere,
Where some I meet perchance may pause
and ask,
What is my name, my purpose, or my task?
My name is 'LIBERATOR'! I propose
To hurl my shafts at freedom's deadliest foes!
My task is hard—for I am charged to save
Man from his brother!—to redeem the slave!

A cartoon of Garrison (right) and South Carolina secessionist Laurence M. Keitt suggests that they conspired to destroy the Union.

Phillips speaking against slavery in Boston.

In the editorial that followed, Garrison promised his readers, "I will be as harsh as truth, and as uncompromising as justice. On this subject I do not wish to think, or speak, or write, with moderation."

Garrison quickly became the leading and most militant voice among the white abolitionists. He was one of the founders of the New England and the American Anti-Slavery Societies. A frequent participant in black conventions and an opponent of African colonization, along with Arthur Tappan, he was burned in effigy in Charleston.

In 1835, a mob raided a meeting of the Boston Female Anti-Slavery Society at which Garrison was speaking. With cries of "Lynch him!" they dragged him through the streets. The scene was witnessed by a young lawyer from a leading Boston family, Wendell Phillips. Phillips was puzzled at the strong emotions Garrison stirred. Two years later, outraged by the murder of editor Lovejoy, Phillips became one of the strongest advocates of the anti-slavery cause.

He gave up the practice of law because he could not support a Constitution legalizing bondage. He ceased to exercise his right to vote—as a protest against a pro-slavery government—and devoted his life to the abolitionist cause. A persuasive and stirring speaker, Phillips ranked with Garrison as an anti-slavery leader. To use his own phrase, he became one of the "men whose words are half battles." Both men were delegates to the World Anti-Slavery Convention in London.

By 1840, the American Anti-Slavery Society listed 250,000 members. It published more than two dozen journals and had about 15 state organizations supervising 2,000 local chapters. Garrison's followers believed moral suasion and passive resistance were the path to emancipation. They shunned political action and denounced churches for their support of slavery.

Garrison's fiery editorials in the *Liberator* and his tracts such as "Thoughts on African Colonization" were effective in arousing antislavery sentiment in the North. But they added fuel to the flames of resentment in the slave states.

Within the antislavery movement, there were differences of opinion. A group headed by Arthur and Lewis Tappan began to disagree openly with Garrison. They felt a more moderate stance might work and favored working through party politics. In 1835, Arthur Tappan decided to appeal to the five-sixths of the South's white population who held no slaves, as well as slaveholders.

Arthur and Lewis Tappan formed the American and Foreign Anti-Slavery Society. It plunged deeply into political action, forming the **Liberty Party**. In 1840 and again in 1844, the party nominated James Birney for President.

Their magazine, the *Anti-Slavery Record;* their paper, *Human Rights;* their official organ, the *Emancipator,* and a magazine for children, *The Slave's Friend,* were all mild in tone. They based objections to slavery on moral and religious grounds. And the publications were regularly posted to a selected list of Southerners.

By virtue of special compact, Shylock demanded a pound of flesh, cut nearest to the heart. Those who sell mothers separately from their children, likewise claim a legal right to human flesh; and they too cut it nearest to the heart.—*L. M. Child.*

On, woman! from thy happy hearth
Extend thy gentle hand to save
The poor and perishing of earth—
The chained and stricken slave!
Oh, plead for all the suffering of thy kind—
For the crushed body and the darkened
mind. *J. G. Whittier.*

FIFTH ANNIVERSARY
OF THE
MASSACHUSETTS ANTI-SLAVERY SOCIETY,
WEDNESDAY, JANUARY 25, 1837.

[☞ The public meetings, during the day, will be held in the SPACIOUS LOFT, OVER THE STABLE OF THE MARLBOROUGH HOTEL, and in the evening, in the REPRESENTATIVES' HALL.]

HOURS OF THE MEETINGS.

Meeting for Delegates at 9 o'clock in the morning, at 46, Washington-Street.
First public meeting at 10 o'clock A. M., in the LOFT OVER THE STABLE OF THE MARLBOROUGH HOTEL.
Second public meeting at 1-2 past 2 o'clock, P. M. same place.
Evening meeting at 1-2 past 6 o'clock, in the REPRESENTATIVES' HALL.

☞ The Committee of Arrangements respectfully inform the ladies that ample accommodations have been prepared for them. The loft is spacious, clean, well warmed, and will accommodate, with ease and perfect safety, at least 1000 persons.

☞ AMOS DRESSER, a citizen of this State, who was 'Lynched' at Nashville, for the crime of being an Abolitionist, will be present, and during the meetings in the afternoon and evening, will give a history of that affair.

Announcement of a meeting where white abolitionist Amos Dresser told about being nearly lynched.

Another major difference between Garrison's followers and those of the Tappans was over the role of women. The American Anti-Slavery Society included a number of women who had equal roles. A Philadelphia Quaker minister, Lucretia Mott, had been one of its organizers. The Tappans and others favoring political action wanted an all-male group. Women, they felt, should form their own groups. They should not appear as public speakers at abolition meetings.

An illustration heading an article describing breeding slaves in the border states for sale in New Orleans.

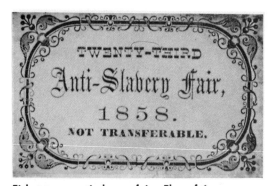

TWENTY-THIRD
Anti-Slavery Fair,
1858.
NOT TRANSFERABLE.

Ticket to an anti-slavery fair. These fairs were a major means of fund-raising.

The South Strikes Back

Words were, after all, only "half battles." The slave forces were accustomed to using the whip and other forms of violence against whites who befriended blacks. In Georgia, a subscriber to the *Liberator* was tarred, feathered, horse-whipped and half-drowned. A number of whites in the South were killed for associating with blacks in public.

In Nashville, Tennessee, in 1835, a vendor of Bibles, Amos Dresser of Lane Seminary, was charged with being an abolitionist. He was whipped by a mob at midnight in the public square. By this time it had become almost impossible to speak openly against slavery in the South or to circulate printed matter concerning abolition.

The South wanted no interference of any sort with slavery, and no discussion, printed or otherwise, of abolition.

CHAPTER CHECK

1. Why do you think the number of people who supported the abolition of slavery increased during the American Revolution?
2. What role did newspapers play in the anti-slavery movement? Why do you think they were so important?
3. Why would the citizens of Boston try to lynch William Lloyd Garrison in 1835?
4. Why do you think the South wanted no discussion of slavery or abolition?
5. Imagine . . . you are (a) a Southern slaveholder, and (b) a Southern slave. How would you react to David Walker's *Appeal*?

The *Amistad.*

CHAPTER 15

Mutiny on the Amistad

One day in the spring of 1839, a handsome young African whose name was Cinque was seized and a carried off to be sold into slavery. The son of a Mendi rice planter, he soon found himself chained in the sitting position in the hold of a Portuguese vessel bound for Cuba. At Havana, Cinque and some 50 blacks in his cargo were purchased by two Spaniards, who chartered the *Amistad* to carry their newly acquired slaves to Puerto Principe, Cuba. Also on board were the ship's captain, two black slaves and two white crewmen. At night, the Africans, seizing weapons from the hold of the ship, killed Captain Ferrer and the cook. With Cinque now in command, they tied the two owners of the cargo to the bridge and ordered them to steer the large ship toward Africa. The white sailors managed to escape in the small boat.

The Spaniards intentionally steered north and west instead of east and south. For 56 days they zig-zagged. Desperate from thirst and lack of food, 10 of the Africans died before *Amistad* arrived off Long Island, New York, one day in August. There a vessel of the United States Navy sighted the strange ship and sent a party of men aboard to find out its business. Astonished to find only Africans in charge, at pistol point they ordered all hands below deck. The *Amistad* was taken to New London, Connecticut. The Africans, except for three little girls, were charged before the United States Circuit

Court at New Haven with the murder of the *Amistad*'s captain. All were imprisoned to await trial.

Excitement in New Haven

The Africans who had taken over the *Amistad* spoke a tongue which no one in New Haven understood. But they acquired many friends, nonetheless, among the towns-people and the teachers and students at Yale. American newspapers were filled with articles about them and their case. Aboli-tionists flocked to their defense. An Amistad Committee was formed, including Lewis Tap-pan, who contributed funds to their defense. Out of this Amistad Committee, the Ameri-can Missionary Association eventually devel-oped to combat "the sins of caste, polygamy and slaveholding." But the language barrier persisted. By learning the Africans' system of counting, Professor Josiah Willard Gibbs of Yale was able to determine some of their language. With this information Gibbs finally located, aboard a British ship in New York harbor, a Mendi sailor named James Covey. He could serve as an interpreter.

Through Covey more details about the story of the *Amistad* captives were revealed. Abolitionists continued to defend them. They charged that the Africans had been kid-napped from their homes. And that they had the right of free people anywhere to em-ploy whatever force was necessary to secure their freedom.

When court proceedings began, there was so much excitement concerning the case that the law students at Yale were dismissed from classes to attend the trial. There were many intricate legal questions involved.

Southern politicians were opposed to the freeing of the *Amistad* mutineers. President Martin Van Buren stood ready to send them into slavery. The court proceedings lasted all winter, and public opinion became in-creasingly divided. A brilliant battery of law-yers was in charge of the Africans' defense.

A drawing that shows the death of Captain Ferrer aboard the *Amistad*.

Captives Are Freed

In court, Cinque testified in his own behalf. He conducted himself with dignity. All of his responses were quickly translated by Covey. The ruling was in his favor. But the decision was appealed to the highest court.

Former President John Quincy Adams, then a Congressman from Massachusetts, was moved by the plight of the captives. He undertook to argue the case before the U.S. Supreme Court. "I implore," he wrote, "the mercy of Almighty God . . . to give me utterance that I may prove myself in every respect equal to the task." On March 9, 1841, after an eight-and-one-half-hour argument by "Old Man Eloquent," the Supreme Court ordered Cinque and his fellow Africans freed. Facing "the insurmountable burden of labor" yet to be encountered in putting down the slave trade, Adams wrote in his diary, "Yet my conscience presses on; let me but die upon the breach."

Under the guidance of abolitionist teachers, Cinque acquired considerable learning before he and his fellows returned to Sierra Leone in 1842. They were accompanied by missionaries, who set up their first anti-slavery mission.

A portrait of Joseph Cinque.

CHAPTER CHECK

1. Why do you think the *Amistad* affair aroused such an interest in the American public?

2. Why do you think that a former president of the United States would defend before the Supreme Court a group of Africans who had committed murder?

3. Imagine . . . you are a Northern abolitionist. How would you react to news of the *Amistad* affair? How could it help your cause?

A Mendi village in Sierra Leone, West Africa.

THE FUGITIVE'S SONG,

WORDS

composed and respectfully dedicated in token of confident esteem to

FREDERICK DOUGLASS

A Graduate from the

"PECULIAR INSTITUTION"

for his fearless advocacy, signal ability and wonderful success in behalf of

HIS BROTHERS IN BONDS.

FUGITIVES FROM SLAVERY in the

FREE STATES & CANADAS.

By their friend

JESSE HUTCHINSON JUN.

CHAPTER 16

Frederick Douglass, Orator and Editor

Frederick Douglass was the foremost black abolitionist. Condensed from his *Life and Times* is this story of his life as a slave in Maryland.

"In Talbot County, Eastern Shore, State of Maryland, near Easton, I, without any fault of my own, was born, and spent the first years of my childhood. From certain events, the dates of which I have since learned, I suppose myself to have been born in February 1817 . . . .

"My first experience of life began in the family of my grandmother. The practice of separating mothers from their children and hiring them out at distances too great to admit of their meeting, save at long intervals, was a marked feature of the slave system. My only recollections of my mother are a few hasty visits made in the night on foot, after the day's tasks were over. Of my father, I knew nothing. Grandmother belonged to a mysterious personage called "Old Master" whose name seemed ever to be mentioned with fear and shuddering, and unhappily for me, all the information I could get concerning him increased my dread of being separated from my grandmother.

"But the time came when I must go. I was less than seven years old. On the plantation of Colonel Lloyd I was left to the tender mercies of Aunt Katy, a slavewoman who, ill-tempered and cruel, was often guilty of starving me and the other children. I had offended Aunt Katy, and she adopted her usual mode of punishing me: namely, making me go all day without food. Sundown came, but no bread. I was too hungry to sleep, when who but my own dear mother should come in. She read Aunt Katy a lecture which was never forgotten. That night I learned as I had never learned before, that I was not only a child, but somebody's child. My mother had walked 12 miles to see me, and had the same distance to travel over before the morning sunrise. I do not remember seeing her again . . . .

"I hardly became a thinking being when I first learned to hate slavery. At the beginning of 1836 I took upon me a solemn vow to gain my liberty. I succeeded in winning to my scheme a company of five young men. Early on the appointed morning we went as usual to the field but I had a sudden presentiment, 'Betrayed!' The constables grabbed me. I was firmly tied. Re-

Cover of sheet music to "The Fugitive's Song," dedicated to Frederick Douglass.

sistance was idle. Five young men guilty of no crime save that of preferring liberty to slavery were literally dragged behind horses a distance of 15 miles and placed in the Easton jail. I wished myself a beast, a bird, anything rather than a slave."

"One Life to Lose"

As a boy of 10, Frederick had learned to read a little from his mistress—until her husband angrily interfered. Then fences and pavements became his copy-books. He picked up what knowledge he could from white children. Then he copied letters and words on walls with chalk. He bought a copy of the popular school book, the *Columbian Orator*. It was his only book, and it contained a great many speeches about liberty and freedom. Douglass learned to read and orate by reading these speeches over and over.

In his early teens, Fred taught at a little country Sunday School. The lessons included instruction in spelling as well as the Scriptures until white men broke it up.

Fred was sent for taming by his master to "a man named Edward Covey, who enjoyed the reputation of being a first-rate hand at breaking young Negroes." The first week under Covey he was flogged so severely that he bore forever the scars upon his back.

One day while working in the broiling sun, Frederick fainted. To revive him, Covey gave him a series of brutal kicks. Then Covey struck him on the head with a hickory slab. That night Frederick struggled seven miles through the dark to his master's house to beg to be removed from Covey's care. But his master ordered him back at once.

Then Fred decided to defend himself in

The last time Fred saw his mother.

Colonel Lloyd whipping old Barney.

The overseer, Gore, shooting Denby.

the future. The next time Covey tried to hit him, he flung the white man to the ground. Covey gave up, contenting himself from then on with simply trying to work Fred to death. Thus it was that Frederick learned "when a slave cannot be flogged, he is more than half free. Men are whipped oftenest who are whipped easiest."

But, a few years later, hired out as a ship-yard worker in Baltimore, Fred could not keep himself from being severely beaten by a gang of white workers. One of the gang members kicked him in the eye out of resentment against a slave working beside him. Frederick's master removed him from the docks because he did not wish his property damaged. All of his pay went to his master. "I worked for it, collected it . . . yet upon returning every Saturday night, this money—my own hard earnings, every cent of it—was taken from me by Master Hugh."

Dreams of freedom were still in his mind. "Why am I a slave? I will run away. I will not stand it. I have only one life to lose. I had as well be killed running as die standing." On September 3, 1838, at the age of 21, Frederick escaped to New York disguised as a sailor. There he was joined by a free black girl he had courted in Baltimore. They were married and together set out for New Bedford, Massachusetts where in freedom they made their home.

Becoming a Public Figure

The abolitionist William C. Coffin happened to hear Douglass speak before a black congregation in New Bedford. Coffin invited him to tell his story at an anti-slavery convention in 1841 in Nantucket. This was Douglass' first appearance before an audience made up almost entirely of white

Frederick Douglass, at the beginning of his public career.

Douglass and his wife arrive in Newport, Rhode Island.

people. He effectively and eloquently told the story of his life under slavery and his escape to freedom. When he finished, William Lloyd Garrison cried, "Have we been listening to a thing, a piece of property or a man?" And the crowd answered, "A man! A man!" From that day Frederick Douglass became a public figure.

John A. Collins asked Douglass to become a speaker for the Massachusetts Anti-Slavery Society. Douglass recalled his first reactions, "I had not been quite three years from my slavery, and was honestly distrustful of my ability. Besides, publicity might discover me to my master. But I finally consented to go out for three months."

Those three months were extended to a half-century of public life. He toured with Collins, with Garrison and with Wendell Phillips. He spoke at Faneuil Hall and at other great auditoriums. He was attacked by mobs in Boston, Harrisburg, (Pennsylvania) and Indiana. But he continued to speak.

Enroute to England in 1845, some Southerners threatened to throw Douglass overboard for a talk he made aboard ship. He lectured in England for two years on slavery,

women's suffrage and other subjects. There he raised enough money to purchase his freedom and to establish a newspaper.

As a believer in equality for women, Douglass was the only male speaker at the first women's rights convention. As a free black opposing all racial restrictions, he declared, "The way to break down an unreasonable custom is to contradict it in practice."

Douglass once clung so hard to his seat in a "white" railroad car, when the conductor tried to eject him, the bench was torn from the floor. Douglass, bench and all were tossed off. Another time, Douglass was refused sleeping quarters on a New York-Newport boat. He had to spend the night on deck. Wendell Phillips remained with him, unwilling to allow Douglass "to bear the burden of insult and outrage alone."

But neither Phillips nor Garrison believed that Douglass should start a black paper. They felt the *Liberator* and other established papers fighting the cause of abolition were enough. Also, Douglass was too valuable as a speaker. On this issue, and the question of political action through the ballot, Douglass and Garrison began to disagree. In 1847,

Masthead for the *Frederick Douglass' Paper,* first published as *The North Star.*

Frederick Douglass.

Douglass founded *The North Star*.

From addressing white people about blacks, he turned to addressing blacks themselves. Douglass believed that "the man struck is the man to cry out." And that "he who has endured the cruel pangs of Slavery is the man to advocate Liberty . . . in connection with our white friends." *The North Star* was printed for all to read. Its slogan was, "Right is of no sex—Truth is of no color— God is the Father of us all, and all we are Brethren."

C H A P T E R   C H E C K

1. What can you learn about slavery from reading Frederick Douglass' account of his life?
2. Why do you think Douglass was so effective as an abolitionist?
3. Imagine . . . you are a Northern white. How would listening to Frederick Douglass effect your opinion about slavery?

Harriet Tubman and a map
of the Underground Railroad route.

CHAPTER 17

Truth, Tubman and the Underground Railroad

Two women who had been born slaves devoted all their energies to freeing others. Both were deeply religious. One, Sojourner Truth, was termed a **mystic** (spiritual seer). The other, Harriet Tubman, was a woman of action. But in times of stress Tubman's favorite prayer was, "Lord, you have been with me through six troubles. Be with me in the seventh."

Both women were so famous that books were written about them during their lifetimes. Neither of them could read nor write. Both women had been married, but most of their lives each walked alone. Each covered wide areas in her travels. Each faced danger and possible death.

Sojourner Truth was born Isabella Baumfree about 1797. The property of a Dutch master in New York, she spoke English with a Dutch accent all her life. Her childhood home was a hotel cellar where her parents and a number of other slaves were quartered. While Isabella was still a child, her parents died. She was sold and resold, finally becoming the property of John Dumont. He promised to free her in 1826, if she worked hard. Then he changed his mind.

New York State freed all its slaves in 1827. Isabella walked away, taking only her youngest child. Her five-year-old son Peter was sold to an Alabama slave-owner. Isabella went to court and succeeded in getting Peter back.

In 1834, Isabella was living in a commune in New York City. She was accused, with a new leader, of murdering the commune's original leader. Her accuser was a white man who had no proof. She sued for libel and won a judgment of $125.

One day in 1843, Isabella decided to leave her job as a domestic servant to travel. "The Spirit calls me," she said, "I must go." With only a few coins in her purse, Isabella departed. Although free herself, she felt called to preach and teach against slavery.

Isabella adopted a symbolic new name, Sojourner Truth. She declared, "The Lord gave me Sojourner because I was to travel up and down the land showin' the people their sins and bein' a sign unto them. Afterwards I told the Lord I wanted another name, cause everybody else had two names; and the Lord gave me Truth, because I was to declare truth unto people."

Sojourner Truth became a famous figure at anti-slavery meetings. Once she said about her work, "I think of the great things of God, not the little things." She was a very tall and very dark woman with a deep voice like a man's. She electrified many audiences. And she irritated those who did not agree with her. A man told her that he cared no more about her speeches than he would about a flea bite. Sojourner replied, "Maybe not, but the Lord willing, I'll keep you scratchin'."

Sojourner Truth, mystic abolitionist.

Conductor Tubman

Harriet Tubman was an even greater irritant to the slave-owners. Not only did she make speeches in the North but, time after time, she went into the South and brought slaves out to freedom. At one time $40,000 was offered for her capture. When she was about 28 she had run away herself from a Maryland plantation. She had to leave her husband, parents, brothers and sister behind. Two brothers started out with her, but became frightened and went back. To prevent this from ever happening again, Harriet Tubman carried a pistol on her freedom forays. If any slave heading North in her parties faltered, she drew her gun and said, "You'll be free or die!" Strength to go on was always forthcoming.

Up creek beds, through swamps, over hills in the dark of night, on 19 secret trips into the dangerous South, Tubman guided more than 300 slaves to freedom. This included her aged parents. Once in 1851 she took a party of 11—including two of her brothers—all the way to Canada. The Fugitive Slave Law had, by then, made it dangerous to stop short of the border.

One slave in the party had a $1,500 reward on his head. He was so frightened he would not a say a word. On the train crossing from Buffalo, New York, to Canada, he wouldn't even look out the window at the scenery. But when he found himself on free soil, he sang and shouted so much no one could shut him up. Tubman said, "You old fool, you! You might at least have looked at Niagara Falls on the way to freedom!"

Friendless and without work in Canada, Tubman herself prayed, cooked and begged for these **refugees** all winter. Then, in the spring, she went back South to free more.

She went alone. But once she got her slaves started, Tubman had help. There were secret stations of the Underground Railroad from Wilmington, Delaware, to the Great Lakes. (The **Underground Railroad** was not a real railroad but a network of people and places.) There were hiding places in barns, cellars, churches, woodsheds and caves. There were white friends to help with food and warm clothing.

Travel on the Underground Railroad was mostly at night. The runaways had to remain in hiding by day. Way stations were 10 to 20 miles apart. Conductors sometimes used covered wagons or carts with false bottoms to convey slaves from one station to another. Quakers did not believe in violence. But conductors of other faiths often secreted arms to use for defense, if need be.

Tubman was one of the most famous "conductors" on the Underground Railroad. She once said, "I nebber run my train off detrack, and I nebber lost a passenger."

The Underground Railroad

There were also white "conductors" on the Underground Railroad. John Fairfield, of a Virginia slave-holding family, was one. Sometimes posing as a peddler or a slave-trader, sometimes as a traveling evangelist, he brought many slaves out of the South.

The majority of slaves who escaped did not have guides to help them. However, some slaves knew that if they reached Wilmington, Delaware, the Quaker Thomas Garrett would feed and hide them. In Camden, New Jersey, John Hunn would help. In Philadelphia was William Still, the black secretary of the Vigilance Committee. (The **Vigilance Committee** was a loose organization with chapters in many Northern cities.

A runaway protects his family from bloodhounds.

William Still, author of *Underground Railroad*.

Levi Coffin, "President" of the Underground Railroad.

Its purpose was to protect the rights of black people.) Still kept a record of all the "passengers"—sometimes called "merchandise"—passing through his station.

In New York City, many white sympathizers and free blacks like Charles Ray stood ready to help a refugee. In upstate towns were Gerrit Smith, Stephen Myers and the Reverend J. W. Loguen, himself an escaped slave. When runaways got as near the border as Rochester, Frederick Douglass or Susan B. Anthony would shelter them until they could make the "last jump" into Canada. On the western escape route that ran

Henry Brown, a Virginia slave who escaped by shipping himself to freedom.

A page from Daniel Osborn's diary in which he noted fugitives he aided.

through Cincinnati, Ohio, Levi Coffin helped around 3,000 blacks to continue northward.

The Great Escape

It is estimated some 50,000 slaves escaped to freedom in the decade preceding the Civil War. So many slaves were running away that some masters met to see what could be done to stop them. Methods of escape for slaves varied. Generally, it was on foot, wading in streams as much as possible to throw bloodhounds off the scent. Sometimes a slave "borrowed" his master's horse. Very daring slaves even rode on trains. And one had himself nailed in a box with some biscuits and a "bladder" of water and shipped from Richmond to Philadelphia. When William Still opened the box, out popped Henry Brown.

Still, who later wrote a book entitled *Underground Railroad*, was known as a brakeman. His Philadelphia home was a busy station. Many Underground Railroaders went to jail. Some, like John Fairfield, were killed.

CHAPTER CHECK

1. What are some of the traits that made Sojourner Truth so effective as an anti-slavery lecturer?
2. Why do you think $40,000 was once offered for the capture of Harriet Tubman? What threat did she pose to the South?
3. Imagine . . . you are a fugitive slave. How would you try to escape? What are some of the dangers you would face?

VOL. III. No. VII.   JULY, 1837.   WHOLE No. 31.

This picture of a poor fugitive is from one of the stereotype cuts manufactured in this city for the southern market, and used on handbills offering rewards for runaway slaves.

THE RUNAWAY.

One of the handbills offering rewards for runaway slaves.

CHAPTER 18

Resisting Recapture

The Fugitive Slave Law of 1850 provided that any federal marshal who did not arrest on demand an alleged runaway might be fined $1,000. It also offered to federal officers in the North a fee for captured slaves.

The abolitionists had the double task of rescuing slaves, first from slavery, then from federal officials. Unfortunate refugees and free-born women and men had no opportunity to defend themselves legally. Their only chance to maintain freedom lay in escape or rescue by force from the clutches of constables, marshals or jailers. The Fugitive Slave Law, abolitionists contended, was made to be broken.

William Parker and other free blacks drive out slave-catchers at Christiana, Pennsylvania.

In 1851, a group of Boston blacks led by Lewis Hayden, forcibly took a refugee, Frederick Wilkins, known as Shadrach, from federal officers. In that same city, citizens had hidden William and Ellen Craft until the slave-catchers, with their federal warrants, were driven out of town. The Crafts had earlier escaped from the South. Ellen, very light in complexion, had dressed as a man and posed as William's owner on the train.

During a meeting of the Liberty Party in Syracuse, Jerry McHenry was seized by slavers to be returned South. McHenry was a runaway slave who had been living as a free man for several years. McHenry was rescued by an indignant group in such open defiance of the law that prosecution was deemed futile.

In 1858 near Oberlin, Ohio, three U.S. marshals seized an escaped slave, John Price. A large group of Oberlin citizens almost instantly rescued him. When 37 of the rescuers were indicted by a federal grand jury, the case became front-page news throughout the country. Charles H. Langston, a black, and Simeon M. Bushnell, a white, were the first of the group convicted. They served time in the county jail, but on their release were greeted with a brass band and hailed as heroes.

Trouble at Christiana

Frederick Douglass writes in his *Life and Times*: "The thing which more than all else destroyed the fugitive slave law was the resistance made to it by the fugitives themselves. A decided check was given to the execution of the law at Christiana, Penn., where three colored men, being pursued by Mr. Gorsuch and his son, slew the father, wounded the son, and drove away the officers, and made their escape to my house in Rochester. The work of getting these men safely into Canada was a delicate one. They were not only fugitives from slavery but charged with murder, and officers were in pursuit of them. There was no time for delay . . . .

"Happily for us the suspense was not long, for it turned out that that very night a steamer was to leave for Toronto, Canada." Douglass himself put these blacks on the northbound boat.

Thirty-one blacks and five whites were arrested at Christiana. Some were indicted for treason, murder and rioting. One white man was tried for treason first. He was defended by Pennsylvania lawyer Thaddeus Stevens and **acquitted** (found not guilty). Because of this legal victory, the charges against the others were dropped. Abolitionists felt that they had acted rightly against the slave-catchers.

"This affair, at Christiana," Douglass continued, "and the Jerry rescue at Syracuse, inflicted fatal wounds on the fugitive slave bill. It became thereafter almost a dead letter."

The rescue of the three men at Christiana, like that of Shadrach in Boston and Jerry in Syracuse, took place in the year 1851. Such open disobedience to federal law and such widespread assistance to fugitive slaves caused Southerners to lose faith in the Compromise of 1850 and the Fugitive Slave Law.

The Burns Case

Still many runaways were returned. The most famous case is that of Anthony Burns. On May 24, 1854, he was arrested and placed under guard in the federal jury room of the Boston courthouse. His former master was Charles Suttle of Alexandria, Virginia. Although an attempt was made to keep it secret, news of Burns' arrest spread quickly. The next morning three distinguished lawyers were in court to defend him. They were Charles M. Ellis, a member of the Boston Vigilance Committee, Richard Henry Dana, Jr., author of *Two Years Before the Mast*, and Robert Morris, the city's most prominent black attorney.

The following evening, Faneuil Hall was filled to overflowing with citizens gathered to

A cartoon entitled "Rocking Slaves in Faneuil Hall." It commemorated the rescue of Shadrach.

KIDNAPPING AGAIN!!

A MAN WAS STOLEN LAST NIGHT BY THE

Fugitive Slave Bill COMMISSIONER!

HE WILL HAVE HIS

MOCK TRIAL

ON SATURDAY, MAY 27, AT 9 O'CLOCK,

In the Kidnapper's 'Court,' before the Hon. Slave Bill Commissioner,

AT THE COURT HOUSE, IN COURT SQUARE.

SHALL BOSTON STEAL ANOTHER MAN?

Thursday, May 25, 1854.

A Boston poster announcing Anthony Burns' seizure.

protest Burns' arrest. On the platform that night, after Wendell Phillips and Theodore Parker had spoken, a man cried, "When we go from this Cradle of Liberty, let us go to the tomb of liberty—the courthouse!" The crowd broke for Court Square, where the Reverend Thomas Wentworth Higginson and Lewis Hayden were already leading a group of abolitionists in battering down the door of the courthouse to rescue Burns. Inside the courthouse, constables and deputies were ready with pistols and clubs. Reverend Higginson was wounded and in the scuffle one of the deputies was killed. Military reinforcements arrived, the abolitionists were routed and many were arrested.

Despairing of freeing Burns by force or by legal means, the friends of freedom raised $1,200 and negotiated to purchase his freedom. But the U.S. Attorney refused to permit this transaction, insisting that in keeping with the Fugitive Slave Law, the refugee must be returned to Virginia.

When Burns came to trial on Monday, police and soldiers surrounded the courthouse. They guarded every door and window and lined the staircase leading to the courtroom. From Washington, President Franklin Pierce wired to spare no expense in having the military protect the court "to insure execution of the law." On Friday, when Burns was sentenced to return to slavery, 22 military units were assembled in Boston to see that he did not escape. Besides the police of Boston, 1,500 dragoons (soldiers on horses), marines and calverymen, with Burns in their midst, marched to the dockside. They moved through streets lined by a crowd of 50,000 persons hissing and crying, "Shame!" At one point, the populace tried to break through the police and rescue Burns. Several were injured.

The cost of returning a slave to the South in some cases amounted to many times the slave's price. Estimates of the cost of returning Burns reach $100,000. Newspaper headlines were given to each sensational case. Violent arguments arose for and against the return of fugitives. The gulf between those who bought and sold human beings and those who opposed such practices widened. The federal government, though hard put to uphold the Fugitive Slave Law, was yet determined to do so.

CHAPTER CHECK

1. How did the Fugitive Slave Law help anger Northerners against the Southern slaveholders?
2. What were some of the ways that Northerners helped fugitive slaves escape?
3. Imagine . . . you are a fugitive slave living in a Northern city. How would you react to the passage of the Fugitive Slave Law? How would this law change your life?

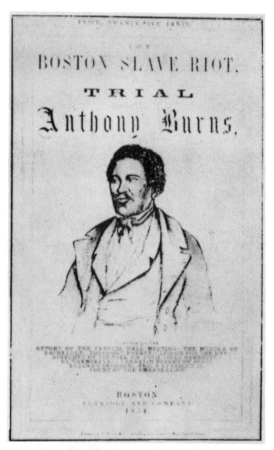

The cover of a pamphlet that tells the story of Burns.

Federal and state troops returning Burns to slavery.

CHAPTER 19

Daring Words, Then a Raid

Anti-slavery sentiments were expressed in many ways. In this chapter you will read about three white 19th century American citizens who hated slavery. Each one had an impact on its abolition. One was a professional writer, who was also a teacher and the wife of a minister. One was the only prominent Southern author to attack slavery before the Civil War. And the third was a man who became obsessed with the idea of taking direct action to win justice for black people.

Cover of a children's edition of *Uncle Tom's Cabin*.

Uncle Tom's Cabin

"In the midst of these fugitive slave troubles," wrote Frederick Douglass, "came the book known as *Uncle Tom's Cabin*, a work of marvelous depth and power . . . Its effect was amazing, instantaneous and universal."

Uncle Tom's Cabin was first published in 1851 in the *National Era*. It was printed just as each chapter came fresh from the pen of Harriet Beecher Stowe. Stowe had six children, including a new baby, and little time for careful writing. Her husband, a Biblical scholar, had been teaching at Lane Seminary in Cincinnati. She had seen slavery just across the Ohio River and had wanted to do something about it.

The Stowes moved to Brunswick, Maine, after he had been asked to teach at Bowdoin College. The beginnings of a story came to her one Sunday in church. She went home and sat down to write *Uncle Tom's Cabin*. The novel was turned down by one publisher then accepted doubtfully by another.

It was published in March 1852, in Boston. Before the first week was up, 10,000 copies had been sold. Before the summer, Mrs. Stowe's earnings from the sale of the book had amounted to $10,000. Eighty printing presses, going day and night, could not supply the demand for copies. Three hundred thousand copies were sold during the first year.

It appeared in England, France and Germany, and was soon translated into many languages. However, its circulation was forbidden in the South. The character of Uncle

Mary E. Webb, a free black women, reading from *Uncle Tom's Cabin* in London in 1856.

Harriet Beecher Stowe, author of *Uncle Tom's Cabin.*

Tom was based in part on the life of Josiah Henson. He was an escaped slave whose narrative Mrs. Stowe had read. He had described how, as a punishment, an overseer had cut off his father's ear. One day, Mrs. Stowe received a package. When her husband opened it, out fell the ear of another slave—a tribute from the South.

A Book and a Play

"The object of these sketches," wrote Harriet Beecher Stowe in her preface to *Uncle Tom's Cabin*, "is to awaken sympathy and feeling for the African race, as they exist among us; to show their wrongs and sorrows, under a system so necessarily cruel and unjust as to defeat and do away the good effects of all that can be attempted for them, by their best friends."

But her book awakened more than a sympathy. According to Frederick Douglass, it lighted "a million campfires in front of the embattled hosts of slavery." *Uncle Tom's Cabin* became a best-seller second only to the Bible. To Mrs. Stowe came hundreds of abusive letters from the South. But thousands of letters of praise arrived from all over the world.

When in the fall of 1852, a dramatization of the book opened in Troy, New York, it ran for 100 performances. At the National Theater in New York City, it remained a year. Later, four companies were performing the play nightly in Manhattan. And for more than half a century thereafter, all across the country, whole generations wept over Little Eva's ascension into Heaven and Uncle Tom's death at the hands of Simon Legree.

"The theater," Wendell Phillips said, "has preached immediate emancipation and has given us the whole of Uncle Tom, while the pulpit is either silent or hostile."

Helper's Book

In 1857, another book appeared which infuriated the South. It was written by a poor white North Carolinian named Hinton R. Helper. The book was called *The Impending Crisis of the South*. It attributed the backwardness of that region and the poverty of the poor whites directly to the slave system. He quoted government statistics to prove his economic points. He showed how cotton culture had exhausted the land, limited diversified crops and starved the masses.

"There is no legislation except for the benefit of slavery, and slaveholders," he said. Of the treatment of the poor whites by wealthy slavers, he wrote, "Never were the poorer classes of a people . . . so basely duped, so adroitly swindled, or so damnably outraged." With his book banned in the slave states, Helper wrote, "The South can never have a literature of her own until after slavery shall have been abolished."

Helper did not oppose slavery because he wanted freedom for blacks. He opposed it because he felt that the institution of slavery was damaging to the South.

John Brown's Raid

As the impending crisis developed, American writers devoted more and more attention to the conflict between slavery and freedom. In 1859, a man who had never written a book seized a government arsenal. (An **arsenal** is a place where weapons are stored.) His intention: to arm the slaves.

In July 1859, under the name of Isaac Smith, John Brown rented an old house on a farm in Maryland. The farm was across the Potomac River from Harper's Ferry. He began to store arms and lay careful plans. About a dozen men drilled in a secluded field. Visitors were unwelcome. In the house, Brown's 15 year-old daughter Annie and 17 year-old Martha, wife of his son Oliver, kept a lookout as they cooked and washed dishes for the men. Oliver and his brother Watson aided their father.

Meanwhile, Brown went to keep an appointment with Frederick Douglass in a stone quarry in Pennsylvania. There Douglass tried to discourage him. Douglass felt the plan was bound to fail. Brown returned to his farm without Douglass. But Shields Green, a runaway slave from Charleston whom Douglass had sheltered, came with Brown. They found Dangerfield Newby, a former Virginia slave, already there. Later that summer, other blacks began to arrive at the

Hinton R. Helper.

farm. They included two students from Oberlin College, Lewis Sheridan Leary and John Armstrong Copeland, as well as Osborn Perry Anderson from Pennsylvania.

With a group of 21 men, on the rainy Sunday night of October 16, 1859, John Brown attacked the federal arsenal at Harper's Ferry. His objectives were to take the town, distribute arms to the slaves in the vicinity and spread the revolt from there across the South. The arsenal was taken, but the plan failed. President James Buchanan called out the marines and the cavalry under the command of Colonel Robert E. Lee. Brown was wounded and taken prisoner. In the early fighting, Brown's two sons were killed, as were Leary, Newby and six others. Anderson escaped. Copeland and Green were hanged for treason.

John Brown.

In all, seven of the raiders died on the gallows, including John Brown. But while they were awaiting trial, the whole country was in a state of excitement. Southern cities called out troops for fear of slave uprisings, and Washington itself was patrolled by the military. Brown, lying wounded and bloodstained a few hours after his capture, warned, "You may dispose of me very easily. I am nearly disposed of now, but this question is still to be settled—this Negro question, I mean—the end of that is not yet."

No one among Brown's band implicated anybody else. On December 2, the day of his execution, Brown scrawled a message on a piece of paper which he left with his jailer. "I, John Brown, am now quite certain that the crimes of this guilty land will never be purged away but with blood. I had, as I now think vainly, flattered myself that without very much bloodshed it might be done."

On a clear, cool, sun-bright morning, they rode John Brown to the scaffold in an open cart. The old man looked at the Blue Ridge Mountains in the distance and said, "This is a beautiful country."

CHAPTER CHECK

1. Why do you think that *Uncle Tom's Cabin* was so successful?
2. How did Hinton Helper's book threaten the Southern slaveowners?
3. What is your opinion about John Brown's decision that only armed revolt would free the slaves? Was he right? Why do you think his plan failed?
4. Imagine . . . you are a Southern slaveowner. How would you react to the news of John Brown's raid?

FREE SPEECH.
FREE HOMES,
FREE TERRITORY.

PROTECTION TO AMERICAN INDUSTRY

FOR PRESIDENT
ABRAHAM LINCOLN
OF ILLINOIS

FOR VICE PRESIDENT
HANNIBAL HAMLIN
OF MAINE

CHAPTER 20

The House Divides

"**A** house divided against itself cannot stand," declared Abraham Lincoln in accepting the Republican nomination for senator from Illinois in the spring of 1858. "I believe this government cannot endure, permanently half *slave* and half *free*. I do not expect the Union to be *dissolved*—I do not expect the house to *fall*— but I do expect it will cease to be divided. It will become *all* one thing, or *all* the other."

In the fall of 1858, Lincoln and his Democratic opponent, Stephen A. Douglas, had a series of seven debates in small Illinois towns. Lincoln said, "You say slavery is wrong; but don't you constantly object to somebody else saying so? Do you not constantly argue that this is not the right place to oppose it? . . . It must not be opposed in politics, because that will make a fuss; it must not be opposed in the pulpit, because it is not religion. Then where is the place to oppose it?"

Lincoln lost this election to Douglas. But he won wide support in the West and North for his resistance to the spread of slavery. Early in 1860, politicians in the deep South openly threatened that the election of a "Black Republican" would be grounds for secession. As the presidential campaign began, the Democratic Party split into two factions at Charleston.

Lincoln Elected

The extreme pro-slavery elements later nominated John Breckenridge of Kentucky. The regular Democratic nomination went to Douglas. In Chicago, the Republicans nominated Lincoln. Their party platform stood resolutely for no further extension of slavery.

Southerners called the Republican Party a "party of destruction and rebellion." The campaign was a bitter one. But on November 6, 1860, Lincoln was elected President. He had won a majority of the electoral vote but only about 40 percent of the popular vote.

The South Secedes

Six weeks after the Lincoln victory, South Carolina, at a popular convention called by the state legislature, voted unanimously to sever all connections with the Union. It voted to adopt a flag of its own, and to take over all federal buildings. There was dancing in the streets of Charleston. Within a few weeks, Mississippi, Florida, Alabama, Georgia, Louisiana and Texas had all declared themselves no longer a part of the United States. Under the doctrine of states' rights, long preached by John C. Calhoun and other Southern leaders, they felt they had the right to withdraw, or **secede**, from the Union.

In February 1861, at Montgomery, Alabama, a provisional government was established. It was called the Confederate States of America. Jefferson Davis of Mississippi was elected president. In Washington, many Southern residents packed their bags and left for the Confederacy.

Garrisonian abolitionists had long felt the slaveholding South had no right to be in the Union. They agreed with Wendell Phillips when he said, "Let the South march off with flags and trumpets, and we will speed the parting guest . . . and rejoice that she has departed."

In such a climate of defiance and disunity, on March 4, 1861, Lincoln took the oath of office. On April 12, Confederate forces bombarded Fort Sumter, South Carolina. The Civil War had begun.

A cartoon showing the black man supporting the cotton economy of the Confederacy.

Workers at a government blacksmith shop.

Dockworkers unloading Army supplies.

Work, Yes; Fight, No

During the first year of the Civil War, participation by blacks was limited almost entirely to non-military service. The government feared that the border states might join the rebels if blacks were enlisted. They also felt that white troops might refuse to fight alongside black troops. The blacks, for whom to a large degree the war was being fought, could not engage in the fighting.

From the beginning, men of color stood ready to enlist. In Boston, Providence, New York and other cities, blacks, at their own expense, organized and equipped drill units. In response to the offers to volunteer, the War Department replied that it had "no intention to call into the service of the government any colored soldiers."

Black activities were limited to labor behind the lines. They worked as teamsters, camp attendants, waiters and cooks. However, the first man to be honorably discharged from the Union Army was black. Without mentioning his heritage, this man, who had a very light complexion, enlisted in New York City. But, after a few days, his race was discovered and he was handed his walking papers.

The first black in uniform to be wounded was Nicholas Biddle. He was an escaped slave who settled in Pottsville, Pennsylvania. Two days after the call for volunteers, Biddle had attached himself to a troop unit heading for the defense of Washington. The white soldiers gave him a uniform. The company marched through the slaveholding city of Baltimore on April 18, 1861. They were taunted by white onlookers in the streets. The one black among them was especially singled out for abuse. The rabble turned into a jeering, stone-throwing mob. Biddle was felled by a rock. It cut his scalp to the bone, leaving blood on the cobblestones as his comrades supported him.

Freedom Through Invasion

At Bull Run, on Virginia soil about 25 miles outside of Washington, was the first great conflict. The Union troops were routed and the Confederates headed into Maryland.

Black peddlers trade with soldiers in South Carolina.

A federal naval blockade of the entire Eastern seaboard had proved successful. By the end of 1861, the Northern armies had invaded portions of the coast as far as the Sea Islands of South Carolina.

These islands were used as supply stations for the blockading fleet. On the island of Hilton Head, military headquarters were set up. To these islands, especially to Hilton Head and Port Royal, on which the town of Beaufort was located, flocked thousands of runaway slaves to cast their lot with the Yankees.

By September, an alarmed Confederacy estimated that as many as 10,000 slaves had absconded to the enemy in that region. Sometimes the refugees brought useful information to the Union lines. Familiar with the countryside, many became **foragers** (people who search for food) for the troops. They brought in fruits, vegetables, chickens and pigs. They sold them to the soldiers. When Army hospitals and barracks had to be built, blacks went into the forests and chopped down trees for lumber. By night, from neighboring Confederate plantations, they stole horses, mules and cows, which they turned over to the Yankees.

One ex-slave knew where a large number of bales of cotton had been hidden up the river. He was provided with a boat and some soldiers to secure it. The cotton turned out to be worth several thousand dollars.

Meanwhile, Union troops continued southward to the mouth of the Savannah River. And they went into Florida as far as St. Augustine. The Department of the South was created. During the second year of the war, the new Confederate General Robert E. Lee's attempt to invade the North was checked at Antietam, Maryland. Nashville fell. Union General Ulysses S. Grant captured Fort Donelson on the Cumberland River. This forced the Confederates out of Kentucky and western Tennessee. And General Benjamin Butler entered New Orleans. In these areas, too, in ever-increasing numbers, bondsmen flocked to the Union camps.

Education Behind the Lines

In the East, Douglass and others were trying to get the government to enlist black troops. The old abolitionist societies had begun to support the war effort with vigor. From their groups and from the American Missionary Association grew various movements to aid the blacks who found themselves within the Union lines in the liberated areas. Churches and clubs were persuaded to send clothing, medicine, seed, farming tools and other necessary items to the blacks.

And, of far greater import, teachers were sent to the South. A free black woman, Mary S. Peake, with the help of Lewis C. Lockwood, set up a school at Hampton, Virginia, in the fall of 1861. The following spring, some 50 men and women sailed from New York to teach in the Port Royal area. They set up 30

Slaves mounting a Confederate cannon at Fort Sumter.

Teamsters with General Butler (at Bermuda Hundred).

Dock laborers at a Southern port in Union hands.

schools in the Sea Islands for the black followers of the Union armies, the workers and their families. Vincent Colyer opened a school in two small black churches in New Bern, North Carolina. More than 600 black men and women appeared the first night. During the day, Colyer taught poor whites. In Lawrence, Kansas, a night school was started with volunteer white teachers.

Freedmen's relief societies came into being in many Northern cities. They raised funds for books and teachers' salaries. They raised funds to help supply the physical needs of the former slaves, many of whom reached federal territory in rags and were weak with hunger. These latter needs were temporary. But the need for educational opportunities grew.

The foundation laid by the abolitionists in this field marked the beginnings of free education in many Southern communities. And the specialized training given some of the escaped slaves as mechanics, gunsmiths and hospital orderlies gave them skills for earning a decent living for the rest of their lives.

CHAPTER CHECK

1. What did Abraham Lincoln mean when he said "A house divided against itself cannot stand?"
2. Why do you think that blacks were limited to non-military roles at the beginning of the war?
3. How did the old abolition societies help the newly freed slaves during the Civil War?
4. Imagine . . . you are a Southern slave. How would you react to news that the Union army was in your area? What are some actions you would take?

The Emancipation Proclamation.

CHAPTER 21

War's End Brings Freedom

A recruiting poster for black volunteers.

One of the most amazing escapes from Confederate to Union jurisdiction was led by the young South Carolina slave Robert Smalls. Smalls was a seaman on the *Planter*, a cotton steamer. The Confederates had converted it into a gunboat. Its crew was black, its officers were white.

One spring night in 1862, Smalls smuggled his wife, his children, his sister-in-law and his brother's wife and child aboard. The white officers were sleeping ashore at their homes in Charleston. Smalls fired the boiler and hoisted the Confederate flag. Just before dawn, he steamed out to the open sea. As he came within sight of the blockade vessels of the United States Navy, he hauled down the Confederate colors and hoisted a white flag of truce.

The Union sailors boarded the *Planter*. They found Smalls and his black crew. Smalls promptly turned the ship over to the Union as their gift from the Confederacy. This daring exploit was widely publicized in the North. Congress voted Smalls a sizable sum of money. Lincoln signed the appropriation.

That same year in Mississippi, Jefferson Davis' plantation fell within federal lines. The President of the Confederacy lost a sizable amount to the Union encampment at Chickasaw Bayou. By this time, the government had set up camps from Washington to Memphis to care for blacks who had escaped or who had been abandoned by their owners. They fed and clothed them and assigned work.

Unofficial Fighters

In the spring of 1862, Union General David Hunter called for the creation of a black regiment in South Carolina. Because few blacks volunteered, Hunter instituted a draft. He went from plantation to plantation and forceably removed about 500 able-bodied black men. The uproar among the blacks that resulted, forced him to offer the men a choice. Hunter said they could return to their owners or remain with him. Many chose to stay. From this group was born the First South Carolina Volunteers. In the late summer of that year, one of its companies was sent to an island off the Georgia coast for patrol duty. This unit, with the men ragged and still unpaid after three months of service, was disbanded without ever having been officially **mustered** (formally enrolled) into the army.

Another such luckless group was the First Regiment of Kansas Colored Volunteers. They were under General Jim Lane. They were formed in the fall of 1862 in defiance of the officials in Washington. They saw action twice against rebel fighters. On the Osage River in Missouri, one of their soldiers was killed. Several more were wounded, battling some 600 of the enemy. They, too, had gone unpaid for months. Their commander sought to persuade the Secretary of War to make their standing official, but they were ordered to disband.

In New Orleans, General Ben Butler, acting entirely on his own, issued a call for colored vounteers in August 1862. The response was enthusiastic. And the First Regiment Louisiana Native Guards was formed. Composed of both former slaves and free men of color, many of them French-speaking, this became the first black unit actually mustered into the Union armies. For the duration of the war it was used to guard the approaches to New Orleans.

In November, the formerly disbanded and ill-treated regiment of the First South Carolina Volunteers was mustered in. Shortly thereafter, the First Kansas Colored Regiment was given official standing. They became the initial all-black regiment in a Northern area. But the bar to the general enlistment of blacks remained until the proclamation of an eventful document in January 1863. The President put his hand and seal to their freedom warrant.

A regiment of black soldiers receiving the flag.

Blacks celebrate in New Bern, North Carolina when they learn that units of black troops will be formed.

The Emancipation Proclamation

"... On the first day of January, in the year of our Lord one thousand eight hundred and sixty-three, all persons held as slaves within any State or designated part of a State, the people whereof shall then be in rebellion against the United States, shall be then, thenceforward, and forever free; and the Executive Government of the United States, including the military and naval authority thereof, will recognize and maintain the freedom of such persons, and will do no act or acts to repress such persons, or any of them, in any efforts they may make for their actual freedom .... And I further declare and make known, that such persons of suitable condition, will be received into the armed service of the United States to garrison forts, positions, stations, and other places, and to man vessels of all sorts in said service. And upon this act, sincerely believed to be an act of justice, warranted by the Constitution, upon military necessity, I invoke the considerate judgment of mankind and the gracious favor of Almighty God. In witness whereof, I have hereunto set my hand and caused the seal of the United States to be affixed. Done at the City of Washington, this first day of January, in the year of our Lord one thousand eight hundred and sixty-three, and of the Independence of the United States of America the eighty-seventh."

—By the President:
Abraham Lincoln

The war ends and soldiers are allowed to return home.

The War Ends

That fall, the Union General William T. Sherman began his devastating march through Georgia. On April 2, 1865, the capital of the Confederacy, Richmond, was abandoned to the Union forces. The government again occupied Fort Sumter. On April 9, General Lee surrendered to General Grant at Appomattox, Virginia. And on May 10, the rebel president, Jefferson Davis, was captured. He was imprisoned at Fortress Monroe, the former haven of escaped slaves.

Although the war was over, the 62nd U.S. Colored Infantry engaged in a minor skirmish in Texas on May 13 with rebel holdouts. Sergeant Crocket is believed to have been the last black man to shed blood in the Civil War.

When Richmond fell, President Lincoln went to the city by boat. As he walked through the streets, he was surrounded by weeping blacks to whom his name had come to mean "Saviour." Ten days later, Lincoln was dead, assassinated by a fanatic actor who wished to avenge the cause of the South.

Some 186,000 blacks had enlisted in the Union Army. Ninety-three thousand came from the seceded states. Forty thousand came from the border states, and 52,000 came from the free states. At least 38,000 black soldiers died to save the Republic and to put an end to slavery.

The Thirteenth Amendment

Lincoln's Emancipation Proclamation had been issued as a military edict. It affected only the slaves in those portions of the commonwealth then in rebellion.

It was the Thirteenth Amendment to the Constitution which finally abolished slavery

President Lincoln enters Richmond, April 4, 1865.

everywhere in the United States. Before his death, Lincoln had urged Congress to act. On January 31, 1865, the Thirteenth Amendment passed the House of Representatives. It was ratified during the year by the required number of states. On December 18, it was proclaimed in effect. Slavery was now no longer legal anywhere in America.

The long fight of the white abolitionists, the black runaways, the black and white Underground Railroad workers had at last been won. The Thirteenth Amendment declared, "Neither slavery nor involuntary servitude, except as a punishment for crime whereof the party shall have been duly convicted, shall exist within the United States, or any place subject to their jurisdiction. Congress shall have power to enforce this article by appropriate legislation."

The struggle that had begun ostensibly over states' rights, and only secondarily over slavery, had culminated in the freedom of the slave.

As for the slaves themselves, newly set free, a new world came into existence. A new way of life began. Eventually each freed slave had to stand on his or her own. And there were grave problems in the South for both former slave and master.

"What I likes best, to be slave or free?" said one old black man. "Well, it's this way. In slavery I owns nothing and never owns nothing. In freedom I owns the house and raise the family. All that causes me worriation—and in slavery I has no worriation—but I takes the freedom."

CHAPTER CHECK

1. What military contributions did blacks make to the war effort?
2. Why do you think that the Civil War changed from a struggle over states rights to one of freedom for the slave?
3. Imagine . . . you are (a) a Southern slave, and (b) a Southern slaveowner. How would you react to the Emancipation Proclamation?

Blacks heading for Hilton Head, South Carolina, to join the First South Carolina Volunteer Regiment.

Main Events

1. During the American Revolution blacks petitioned for their freedom and the first antislavery societies were formed.

2. In the 1820s, both black and white antislavery newspapers began publication. *The Liberator* first appeared in 1831.

3. In 1829, David Walker's *Appeal* called for violence if necessary to overthrow slavery.

4. In 1839, a cargo of Africans killed the captain of the *Amistad* and sailed the ship to freedom.

5. In 1841, the escaped slave Frederick Douglass made his first appearance before an abolitionist audience. He soon became one of the most important abolitionists in the world.

6. In the period before the Civil War, thousands of Southern slaves escaped to freedom on the Underground Railroad.

7. The Fugitive Slave Law of 1850 made it easier to capture escaped slaves in the North, and angered both sections of the country.

8. In 1852, the novel *Uncle Tom's Cabin* was published.

9. In 1859, John Brown attempted to start an armed slave rebellion at Harper's Ferry.

10. On January 1, 1863, the Emancipation Proclamation was issued.

11. During the Civil War some 186,000 blacks enlisted in the Union Army. Many thousands more helped in other ways.

12. In 1865, the Thirteenth Amendment to the Constitution abolished slavery in the entire United States.

Words to Know

Match the following words with their correct definitions. Number your paper from 1 to 12, and write the correct word beside each number.

acquit
arsenal
Fugitive Slave
  Law
Liberty Party
manumission
moral suasion

mustered
mystic
refugee
secede
Underground
  Railroad
Vigilance Committee

1. a person who flees for safety or freedom
2. having enlisted in the military service of a country
3. a place for storing weapons and military equipment
4. the first anti-slavery political organization
5. a network of places and people who helped escaping slaves

6. to find someone not guilty in a court case
7. freeing someone from slavery
8. someone who experiences a direct communion with God
9. an organization set up to protect the rights of blacks
10. to withdraw from a political organization
11. to persuade someone by appealing to their principles
12. made it a crime to harbor escaped slaves

Thinking and Writing

A. Using Your Powers of Persuasion

People use their powers of persuasion to convince other people to think as they do. Sometimes, they state facts very clearly. Sometimes, they appeal to other people's feelings. Both facts and feelings are important means of persuasion.

One way of persuading people is through an editorial. Imagine that you are an anti-slavery newspaper editor. Write an editorial for your paper. Convince your readers that slavery should be abolished now.

B. Putting Yourself in Another Person's Place

You are a former slave in the South. The Civil War is over. You are now free. You have dreamed of this all your life. Write a paragraph or two telling how you feel and what you plan to do. Think about the following questions:

1. How will your life be different now?
2. What does it mean to be free?

A black soldier on guard duty.

PART FIVE

UP FROM SLAVERY

1865–1900

A drawing of a school for blacks in the South, attended by young and old.

LOOKING AHEAD · PART FIVE · 1865–1900

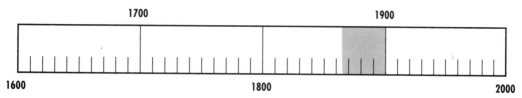

Following the Civil War, the South was a shambles. Its farms were neglected and its economy was in ruins. And many of its citizens had been killed or wounded. For both blacks and whites there were prospects of desolation and starvation. But the immediate future looked bleaker for the four million newly freed slaves, often called **freedmen**.

To cope with this situation, Congress set up the Freedmen's Bureau. Among its accomplishments, the Bureau helped blacks and poor whites find jobs and gain an education. Thousands of Northern white teachers and black churches also aided in setting up schools.

In an effort to restore as much of the slave system as possible, each former Confederate state passed a set of Black Codes. These laws tried to regulate the movements and activities of the newly freed slaves.

These actions outraged many Northerners, especially Republicans in Congress. In 1866, Congress passed the first Civil Rights Act. Soon it also passed the Reconstruction Acts and the Fourteenth and Fifteenth Amendments. These guaranteed basic civil rights to blacks, including the right to vote.

Federal troops stationed in the South helped to protect the rights of blacks. During this time some 700,000 freedmen were added to the voting rolls. Many blacks par-

Blacks lining up for aid at the Memphis Freedmen's Bureau.

ticipated in local and state governments. Some even served in the United States Congress. These black officeholders took their jobs seriously and helped make many improvements.

The numerous changes during Reconstruction angered many Southern whites. They tried to deny black Americans their civil rights. The Ku Klux Klan and other malicious gangs of hooded night riders attacked blacks and their white supporters. They were dedicated to seeing the old social arrangements return. They created a reign of terror: frightening, punishing, and killing blacks who wanted to change the old ways.

Eventually, many of the radical leaders in Congress left. Other issues became more important for the Northern supporters of black equality. By 1877, all Federal troops had been pulled out of the South, and Reconstruction came to an end.

Following Reconstruction, a system of rigid segregation developed in the South. Blacks were legally separated from whites through a series of Jim Crow laws. In 1896, the Supreme Court declared that these "separate but equal" laws were constitutional.

Blacks were also denied their legal rights through an increased wave of racial violence. The biggest problem was the growing number of lynchings, which reached a peak at the end of the 19th century.

One of the rights which blacks lost was the right to participate in politics. Those who wanted to enter the new political organizations, such as the Southern Farmers' Alliance or Populist Party, were denied equal access. Blacks who tried to vote were beaten or killed. Southern states began legally barring blacks from voting through constitutional conventions and use of the grandfather clause. By the turn of the century, most Southern blacks could no longer vote.

One basic post-war problem was jobs. Few Southerners, black or white, had any money. Most owned no land and were forced to take whatever work was available. Eventually, a system known as **sharecropping** developed. In it, the landowner and the farmer shared in the profits of the crops. However, in practice, most blacks saw little profit and became tied by debt to the land.

Major Northern businesses moved into the South after the war. However, almost all the new jobs went to whites. Also, the old skilled black artisans of **antebellum** (before the war) days found their places increasingly filled by white workers. By 1900, less than five percent of all blacks held skilled jobs.

Blacks were generally barred from white labor organizations. Separate groups, or no union at all, was often the dilemma of the black worker. In both the North and the South, blacks formed their own separate locals. But white laborers often refused to recognize black labor organizations. Having no protection, black workers were often forced to accept lower wages in order to live.

Although suppressed as a race, a few blacks did manage to succeed. Some created important inventions for American industry. By the end of the nineteenth century, Booker T. Washington had become the most powerful representative of his people. Backed by high government officials, this former slave led a new cause for black people at his school, the Tuskegee Institute. Washington's philosophy was that blacks should work hard and make the most of the opportunities that whites left for them. Eventually, he would be challenged by other black leaders. But in a time of rigid segregation and heavy racial violence, he was the most influential black leader in America.

Booker T. Washington.

A cabin (right). Below, squatters among the ruins of Columbia, South Carolina.

CHAPTER 22

Rebuilding the South

"The Yankees freed you. Now let the Yankees feed you." This was the dominant attitude of the former Confederacy toward black people.

"When the Hebrews were emancipated," said Frederick Douglass, "they were given three acres of ground upon which they could live and make a living. But not so when our slaves were emancipated. They were sent away empty-handed, without money, without friends and without a foot of land to stand upon."

Rootless blacks roamed Southern roads like bands of gypsies. Caught "in a hazy realm between bondage and freedom," they received no payment for a lifetime of slave labor. After testing their new-found freedom and looking for family members, many returned to the places they had left. Sometimes, they returned to their old plantations.

The South was a shambles. Its major cities were gutted or shelled. Its farms were neglected. Crops were ungathered. Banks had closed, and Confederate money was worthless. About one-third of white male citizens had been killed or wounded, and slaveholders had lost some $2.5 billion in human property.

For both blacks and whites there were prospects of desolation and starvation. But the immediate future looked bleaker for the 4 million newly freed slaves. To cope with this situation, in March 1865, Congress set up the Freedmen's Bureau under the Army.

"Slabtown," near Hampton, Virginia, built largely of barrel staves by ex-slaves.

A New England schoolteacher holds primary classes for black students in Vicksburg, Mississippi.

Free Schools for All

Against violent Southern opposition, the Freedmen's Bureau distributed rations and medicine to both blacks and poor whites. The bureau's activities were supported by federal troops. It attempted, without much success for lack of land, to resettle blacks in rural areas. It found them jobs, supervised work contracts and sought fair wages. It acted as the freed black's friend in court or set up courts of its own.

The bureau built or aided in the creation of more than 4,000 schools. These schools had some 9,000 teachers and almost 250,000 students. It was the first widespread free public school system in the South. And it led to free education for whites as well as blacks. Perhaps one black in 20 among the newly freed could read and write. By the time the bureau ended its work in 1869, about two in 10 newly freed blacks were literate.

Encouraged by the Freedmen's Bureau and sponsored by Protestant churches, thousands of Northern white teachers came South. Some communities were so hostile that the Northerners risked their lives daily to teach black people. The Northern black churches also sent teachers and money to their brethren.

Many schools and colleges were set up

for black youth. Among them were Shaw University in Raleigh, North Carolina (1865); Fisk University in Nashville, Tennessee (1866); Talledega College in Alabama and Atlanta Baptist College, later renamed Morehouse, (1867) and Clark College, also in Atlanta, (1869).

Rejoining the Union

The political and economic picture of the South was complicated. How could a South, long used to slavery's ways, be rebuilt? How could the seceded states be brought back into the Union without handing over political power to ex-Confederates? What could be done about the anger and violence of whites towards blacks?

It was President Lincoln's opinion that the states of the South should be considered never to have left the Union since they had no constitutional right to secede. Andrew Johnson, the Republican vice president who took office upon Lincoln's death, agreed. He liberally granted pardons to ex-Confederates. He rapidly restored home rule in the South.

In an effort to restore as much of the slave system as possible, each former Confederate state passed a set of Black Codes.

In some places, any black caught without visible means of support could be indentured to an employer. In other communities, black orphans were bound over to white people to work out their childhood. Curfew laws forced black citizens off the streets after sundown. Black witnesses could not testify in court against whites.

Blacks migrating to some Southern states had to post bond or be declared vagrants, subject to arrest. Other states required black travelers to carry passes. Still others

The Abraham Lincoln School for Freedmen in New Orleans, Louisiana.

A group of freedmen discussing their political rights.

The burning of a freedmen's school during a riot in Memphis, Tennessee in 1866.

Masked Ku Kluxers in Mississippi. The Klan was formed in 1865, with General Nathan Bedford Forrest as Grand Wizard.

prohibited assembly unless a white man were present to monitor the meeting. Police courts often sentenced blacks found guilty of crimes to work for planters who had paid their fines. Excessive fines were levied for minor offenses.

These actions outraged many Northerners, especially in the Republican Party. They held that the Southern slaveholders had abandoned and betrayed the Union and its Constitution. They should be made to pay for their actions under the laws of war. What was needed, they argued, was a complete reorganization—a **reconstruction**—of the South. The sternest faction in Congress came to be known as Radical Republicans. They were led in the House of Representatives by Thaddeus Stevens of Pennsylvania and in the Senate by Charles Sumner of Massachusetts.

Meeting in December 1865, Congress moved to take over the reconstruction program. It set up a joint committee headed by Senator William P. Fessenden of Maine, a moderate. President Johnson vetoed the committee's bills which would extend the Freedmen's Bureau for five years and guarantee civil rights to blacks. When Congress overrode his vetoes, the President took his case to the voters. But in the 1866 Congressional elections, overwhelming Republican majorities were elected to both houses. The President had lost his power.

In 1866, Congress passed the first Civil Rights Act. Military commanders in the South were instructed to prevent abuses of blacks' rights. This federal action infuriated the South. Race riots broke out. Julia Hayden, a 17 year-old black teacher, was murdered for running a school for free blacks in Tennessee.

In Memphis, large numbers of armed citizens "commenced firing upon every Negro who made himself visible," the New York *Times* reported. "One Negro on South Street, a quiet, inoffensive laborer, was shot down almost in front of his own cabin, and after life was extinct from his body was fired into, cut and beat in a most horrible manner. . . . So far as I have been able to learn, not a white man was fired on by a Negro."

When it was over, 46 blacks and two white liberals were dead. About 75 other people were wounded.

The same year, the Ku Klux Klan was formed in Tennessee to block the federal government's efforts on behalf of Southern blacks. Hooded nightriders began to terrorize black people. They used arson, beatings, and murder.

In Congress, the joint committee sought and won approval for the Reconstruction Acts of 1867. They divided the South into five districts controlled by martial law. They required that new state constitutions be drawn up and that black men were guaranteed the right to vote. Whenever possible, abandoned lands were to be sold or leased to freedmen. Also, all states seeking readmission to the Union had to ratify the Fourteenth Amendment.

This amendment said that no state shall

A cartoon questioning whether slavery was dead. The box on the left tells of a court-ordered sale of a convicted black man in Maryland. The box on the right tells of the whipping of a black in North Carolina.

A cartoon presenting the labor question from a Southern point of view. The seated man is saying, "My boy we've toiled and taken care of you long enough. Now you've got to work."

"deprive any person of life, liberty or property without due process of law." In short, it guaranteed equal rights to all Americans. The orderly system of justice known as "due process of law" would become one of the most important ideas in constitutional law. In the decades ahead, many civil rights cases would hang on this issue. The amendment was ratified in 1868.

This, along with the passage of the Civil Rights Act, the Reconstruction Acts, and the ratification of the Fifteenth Amendment guaranteeing that voting could not be denied "on account of race, color, or previous condition of servitude," gave Southern blacks some legal protection. It also gave rise to bad feelings among many Southern whites which have festered until this day.

Sharecropping Develops

By the war's end, most Southern planters had little or no money left. With their slaves freed, their problem was how to secure labor for the great plantations.

Freedmen had even less money and barely a change of clothing. The majority were rural workers, accustomed to growing cotton. They were driven by hunger to work for little or nothing. At first, the Freedmen's Bureau urged them to work for former slaveholders under contract, usually for a year at a time. This idea was not popular with newly freed blacks.

Eventually, a system took hold that was more acceptable to planters and blacks. Planters got their crops, and blacks had a certain amount of autonomy. Under the system of tenant **sharecropping**, workers produced a crop in return for housing, seed and credit at a company store.

In theory, when the crop was sold, workers would share the profits. But usually debt, sometimes combined with dishonest bookkeeping, left the worker owing the planter at the year's end. So the black peasant became bound to the soil. Under penalty of arrest for debt, he could not leave. To add to the misery of the landless blacks, the courts leased convicts to work on plantations, on turpentine flats, mines and in building railroads. In time, blacks also had competition from poor whites for whom sharecropping was the only alternative.

Cotton was no longer as profitable as it once had been. Southern fields had not been revitalized by crop rotation or fertilizer. After 1873, the price of cotton dropped sharply and continued to decline until the end of the century. Farm workers, black and white, had a hard row to hoe.

Women, as well as men, worked in the rice paddies.

Women and children at work in a cotton field.

CHAPTER CHECK

1. Describe the condition of the South at the end of the Civil War.

2. What was the Freedmen's Bureau? List at least two of its accomplishments.

3. How did President Andrew Johnson and the Republicans in Congress differ in their attitudes towards Reconstruction?

4. Imagine . . . you are a Northern war veteran. How would you react to news of the Southern Black Codes? What would you like to see done?

Lieutenant Governor O. J. Dunn of Louisiana and black members of the state legislature in 1868.

CHAPTER 23

Blacks in Politics

Under federal military occupation of the South, some 700,000 blacks were added to the voting rolls. They flocked to the polls. Many freedmen participated in municipal and state governments. There were black majorities of registered voters in Alabama, Louisiana, South Carolina, Florida and Mississippi. The Republicans took full advantage of this situation to break the former Democratic stranglehold.

With the aid of some Southerners and the sometimes sincere, sometimes opportunistic help of Northerners, the Republican Party controlled the vote within most Southern states. Southern Democrats called local whites who helped Republicans, **scalawags**. The term they used for Northern newcomers was **carpetbaggers**.

The government helped to protect black voters through the Force Bills of 1870-71. These bills provided, among other things, for the use of federal troops at the polls. The Union League also helped protect black voters.

The **Union League** was a patriotic organization established in the North during the Civil War. Following the war, local chapters were established throughout the South. It soon became an interracial political organization. It provided a vehicle for black political leaders and a structure they could use to express their aspirations.

The last rebel state was readmitted to the Union in 1870. The last federal troops were withdrawn from the South in 1877. After this, blacks began to lose political ground. The terror of the more powerful Klan prevented the freedmen from voting. Their political activity in the South was short-lived, but while it lasted, many offices were for the first time filled by blacks.

Makers of Good Laws

Not all the blacks in Southern politics were illiterate former slaves. Many had been born free. Some were highly educated. In general, they were not vindictive toward their fellow white Southerners or former masters.

Beverly Nash addressed this issue at the constitutional convention of South Carolina. He said, "We recognize the Southern white man as the true friend of the black man. . . . In these public affairs we must unite with our white fellow citizens." Together blacks worked willingly with whites at lawmaking.

Black officeholders lacked political experience. But the law-making bodies in which they sat during Reconstruction made a number of social advances unknown before the war. Uneducated black legislators wanted education themselves. They helped write into the new state constitutions provisions for free public schools. Black men wanted equality before the law. So liberal measures upholding this concept were introduced by them and passed. The freedmen wished to maintain federally-granted suffrage. So they saw to it that it was written into the official codes of their states. Since they were poor, black lawmakers proposed no property qualifications for voting or for holding office.

Senator Blanche K. Bruce of Mississippi.

A cartoon depicting Hiram Revels seated in Jefferson Davis' former seat in the U. S. Senate.

"They opened the ballot box and jury box to thousands of white men who had been debarred from them by lack of earthly possessions," wrote Albion W. Tourgee, a carpetbagger who moved to North Carolina. "They introduced home rule in the South. They abolished the whipping post and branding iron."

New state constitutions were drawn up by these Reconstruction assemblies. And they were the most progressive the South had ever known. Many of their provisions remain in effect today.

Tourgee helped write the new constitution for North Carolina. Later, he became a judge well-known for his opposition to the Ku Klux Klan. He was often threatened.

Blacks in Congress

The first black elected to the U. S. House of Representatives was John Willis Menard of Louisiana. He was chosen to fill a vacancy caused by death. But his seat was challenged and he never served.

The first black Representative to be seated in Washington was Jefferson F. Long of Georgia. He served from 1869-1871. Between that time and 1876, 13 other black men were elected to the House from the Southern states.

Two black Senator were elected. They were Hiram Rhoades Revels, 1870-71, and Blanche Kelso Bruce, 1875-81. Both men were from Mississippi. Revels was elected to fill out the uncompleted term of Jefferson Davis. Revels served for one year. Free-born in North Carolina, he had studied at a Quaker seminary in Ohio and at Knox College. As a minister of the A. M. E. Church, Revels had been an Army chaplain in Mississippi.

Bruce followed Revels in the Senate.

Electioneering in the South, as blacks sought public office.

Bruce had been a Virginia slave who escaped to the North. He studied at Oberlin and later became a planter in Mississippi. In all, from the states of Mississippi, Alabama, Georgia, Florida, Louisiana, Virginia, North Carolina and South Carolina, 22 blacks were elected to Congress before 1901. Eight were from South Carolina. J. H. Rainey and Robert Smalls of that state each completed five terms.

Most of these men had been state or local officials before going to Congress and were not without parliamentary experience. Their education was on a par with that of most other politicians of their day. They took their positions seriously, and their voting records show that they were not only interested in civil rights for blacks but in all of the leading issues of the times. Few became involved in the scandals of graft and corruption which swept the country during those years. The Republican leader James G. Blaine said of them, "They were as a rule studious, earnest, ambitious men, whose public conduct . . . would be honorable to any race."

Nevertheless, these legislators were often blamed for the ills which beset the defeated states. Many biased historians of the period recorded unsubstantiated charges against the black legislators. But the same historians ignored the good things done by the legislatures in which blacks served.

Fruits of the Ballot

During Reconstruction, blacks were elected to a number of high offices in the South. In Little Rock, Arkansas, Mifflin W. Gibbs became the first black municipal judge in the United States. Louisiana had three black lieutenant governors. They were C. C. Antoine, Oscar J. Dunn and P. B. S. Pinchback. The last, in 1873, became acting governor of the state after the removal of the white incumbent. Pinchback was elected to the United States Senate but was never seated.

Jonathan Gibbs, a graduate of Dartmouth College, was secretary of state and superintendent of public instruction in Florida. In South Carolina, Glasgow and London-educated Francis L. Cardozo was, from 1872 to 1876, state treasurer. In Mississippi there were many black officials. John R. Lynch became the speaker of the house, A. K. Davis was lieutenant governor, James Hill was secretary of state. South Carolina had two black lieutenant governors, Alonzo J. Ransier and Richard H. Cleaves.

Many black conventions were held in the North and South in which black citizens were urged to political action. In the North, just after the passage of the Thirteenth Amendment, abolishing slavery, John S. Rock was the first black lawyer to be admitted before the U.S. Supreme Court.

CHAPTER CHECK

1. What were some of the ways that the newly freed slaves participated in their government?
2. How did black politicians change Southern society?
3. Imagine . . . you are a newly elected black politician from the South. What are some of the issues you would be interested in working on? What kind of special problems would you face?

John R. Lynch.

P. B. S. Pinchback.

Oscar J. Dunn.

John S. Rock.

A cartoon of a murdered black man in Richmond, Virginia, with the letters "K.K.K." scratched on the wall.

CHAPTER 24

Reaction Sets In

The Republicans utilized the interests of the freedmen to strengthen their party in the South. This angered the Democrats. Secret orders were organized in addition to the Ku Klux Klan. They included the White Brotherhood, the Rifle Clubs, the Council of Safety, the Pale Faces and the powerful Knights of the White Camellia. The whip, the gun, the rope and fire were their instruments, and **lynching** their common method.

In South Carolina, in 1871, various legally elected black officeholders were ordered to resign immediately on pain of "retributive justice." Night raids on the homes of blacks active in politics were frequent. Women and children as well as men were tortured and whipped. A petition to Congress signed by the black citizens of Frankfort, Kentucky, in 1871, asked for relief from "the Ku Klux Klan riding nightly over the country." It listed by name, place and date more than a hundred outrages.

In the summer of 1876, in Hamburg, South Carolina, the "disgraceful and brutal slaughter of unoffending men . . . for opinion's sake or on account of color" so shocked President Ulysses S. Grant that he wrote a letter to the governor of South Carolina. President Grant continued to describe the scene at Hamburg as "cruel, bloodthirsty, wanton, unprovoked . . . a repetition of the course that has pursued in other states within the last few years, notably in Mississippi and Louisiana." During the elections that fall, South Carolina blacks were frequently beaten and shot to death.

Violence still failed to keep some blacks from going to the polls. In Edgefield, South Carolina, white men blocked the courthouse steps. Blacks voting the Republican ticket could not reach the ballot boxes. The Democrats won the election.

Massachusetts Senator Charles Sumner had tried for several years to get a new civil rights bill through Congress but without success. Finally, the year after his death, a watered-down version of his bill passed both houses of Congress. It was the Civil Rights Act of 1875. Little attention was paid, however, to its provisions. In 1883, it was declared unconstitutional by the Supreme Court.

Representative Thaddeus Stevens died in 1868. Without him or Sumner, there was no voice of power left in Congress to defend black rights. During the Reconstruction period many discouraged planters sold their acreage and moved to the cities. Whatever graciousness there had been in plantation life began to disappear. Few freedmen were able to buy land. After 10 years of freedom, only about five percent of the blacks in the South had acquired farms. None were owners of large plantations.

Jim Crow Laws

During slavery, blacks and whites in the South mingled freely. But the institution of slavery made clear each person's social status. Once slavery ended, many whites felt uncomfortable meeting blacks on equal footing, for example, while waiting for a train or in a public restaurant. To make sure blacks "stayed in their place," many communities set aside "white" and "colored" seats in public places and on public transportation. Drinking fountains, waiting rooms—even cemeteries—were set apart or **segregated** in this way.

This was the custom in many cities and towns across the nation, but in the South, it became law. Nicknamed for the comedian

Federal troops leaving New Orleans, Louisiana, April 24, 1877.

Jim Crow (see Chapter 8), these laws were put in place beginning in the 1870s.

In 1873, a financial panic left depression in its wake. Cotton prices slumped. By 1875, it had dropped to 11 cents a pound, and continued to decline. By the 1890s it was less than five cents a pound.

Party Politics

The Republican Party no longer cherished the idealistic war aims of freeing and protecting blacks. It was now the party of the new industrialists and businessmen. Republicans were open to urgings that blacks be abandoned to their former masters. And they were open to suggestions that the South be given a share of the economic future.

The presidential election of 1876 was in dispute. Democrat Samuel Tilden of New York had won the popular vote. But the returns for the Electoral College were conflicting. Both Democrats and Republicans claimed victory in South Carolina, Louisiana and Florida.

A behind-the-scenes caucus of supporters of Republican Rutherford B. Hayes of Ohio and Southern Democrats eventually came to an agreement. It included several provisions, if the vote swung to Hayes. The provisions were that federal troops would be withdrawn from the South. Substantial subsidies for Southern improvements, such as railroads, would be appropriated. And more federal jobs would go to Southerners.

By a vote of eight to seven, the commission awarded the election to Hayes. He promptly appointed a former Confederate general to his Cabinet as postmaster general. He moved to end military protection of black suffrage. On April 10, 1877, federal troops were withdrawn from South Carolina. On April 24, those stationed in New Orleans left. And in 1878, an order was issued forbidding the use of government troops in elections.

By a combination of illegal terror and state laws limiting black suffrage, the Democratic Party returned to power below the Mason-Dixon line.

A chain gang cleaning Richmond, Virginia streets in preparation for a reception for President Hayes.

Exodus to Kansas

With the former Confederates again in the saddle, thousands of blacks from the Deep South fled to the North and West. They were seeking livelihoods without the chicaneries of the sharecropping system. They were also seeking personal safety from the terror of mobs by day or the Klan by night. But the South did not want to let its black laborers go. Transportation companies were forbidden to sell them tickets. Vagrancy laws were invoked to arrest travelers. And black "agitators" who preached migration were horsewhipped and driven away.

Two black men succeeded in organizing large mass migrations. One was Henry Adams of Louisiana. The other was "Pap" Singleton of Tennessee. Both set Kansas as a goal—the Kansas of old John Brown. Southern Democrats accused Northern Republicans of enticing blacks in order to add their names to Republican voting rolls in the North. Democratic Senator Voorhees of Indiana, in 1878, asked Congress to appoint a committee to investigate the matter.

Both Singleton and Adams were called to Washington to testify. Each gave evidence of the ill-treatment of black people. They told

This illustration shows blacks leaving the South in two different periods of history. The circled inset shows a slave escaping. The other part of the illustration shows freed people waiting for transportation.

of how schools were burned. They told of how children were forced to work in the cotton fields. And they told of how black tenants were kept in debt by plantation trickery and high commissary prices. Despite 1,700 pages of such testimony, the Democrats still contended that Republicans had instigated the mass migration of blacks.

Freedmen continued to leave the South by the thousands. Some of them settled on the public lands that the government had opened up to squatters. Some went into the Native American territories. The largest number went to Kansas. Soon messengers were sent South from Kansas to advise that no more blacks should come there. Under the Homestead Law, some of the migrants acquired land. But most of them had no funds for livestock or farming tools.

The Freedmen's Relief Association and Eastern philanthropists aided the new settlers, to some extent. But although schools were built, neither the state of Kansas nor the federal government gave the blacks any direct help. Western winters were cold and the snow deep and some of the blacks arrived barefoot. But few returned to the South.

A Lexington, Kentucky handbill of 1877.

Louisiana freedmen enroute to Kansas after the great yellow fever epidemic.

CHAPTER CHECK

1. Why do you think most white Southerners were opposed to letting blacks vote?

2. Why do you think that many of the changes made by the Reconstruction governments did not last?

3. Imagine . . . you are a Southern black. What would you do after the collapse of Republican rule in 1876? Would you stay, or would you move to the North or West? What are the advantages and disadvantages of each?

Henry W. Grady.

CHAPTER 25
Segregation Upheld

Henry W. Grady, part-owner and editor of the Atlanta *Constitution*, became the South's most famous white voice through a speech called "The New South." He made the speech first before the New England Society of New York in 1886. He repeated it on many platforms until his death. His objective was to encourage Northern investments in the South and to pacify the Northern conscience concerning black people.

Grady claimed that black workers pros-

pered in the South. He claimed that blacks shared equitably in school funds. And that they had the "fullest protection" of the laws. Therefore, he argued, the problem of black people should be left in the hands of the South. Left "to those among whom his lot is cast, with whom he is indissolubly connected and whose prosperity depends upon their possessing his intelligent sympathy and confidence." As to relations between the North and South, Grady declared that he stood upon "the indissoluble union of American states and the imperishable brotherhood of the American people."

When Grady sat down, the band played "Dixie." Among the 240 guests who lustily applauded his speech were such leaders of American industry and opinion as J. Pierpont Morgan, Charles L. Tiffany, Elihu Root, Russell Sage and the editor of the New York *Times*, Charles R. Miller.

The *Times*, like most of the country's leading papers, extolled the speech to the highest. But it neglected to comment upon its gross untruths regarding blacks. The Boston *Transcript* approvingly quoted the Springfield *Republican*, "New England rejoices in the New South most heartily."

The black press, however, did not think so highly of Grady's oration. The *Christian Recorder* commented, "In that address, beneath the glamour of eloquence, the old rebel spirit and the old South are seen throughout."

Court Approves Separation

The Supreme Court, made up mostly of Northerners and Republicans, strongly sup-
ported the growing national opinion that black people were not entitled to the same civil rights as whites. The 1883 Supreme Court decision on civil rights written by Justice Joseph Bradley, a New Jersey Republican, gave approval to the Jim Crow segregation of blacks by individuals in all states.

The *Plessy v. Ferguson* decision of 1896 upheld the constitutionality of state laws providing "separate but equal" accommodations for blacks. This precedent greatly aided the spread of segregation on public transportation and in public places throughout the nation. Lower federal courts and the Interstate Commerce Commission had already approved such segregation. Blacks correctly contended that separate accommodations were rarely, if ever, equal.

When Homer Plessy was forced from a "white" railway coach in Louisiana, the Supreme Court upheld the state segregation statute. It declared that the Fourteenth Amendment "could not have been intended to abolish distinctions based on color, or to enforce . . . a co-mingling of the two races upon terms unsatisfactory to either."

Justice Joseph Bradley.

Justice John Marshall Harlan.

Southern Senators confer in a cloakroom.

Justice John Marshall Harlan wrote a strong dissent.

"In view of the Constitution, in the eye of the law, there is in this country no superior, dominant, ruling class of citizens. There is no caste here. Our Constitution is color-blind, and neither knows nor tolerates classes among citizens. . . . It is therefore to be regretted that this high tribunal . . . has reached the conclusion that it is competent for a State to regulate the enjoyment by citizens of their civil rights solely upon the basis of race. In my opinion, the judgment this day rendered will, in time, prove to be quite as pernicious as the decision made by this tribunal in the Dred Scott case. . . . The thin disguise of equal accommodations for passengers in railroad coaches will not mislead anyone, nor atone for the wrong this day done."

CHAPTER CHECK

1. Why do you think that many white Northerners found Henry Grady's message so appealing?
2. Why do you think that segregation became the dominant trend in the South after Reconstruction?
3. Imagine . . . you are the leader of your local black community in the South. How would you react to the *Plessy v. Ferguson* decision of 1896? What are some actions you might take?

Sewer diggers in Savannah, Georgia.

CHAPTER 26

Blacks Pushed Aside

The end of Reconstruction found poor white farmers in worse condition than after the war. Out of their discontent grew the Southern Farmers' Alliance. By the 1890s, the Alliance had acquired considerable political influence. It attempted to force agricultural reforms in Washington.

In South Carolina, the poor whites elected to the governorship a one-eyed farmer, Benjamin R. Tillman. Later, they sent him to the Senate. In Georgia, the Farmers' Alliance elected the governor. Then it gained control of the state legislature and sent Thomas E. Watson to Congress.

As the white Alliance spread rapidly through the South, the Colored Farmers'

National Alliance moved with it. The agrarian radicalism of the whites was shared by the blacks. But Jim Crow kept their organizations separate. Each at its peak was reported to have more than 1,250,000 members. At first, through the Colored Alliance, Tillman and Watson made overtures for the black vote. Later, they became violently anti-Catholic, anti-Jewish and anti-black.

Battle over Ballots

A new political party called the People's, or Populist, Party developed out of the Farmers' Alliances. It demanded relief for the farmers. It called for government ownership of railroads and communications and graduated income taxes. In 1892, this new party polled more than a million votes for the presidency. They sent 15 men to Congress and elected two governors. In North Carolina, the Populists and the Republicans combined forces. In 1894, with blacks voting, they gained control of the legislature. A large number of local offices went to black men. In various cities blacks became policemen, sheriffs and aldermen.

This, in turn, aroused Southern Democrats to allow blacks more access to the polls, provided they voted for Democrats. There was a temporary upsurge of black political influence in some parts of the South. Tom Watson told poor whites and blacks they were being kept apart that they might more easily be robbed by the big land owners. He urged them to vote together on a platform of democratic reform.

But the time when all three parties bid for the black vote was brief. Whites of all parties decided to keep the vote for themselves. The Mississippi politician J.K. Vardaman declared he was against any black man voting, whether he was educated or not. Even before the rise of the Populists his state had **disfranchised** blacks through a constitutional convention. Political demagogues (A **demagogue** is a speaker who plays to popular prejudices.) such as Cole Blease and Hoke Smith, worked with those seeking to disfranchise blacks. Property, poll tax and literacy requirements were eventually incorporated into state constitutions.

In 1898, Louisiana invented a new legal device destined to spread in the South. It was the **grandfather clause**. It exempted from literacy and property tests those men whose grandfathers or fathers had voted prior to 1867. Of course, this meant that most blacks were kept off the registration books. The more than 130,000 registered black voters in Louisiana were reduced within two years to about 5,000. In Alabama, by 1900, only 3,000 blacks remained on the voting lists. Riots broke out, and in Georgia and Virginia elections a number of blacks were killed. In 1898, in Wilmington, North Carolina, 11 blacks died and 25 were wounded.

When the Democratic Party in the South instituted the all-white primaries, blacks were almost totally disfranchised. Because of a fear of the potential of the black vote, the Democrats forestalled the development of a two-party system in the South, lest blacks gain the balance of power. At the turn of the century white supremacy had won its political battle. The high hopes of the blacks which had been born during the Reconstruction era were dashed. The blacks of the South were no better off than slaves again, insofar as their right to the ballot was concerned.

Congressman Robert Smalls.

Resistance Continues

Black leaders throughout the South attempted to turn back the rising tide of disfranchisement. At the South Carolina constitutional convention of 1895, former Congressman Thomas E. Miller proposed that the new state constitution be submitted to the people for ratification. But no popular vote was ever taken. Five other blacks, including former Congressman Robert Smalls, presented the same convention proposals guaranteeing every citizen the right to register and vote. Their proposals were rejected by a vote of 130 to 6. The minority votes were those of the black delegates.

Before complete disfranchisement set in, the last six blacks to represent Southern states in Congress were the Representatives Henry P. Cheatham of North Carolina, 1889-93, John Mercer Langston of Virginia, 1890-91, Thomas E. Miller of South Carolina, 1890-91, George W. Murray of South Carolina, 1893-97, and George H. White of North Carolina, 1897-1901. George White was the last black representative from the old South. All of these men continued active in civic and political affairs after leaving Congress.

Fighting Lynching

On January 20, 1900, George H. White introduced into the House of Representatives the first bill designed to make lynching a federal offense. The year before, 87 blacks and 12 white men had been lynched. During the decade from 1890 to 1900, more than 1,800 mob murders by hanging, burning, shooting or beating were recorded. Of the victims, 1,400 were black. Newspapers from January to October 1900, reported 114 lynchings, all but two in the South. "It is evident that the white people of the South have no further use for the Negro," wrote an Arkansas minister, E.M. Argyle, to the *Christian Recorder* in 1892. "He is being treated worse now than at any other time since the surrender."

But that same year Frederick Douglass said, "Nor is the South alone responsible for this burning shame. ... The sin against the

Congressman George H. White.

Congressman John M. Langston.

Ida B. Wells.

Negro is both sectional and national; and until the voice of the North shall be heard in emphatic condemnation and withering reproach against these continued ruthless mob-law murders, it will remain equally involved with the South in this common crime."

The Cleveland *Gazette* reported in 1898 violence against two black postmasters. They were the shooting of Isaac H. Loftin in Georgia and the burning of the post office and lynching of a Postmaster Baker in Lake City, South Carolina. His wife, three daughters and a son were wounded and a baby was killed. In both of these cases, the paper stated, concerning the mob, "No effort to arrest and punish them has ever been made."

Ida B. Wells

A demand for the arrest and punishment of lynchers became a major black crusade at the turn of the century. The outstanding figure in this movement was a black woman, Ida B. Wells. In 1895, she compiled the first statistical pamphlet on lynching, *A Red Record.*

Wells, born in Mississippi in 1869, taught school in Memphis, Tennessee. Then she became the editor and part-owner of a newspaper, the Memphis *Free Speech*, which circulated throughout the Mississippi Delta. In May 1892, her paper exposed some of the forces involved in the lynching of three young black businessmen in Memphis. Because of those reports, her offices were demolished by white hoodlums and she was driven from the city.

In Chicago, Wells married the militant race leader Ferdinand Barnett. Both became active in the National Equal Rights League. Wells became chairperson of the Anti-lynching Speakers Bureau of the National Afro-American Council. She became a famous speaker on black rights at home and abroad. Statistically, she proved that the "protection of white womanhood," as the South claimed, was not the basis for lynchings. In no given year had even half of the blacks who were lynched been charged with rape or attempted rape. In 1900, less than 15 percent of those lynched had been so suspected. Lynching, she contended, was a form of intimidation to preserve the plantation economy and the white ballot box of the South.

CHAPTER CHECK

1. Why do you think the efforts at cooperation between blacks and whites in the Farmers' Alliances eventually failed?
2. In what ways were blacks disfranchised in the South in the late nineteenth century?
3. Imagine . . . you are a Southern black in the late nineteenth century. How would you react to the lynchings occurring all around you? What could you do to stop it?

Jan Matzeliger, inventor, and a drawing of his patented lasting machine.

CHAPTER 27

Industry and the Black Worker

Early in the 1870s, Jan Matzeliger came to the United States from Dutch Guiana and worked as a shoemaker's apprentice in Philadelphia. When he was 25, he went to Lynn, Massachusetts. There he worked in a shoe factory. He was disturbed by the amount of time it took to last (make or repair) shoes by hand. He began to work at night on a machine to do this exacting labor.

Within a few years, he had made a model for pleating leather at the toe of a shoe. He then perfected a method of attaching the uppers of a shoe to the sole, by machine, as smoothly as hand-lasters could do it.

In 1883, Matzeliger patented his lasting machine. It revolutionized the shoe industry. It was the first machine of its kind "capable of performing all the steps required to hold a shoe on its last, grip and pull the leather down around the heel, guide and drive the nails into place and then discharge the shoe from the machine." The United Shoe Machinery Company of Boston bought the invention. It enabled them to control, within a few years, almost the entire shoe machinery trade and greatly increased their profits. Matzeliger's method of making shoes was adopted in factories around the world.

Other Inventors

During slavery, a bondsman could not take out a patent nor make a contract. But free men of color were not so restricted. The first patent granted a black was for a corn harvester. It was invented in 1834 by Henry Blair of Maryland. In 1846, Norbert Rillieux of Louisiana patented a vacuum pan that revolutionized the sugar-refining process.

In 1872, Elijah McCoy of Michigan, began work on various appliances related to the lubrication of engines. He perfected a cup that became generally used on railroads and ocean steamers. This cup made it unnecessary to stop machines in order to oil them. McCoy was eventually granted some 57 patents. In 1885, John J. Parker set up his own foundry and machine company. He invented and manufactured a screw for tobacco presses. Around 1885, in Cincinnati, Granville T. Woods began work on several inventions. Some of his patents were in telegraphy. One was a system of sending telegrams from a train in motion. His inventions were sold to the American Bell Telephone Company, the General Electric Company and the Westing-

house Air Brake Company before his death in 1910.

So blacks, who were generally denied skilled jobs in factories, aided the increased mechanization of American manufacturing through a number of important inventions.

Factories Move South

Major Northern businesses moved South after the Civil War. They were attracted by its large supply of cheap, non-unionized labor. The South also had plentiful water power and rich coal, iron and oil resources. Mills, plants and foundries were constructed in many Southern communities. In the 1880s, the number of cotton mills in the region grew. New railroads were built. Mining, smelting and lumber industries developed rapidly. Local management was largely in the hands of the Southerners; white workers were preferred.

The only roles for blacks, if any, were as heavy laborers at the lowest wage scales. Except for porters, textile mills were almost 100 percent white. On railroad engines, black firemen were often used to shovel coal but were never promoted to engineer. By 1900, less than four percent of the blacks in the South were employed in skilled jobs. The rest were unskilled laborers.

Road building, sewer digging, street cleaning, brick making, rock quarrying, furnace stoking and mining were jobs allotted blacks. By 1890, one-third of all black workers were female domestic servants, the lowest paid in America. The old skilled black artisans of antebellum days found their places increasingly filled by white workers. They formed guilds barring blacks. And they would strike rather than work alongside black men.

The Rockwood iron furnaces in eastern Tennessee.

Blacks and the New Unions

Blacks were generally barred from white labor groups. However, the Knights of Labor in 1879, appointed black organizers. It announced that it hoped to organize all workers—black and white, skilled and unskilled.

Older unions opposed this plan. They were organized by skill or craft, i.e. mineworkers, plasterers, etc. When, in 1886, the American Federation of Labor (AFL) was formed, each affiliated craft union was allowed to make its own rules regarding race. Needless to say most locals excluded blacks. Meanwhile, the Knights of Labor were denounced as too radical. They declined, but at their peak, they had 60,000 black workers.

Union barriers to black membership, North and South, worked against white labor. In the case of strikes, employers did not hesitate to use blacks as strikebreakers. Blacks were often willing to play this role because their color permitted them no chance to work otherwise.

Separate groups, or no union at all, was often the choice of black workers. In both North and South, blacks formed their own locals. White organized labor often refused to recognize black labor organizations. And they often refused to work with black workers, organized or not. Having little or no protection, black workers were forced to accept lower wages in order to live. Many employers were willing to pay a worker as little as possible, or to secure free labor.

In parts of the South, a system of almost free labor evolved using prisoners, most of them black. In the **convict-lease system**, prisoners were hired out to companies or individuals. These "chain gangs" worked in lumber mills, quarries, mines, brickyards or factories to the profit of state or county, but not

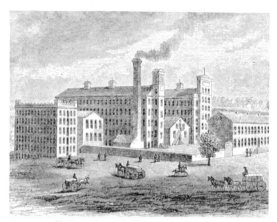

Cotton mills in Columbus, Georgia.

to the gain of the workers. In South Carolina, Governor Ben Tillman made flagrant use of this system.

From the Carolinas to Florida, convicts in striped garb and chains helped to build new roads. The South's growing industries required increased transportation. Farther West, along the Mississippi River, chain gangs kept flood levees repaired. To maintain this source of free labor, men were given long sentences—or heavy fines which they had to work off. Finally, the system reduced the number of paying jobs available for poor whites and blacks.

CHAPTER CHECK

1. How did African Americans contribute to the increased mechanization of American manufacturing? What are some of their important inventions?
2. Why do you think white laborers were opposed to allowing blacks into their unions?
3. Imagine . . . you are a black skilled laborer. What are some problems you would face trying to obtain work? How would this change over time?

Former President Theodore Roosevelt addressing the National Negro Business League.

CHAPTER 28

A School Is Born

As a child, the black man destined to become one of the most famous Americans of his time worked in the salt mines of West Virginia. Booker T. Washington was his name. He was born in bondage on April 5, 1856. Like Frederick Douglass, his father had been a white slaveowner. His mother was a slave. As a small boy he was called one day to the "big house" of the Virginia plantation. There, crowded in among other slaves, he heard a government official read to them the Emancipation Proclamation. He watched the tears stream down his mother's face at the news that they were free.

After rising at 4 A.M. and working all day in the mines, Booker and his mother tried to learn their ABCs at night by the light of the fire. One day in the dark mine, Booker heard the men talking about a Virginia school called Hampton. At Hampton, blacks were taught trades. He made up his mind to go there. The old people of the town helped him with nickels, dimes and quarters. When he was 16, he started out. First he rode a stagecoach until his money ran out. Then through a combination of odd jobs, walking and begging rides, he reached Hampton. He worked his way through college as a janitor.

Young Washington was deeply impressed by General Samuel C. Armstrong, the founder of Hampton, and by the dedicated New Englanders who taught there. "What a rare set of human beings," he later wrote, declaring that their role in the education of blacks in the hard days after the Civil War would "make one of the most thrilling parts of the history of this country." Like them, he wanted to become a teacher. Washington went back to West Virginia where he was the only teacher among many eager learners. He taught children all day and grown-ups at night. Then Hampton asked him to return to supervise a dormitory for 60 Native Americans arriving there to study.

When Washington was 25, a white banker and a black mechanic in an Alabama village wrote to Hampton. They asked for a teacher to open a normal school for rural blacks. (A **normal school** trains teachers.) General Armstrong sent Washington.

A leaky old church was his school. He was the sole teacher. There was a little money for his salary, but none for books, land or a building. The young teacher and his students decided to raise funds for land and to build a school. Between sessions in reading, writing and figuring, they laid the foundations and raised the walls. In this way, in 1881, Tuskegee Institute came into being.

The Spirit of Tuskegee

Tuskegee was destined to become a pioneer example of an independent industrial school. To learn how "to do a common thing in an uncommon manner," Booker T. Washington wanted his first students to build their own school. By doing that they would learn how to build and how to be independent. They bought enough land for a small farm. They learned to cultivate the soil around their school. They raised their own food and took care of livestock. To educate the head, the heart and the hand was his aim. After this, he wanted to transmit the learning to the community.

The idea caught on well with both blacks and whites in the county, then throughout the state. Help came in the form of small gifts of money, food, clothing, quilts. One old ex-slave woman even brought six eggs her hen had laid, for "de eddication of dese boys and gals," since she had nothing else. Eventually, large sums of money came to the school from foundations.

The campus and its farms grew. Presidents and other famous people came to visit. The Tuskegee spirit of practical education for community usefulness spread. Similar institutions were established in the South. Tuskegee also became a model for other schools in far-off lands.

Booker T. Washington's name was a household word by the early twentieth century. This was due, in part, to his agricultural and industrial projects and his part in establishing small businesses by and for blacks. He was also noted for his practical rehabilitation of the rural South, and his efforts toward black-white cooperation under existing conditions.

George Washington Carver, Tuskegee's most famous teacher, conducting a chemistry class.

T. Thomas Fortune.

William Monroe Trotter.

An Atlanta Speech

In his most famous speech, Washington put forward a concept which many blacks accepted but later came to condemn. It was that black people were in a dangerous position and would do well to please whites. Misery sat on black people's doorsteps in the South in the 1890s and the Klan rode its back roads.

"In all things that are purely social," he said, "we can be as separate as the fingers, yet one as the hand in all things essential to mutual progress. ... The wisest among my race understand that the agitation of questions of social equality is the extremist folly. ... The opportunity to earn a dollar in a factory just now is worth infinitely more than the opportunity to spend a dollar in an opera house."

Delivered at the Cotton States' and International Exposition in Atlanta in 1895, this speech later was termed by black critics "The Atlanta Compromise." It was a diplomatic statement in a time of racial stress. But it was hardly a workable formula for the future of a land in which the two races were already greatly intermingled. The speech put Washington on the front pages of papers across the nation. And in the eyes of most

Americans, the speech made him the "official" leader of black people. The "Negro Moses," is what the New York *World* called him. Washington wielded great power nationally in all racial matters, from educational and editorial policy-making to job appointments, high and low. From that time on, Washington was supported by governmental, industrial and educational leaders throughout the nation.

The slave-born editor of the New York *Age*, T. Thomas Fortune, said "It is impossible to estimate the value of such a man as Booker T. Washington." But some younger black intellectuals, who had never experienced slavery, disagreed. The violent objections of the editor of the Boston *Guardian* to his speaking in New England, resulted in William Monroe Trotter's spending some time in jail. In the judgment of the scholarly W. E. B. Du Bois, Washington was "leading the way

President Grover Cleveland visits the Negro Building at the Atlanta Exposition.

The mastheads of four black newspapers published in the United States in the latter part of the 19th century.

backward." A philosophical breach soon widened over the years. It was the Washington school's contention that black people must crawl before they could walk. Industrial education was more necessary than academic learning. And that compromise on suffrage and equal rights might preserve half a loaf.

His opponents claimed such a sacrifice of democratic rights and loss of pride was useless when Southerners like "Pitchfork" Ben Tillman declared they wanted no blacks to vote—not even men like Washington. Governor Vardaman of Mississippi said, "God Almighty created the Negro for a menial."

By the twentieth century, controversy raged among his own people. Washington dined at the White House with President Theodore Roosevelt. He received an honorary degree from Harvard, and was a guest of Queen Victoria at Windsor Castle. Still, he was not indifferent to the barbs of other black leaders. He knew that to "walk the razor's edge between Negro pride and white prejudice" was not always a grateful task. But, of all outstanding blacks, at this Booker T. Washington proved to be most adept.

Until his death in 1915, Washington was the dominant personality in the history of African Americans. And the vast majority of blacks claimed him as their leader.

CHAPTER CHECK
1. What was the spirit of Tuskegee?
2. How do you think Booker T. Washington's background shaped his opinions about race relations in America?
3. Imagine . . . you are (a) a former Southern slave, or (b) a Northern black. How would you react to Washington's Atlanta speech.

A chain gang on a Mississippi levee.

Main Events

1. In 1865, Congress set up the Freedmen's Bureau to help cope with the desolation following the Civil War.

2. In 1866, Congress passed the first Civil Rights Act. White Southerners responded with the formation of the Ku Klux Klan.

3. In 1868, the Fourteenth Amendment was ratified, guaranteeing equal rights to all Americans.

4. In 1869, the first black was elected to the Unites States Congress.

5. In 1876, Reconstruction ends.

6. Following Reconstruction, a system of segregation developed separating blacks from whites through a series of Jim Crow laws and increased violence against blacks.

7. By the end of the 19th century, most blacks in the South had lost the right to vote.

8. By 1900, less than five percent of all blacks held skilled jobs and most were barred from white labor unions.

9. In 1895, Booker T. Washington gave his "Atlanta Compromise" speech.

10. In 1896, the Supreme Court declared that "separate but equal" laws were constitutional in its *Plessy v. Ferguson* decision.

Words to Know

Match the following words with their correct definitions. Number your paper from 1 to 12, and write the correct word beside each number.

carpetbaggers
convict-lease
disfranchise
freedmen
grandfather clause
Jim Crow

lynch
Reconstruction
scalawags
segregation
sharecropping
Union League

1. the newly freed slaves
2. a system where those in prison are hired out to companies or individuals
3. a political organization for Southern blacks following the Civil War
4. Northerners who migrated south after the Civil War
5. a system where workers produce a crop for a share of the profits
6. Southern whites who supported the Republicans
7. the isolation of one group from the main body or society
8. the reorganization of the Southern states following the Civil War
9. to put to death by mob action
10. a legal restriction designed to keep blacks from voting
11. depriving someone of the right to vote
12. a type of law which forces the separation of blacks from whites

Thinking and Writing

A. Writing a Conversation

Review what you read about Reconstruction in the unit. Then write a conversation between a white Southerner and one of his former slaves. How do you think they would feel about each other? What would they think about the actions and events of Reconstruction? Make sure you try to explain both points of view and touch on as many topics as possible.

B. Recognizing Fact and Opinion

Below are eight statements from conversations that may have taken place during Reconstruction. Some of the statements are facts. Some are opinions.

Number your paper from 1 to 8. If the statement is a fact, write "fact" next to the number of the statement. If the statement is an opinion, write "opinion" and explain why.

1. "The Freedmen's Bureau has created more than 4,000 schools."
2. "The Black Codes have restored many aspects of the former slave system."
3. "The government is interfering too much into our lives."
4. "Grant is a much better president than Johnson."
5. "The Ku Klux Klan is needed to protect our rights."
6. "Many blacks were killed in a riot in Memphis."
7. "I voted for the first time yesterday."
8. "Carpetbaggers and scalawags are all corrupt."

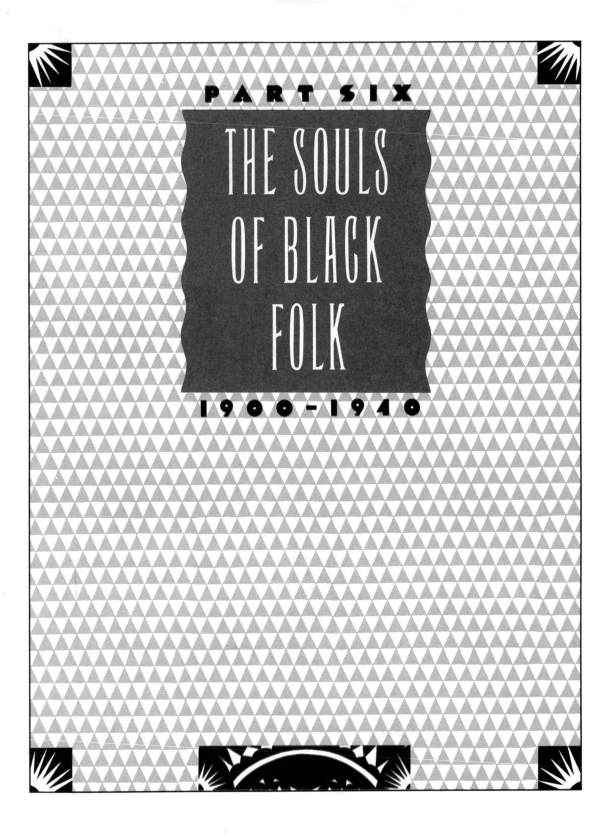

PART SIX

THE SOULS OF BLACK FOLK

1900-1940

Selma Burke, Works Projects Administration (WPA) sculptor, beside her bust of Booker T. Washington.

LOOKING AHEAD · PART SIX · 1900–1940

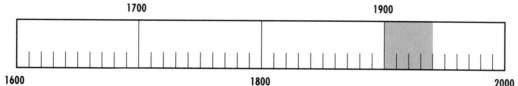

1700

1900

1600

1800

2000

T he problem of the twentieth century is the problem of the color line—the relation of the darker to the lighter races of men in Asia and Africa, in America and the islands of the sea."

So wrote W. E. B. Du Bois in *The Souls of Black Folk* as the new century began. The black population of the United States was 8,833,994. At Atlanta University, a survey indicated that there were 2,500 black college graduates in the country. Four hundred were graduates of leading institutions such as Oberlin, Harvard and Yale.

It was partly due to Booker T. Washington's stress on industrial rather than liberal arts education that the controversy developed between his followers and those of Du Bois.

"Education," said Washington at Tuskegee, "is meant to make us give satisfaction, and to get satisfaction out of giving it. It is meant to make us get happiness out of service for our fellows. . . . There is as much dignity in tilling a field as in writing a poem."

Du Bois, on the other hand, felt "we shall hardly induce black men to believe that if their stomachs be full, it matters little about their brains." Without disputing the values of industrial education, he continued, "So far as Mr. Washington preaches thrift, patience and industrial training for the masses, we must hold up his hands and strive with him. . . . But so far as Mr. Washington apologizes for injustice, North or South, [he] does not rightly value the privilege and duty of voting, belittles the emasculating effects of caste

Scene from "Turpentine," a Federal Theater production at the Lafayette Theater in Harlem, 1936.

distinctions and opposes the higher training and ambition of our brighter minds—so far as he, the South, or the Nation, does this—we must unceasingly and firmly oppose them. By every civilized peaceful method we must strive for the rights which the world accords man."

Some blacks accused Washington of selling out the rights of black people. Few dared say this publicly, however. But the actions of white racists demanded that blacks take a stronger stand. Social unrest brought on by the competition for jobs exploded into race riots, North and South.

Outraged by these events, 29 professional blacks met in 1905 to organize in protest. The meeting was the beginning of the **Niagara Movement**, which led to the organization of the National Association for the Advancement of Colored People (NAACP). The organized demand of equal rights by African Americans had begun.

Washington died in 1915. In that same year, 69 black men were lynched. Two years later, a heavily segregated United States en-tered World War I. While President Woodrow Wilson claimed the nation was fighting to "make the world safe for democracy," the War Department refused to admit all but a few black volunteers. This rejection by the military changed as the war wore on. But, despite the large numbers of black men inducted into service, most were to serve at menial tasks. Among those who saw combat, many won high military honors. All were subjected to the segregation and discrimination experienced by black civilians.

Once black troops returned home, they quickly learned that nothing had changed. During the summer of 1919, race riots spread across the land. Led by the Ku Klux Klan, there were at least 25 riots in which lives were lost. Hundreds were wounded, and families were burned out of their homes.

Some felt new and drastic solutions had to be found to combat American racism, and quickly. Marcus Garvey offered a "Back to Africa" movement. He urged that blacks build a civilization of their own in Africa. Within a few years, Garvey had raised mil-

A former South Carolina sharecropping family and their new house acquired through the Farm Security Administration loan program.

lions of dollars from black workers. But the dream was to die.

Meanwhile, Southerners, black and white, began migrating to the North. They were fleeing a dwindling job market brought on by floods and a failed cotton crop. Incited by the Klan, these racial groups continued their feud, this time over factory jobs in Northern cities. Again, black leaders demanded legal justice.

Black intellectuals fought, using the only weapon they had—the written word. As racial conditions worsened, young African American writers experienced one of their most productive periods. Described as the **Harlem Renaissance**, this movement detailed the lives blacks were forced to live. Claude McKay, Jean Toomer, Georgia Douglass Johnson, Countee Cullen, Nella Larsen and Langston Hughes were a few of these outstanding talents.

The Great Depression of 1929 ended this show of black genius. Among the hundreds of thousands to lose their jobs, none was harder hit nor suffered more than the black

American. For many, public relief stations became the difference between life and death.

In 1932, a President with new ideas was elected. Franklin Delano Roosevelt started various programs designed to benefit millions of financially desperate Americans. A number of black scholars were appointed to important government positions for the first time since Reconstruction. In this improving racial climate, black scholars and artists found opportunities to demonstrate their talents. And unemployed black youths were put to work in public projects.

Federal programs were temporary solutions to an everlasting problem—discrimination against black Americans. In many Northern cities, blacks demonstrated against racist practices until World War II. Then the need for black workers became greater than the determination of whites to keep them out. The change, however, was neither simple nor without great effort on the part of blacks. New laws were not a solution, but they signalled a new beginning.

CHAPTER 29

The Liberation Movement

William Edward Burghardt Du Bois was born of African, French and Dutch ancestry in Great Barrington, Massachusetts, in 1868, the year the Fourteenth Amendment was ratified.

At 16, Du Bois graduated from high school and for the first time went South. He entered Fisk University in Nashville, Tennessee as a scholarship student. There he edited the *Fisk Herald* and wrote many articles. During the summers he taught in log-cabin schools in sharecropping districts. He received a bachelor's degree from Fisk.

In 1888, Du Bois returned to Massachusetts to enter Harvard University in Boston. At Harvard he pursued a second bachelor's degree and was one of six commencement speakers. After studying two years in Germany, DuBois returned to Harvard to receive his doctorate in 1895. It was the first Ph.D. that Harvard had given to a black person.

Du Bois worked briefly at Wilberforce University in Ohio and at the University of Pennsylvania. He then joined the faculty of Atlanta University. For 13 years he headed its department of history and economics. At Atlanta University, Du Bois started annual conferences on the problems of black life.

Meanwhile, the young professor wrote articles on black life for the *Atlantic Monthly*, *World's Work* and other leading publications. These essays were the basis of his most pop-ular book, *The Souls of Black Folk*. It quickly went into many editions and was translated abroad.

Shortly after Du Bois joined the faculty at Atlanta University, a young professor of Latin and Greek came to nearby Atlanta Baptist College (now Morehouse). John Hope was the son of a wealthy Scottish immigrant and a black woman from Augusta, Georgia. With a number of brothers and sisters, he had grown up in a happy home. One of his few unpleasant childhood memories was of the Hamburg race riots across the river from Augusta. Hope had attended Worcester Academy in Massachusetts, and graduated from Brown University in Providence, Rhode Island. He then served as a teacher for the American Baptist Home Mission Society. He and Du Bois were the same age. They became lifelong friends and colleagues in many movements for black advancement.

The Niagara Movement

Both Du Bois and Hope had grave doubts concerning the Booker T. Washington program. Eventually, Du Bois contended, "Things came to such a pass that when any Negro complained or advocated a course of action, he was silenced with the remark that Mr. Washington did not agree."

Washington's power over the black press was tremendous. Only a few black newspa-

William Edward Burghardt Du Bois.

pers dared oppose him editorially. The first to do so was Monroe Trotter's Boston *Guardian*. Hope contributed to the *Guardian*.

Many black intellectuals felt with Du Bois that Washington was a compromiser between the South, the North and blacks. They also disliked his attempts to control anyone who disagreed with him. In July 1905, a group of Washington's opponents held a meeting. The group included 29 black teachers, editors and professional men from 14 states. They formed the base of what would be known as the Niagara Movement. They met on the Canadian side of Niagara Falls, because hotels on the New York side would not rent rooms to blacks.

Masthead of *The Guardian,* founded by Monroe Trotter in 1901.

The meeting answered a call from Du Bois for "organized, determined and aggressive action . . . for the following purposes:

1. To oppose firmly the present methods of strangling honest criticism, manipulating public opinion and centralizing political power by means of the improper and corrupt use of money and influence.

2. To organize thoroughly the intelligent and honest Negroes throughout the United States for the purpose of insisting on manhood rights, industrial opportunity and spiritual freedom.

3. To establish and support major proper organs of news and public opinion."

Among the leaders of the Niagara Movement were editors Trotter and J. Max Barber of Atlanta's *Voice of the Negro.* They were later joined by Hope and a number of others. Hope had become president of Atlanta Baptist College. He was the only high-ranking black educator who dared align himself with this "radical" group which criticized the powerful Washington.

John Hope.

Lynchings and Race Riots

One of the worst of American race riots began on a September Saturday in 1906. In Atlanta, mobs of white people began chasing black people through the streets. There were killings, beatings and torchings of property owned by blacks. Officers of the law gave no protection to blacks. In some cases, law officers assisted the mobs. Seventy people were injured, and 12 were killed.

That same year in Brownsville, Texas, part of the black 25th Infantry was involved in a race riot. Whites went unpunished. When members of the First Batallion refused to testify against their fellow soldiers, an angry President Theodore Roosevelt ordered the whole batallion discharged dishonorably. This was somewhat surprising since blacks had served with distinction under him in the Spanish-American War. Several years later, the discharges were revoked.

Washington continued preaching the virtues of industry and thrift. At the same time, mobs in both the North and the South were burning the homes of black workers and terrorizing black citizens. There were two race riots in Springfield, Ohio, within a few years. In 1904, during the first riot there, a black man was hanged on a telegraph pole and riddled with bullets. The same year in Statesboro, Georgia, two convicted murderers were burned alive, two black women whipped, a young mother beaten and kicked, her husband killed and many black homes wrecked. In the Greensburg, Indiana, riot of 1906, blacks were beaten and driven out of town.

Two years later, in Springfield, Illinois, in spite of the state militia, a mob destroyed black homes and businesses. They strung up an innocent barber after burning his shop. Next they lynched an 84 year-old man within sight of the state capitol. For these public crimes, no one was ever punished. In many communities, blacks felt that they had no legal protection.

A lynching record kept at Tuskegee.

RECORD KEPT BY TUSKEGEE OF LYNCHINGS IN THE FIRST QUARTER OF THE TWENTIETH CENTURY

1900 — 115	1913 — 52
1901 — 130	1914 — 55
1902 — 92	1915 — 69
1903 — 99	1916 — 54
1904 — 83	1917 — 38
1905 — 62	1918 — 64
1906 — 65	1919 — 83
1907 — 60	1920 — 61
1908 — 97	1921 — 64
1909 — 82	1922 — 57
1910 — 76	1923 — 33
1911 — 67	1924 — 16
1912 — 63	1925 — 17

The original leaders of the Niagara Movement in 1905. Du Bois is second from the right in the second row.

Meeting at Harper's Ferry

With shadows of race war and lynching menacing the land, the second Niagara conference met at Harper's Ferry, West Virginia, August 16-19, 1906. Du Bois and Hope chaired a meeting of over 100 black intellectuals. Before beginning its sessions, they paid tribute to the martyred John Brown. They marched at dawn to the engine house where Brown had made his last stand. There they sang "The Battle Hymn of the Republic."

Professor Richard T. Greener, formerly American consul at Vladivostok, Russia, was among those who addressed the conference. A. M. E. Bishop Reverdy C. Ransom also spoke. He had been dragged from a Pullman car and beaten by whites. Another speaker was Lewis Douglass, son of Frederick Douglass and a Civil War veteran.

The resolution passed at Harper's Ferry included the following demands: "First, we want full manhood suffrage and we want it now. Second, we want discrimination in public accommodations to cease. (**Public ac-**

commodations are places like restrooms, waiting rooms and water fountains that often were racially segregated.) Third, we claim the right of freemen to walk, talk and be with them that wish to be with us. Fourth, we want the laws enforced against rich as well as poor, against Capitalist as well as Laborer, against white as well as black. Fifth, we want our children educated. They have a right to know, to think, to aspire. We do not believe in violence. Our enemies, triumphant for the present, are fighting the stars in their courses. Justice and humanity must prevail. We are men, we will be treated as men. And we shall win."

Mary White Ovington covered the meeting for the New York *Evening Post*. She became deeply interested in its objectives. These annual meetings were an impetus for the organization of the National Association for the Advancement of Colored People. On its board of directors were eight members of the Niagara Movement.

Interracial Organizations

The National Association for the Advancement of Colored People developed from a conference of white liberals who met to protest rising violence against blacks. The meeting was held in New York City on Lincoln's birthday in 1909. Ovington, William English Walling, Dr. Henry Moskowitz and Oswald Garrison Villard organized it. Monroe Trotter was invited but he did not attend. He said he did not "trust white folks." But Du Bois, Jane Addams, Francis J. Grimke, John Dewey, Ida B. Wells Barnett, John Haynes Holmes, Bishop Alexander Walters and William Dean Howells were present.

In 1910, offices were set up in New York. Moorfield Storey, a white Boston lawyer who had been Charles Sumner's secretary, was president. Du Bois, who resigned his position in Atlanta, was director of publicity and research and editor of the NAACP's *Crisis*. The *Crisis's* first editorial presented the NAACP's position. The organization stands "for the rights of men, irrespective of color or race, for the highest ideals of American democracy, and for reasonable but earnest and persistent attempts to gain these rights and realize these ideals."

A legal committee was established. It was headed by Arthur B. Spingarn. Distinguished attorneys such as Clarence Darrow, Louis Marshall and Felix Frankfurter gave their services free to this committee. Its first important victory was won in 1915. The Supreme Court declared the "grandfather clause" in the Oklahoma state constitution violated the Fifteenth Amendment and was, therefore, null and void.

In 1917, a Louisville, Kentucky, city ordinance upholding segregated residential areas was declared unconstitutional. And in 1923, concerning an Arkansas case, the Su-

The seal of the National Urban League.

Du Bois (center, standing) in the editorial offices of *The Crisis*.

preme Court held that if blacks were excluded from juries, a fair trial for a black defendant was impossible. The Rosenwald Fund, established by Julius Rosenwald of Chicago, helped build more than 5,000 public schools in the South for blacks. It stimulated local initiative by matching community and state contributions with its own funds. In 1900, the South was spending twice as much for the education of white children as it was for black children. Many rural counties had no schools at all for blacks. The fund also aided in the training of black teachers.

By 1921, the National Association for the Advancement of Colored People had more than 400 branches.

The Urban League

The National Urban League was formed in 1911. It grew out of the Committee on Urban Conditions Among Negroes. The league was formed by George Edmund Haynes and Mrs. William H. Baldwin, Jr. Haynes was a young black graduate student in social work at Co-

lumbia University in New York. Baldwin was a white woman who had been active in the League for the Protection of Colored Women.

The Urban League's objectives were the improvement of the industrial and living conditions of city blacks. There was special attention given to the broadening of job opportunities.

The League's interracial sponsors included Julius Rosenwald, Roger Baldwin, Booker T. Washington, L. Hollingsworth Wood, Kelly Miller and the journalist Fred R. Moore.

With headquarters in New York, the Urban League soon had branches in cities across the country. In 1921, the sociologist Charles S. Johnson became its director of research and investigation. In 1923, he founded the League's magazine *Opportunity, A Journal of Negro Life*. The journal's motto was "Not Alms, but Opportunity."

The League sought to overcome discrimination in employment. It worked to persuade industries employing no blacks to give

Arthur B. Spingarn.

Julius Rosenwald.

them opportunities for work and industrial training. It sought to have those plants and foundries which used blacks only in jobs of unskilled labor to upgrade them according to ability. It tried to ease the difficulties of adjustment between white employers and black employees.

The League developed a program and set up fellowships to train social workers. Some of the most distinguished personalities in that field gained their training and early experience through the League. Its annual conferences became significant gatherings for social workers of both races from all over America.

These two important interracial groups continue to make progress in civil rights. The focus of the NAACP has remained in legal action. And the League's work has focused on urban problems.

CHAPTER CHECK

1. How did W. E. B. Du Bois' education help prepare him for his life as a leader of African Americans?
2. How does the work of the National Urban League differ from that of the NAACP?
3. Imagine . . . you were an admirer of Booker T. Washington during the early twentieth century. How would you react to the Niagara Movement?

The 369th Infantry of the 93rd Division in action.

CHAPTER 30

World War I

In 1913, Woodrow Wilson became the first Southern Democrat in the White House since the Civil War. Half of his Cabinet appointees were Southerners. His first Congress was flooded with anti-black bills. Wilson himself issued orders segregating most black federal employees in Washington.

In 1917, the United States entered World War I under the slogan "Make the World Safe for Democracy." To clarify confusion among blacks concerning such an objective and such a war, Du Bois in the *Crisis* wrote his famous editorial, "Close Ranks." In it he argued that blacks should forget their "special grievances." He said they had more to gain from a society in which democracy was at least an ideal than they would have under German autocracy. (An **autocracy** is a government in which one person has all the power.) He urged black citizens to participate in America's war effort.

Du Bois's position was controversial. Radical black magazines like *Messenger* published strong editorials against black participation in the war. The *Messenger's* editorials were so strong, in fact, that its editors, A. Philip Randolph and Chandler Owen were sentenced in 1918 to two and a half years in jail for opposing the war.

Within a week after the United States entered the war, the War Department stopped accepting black volunteers. The army's quota of blacks was filled. No black men were allowed in the marines or coast guard. In the navy, blacks were allowed to be kitchen workers.

However, when the draft for World War I began, 31 percent of the registered blacks were accepted. Twenty-six percent of the registered white men were accepted. (The **draft** is required participation in the military). Blacks, who then comprised 10 percent of the population, furnished 13 percent of the draftees. During the war, the labor and stevedore battalions were made up almost entirely of blacks. (A **stevedore** is a person who loads and unloads ships.) The commanding officers of these military units were usually white.

In 1917, Emmett J. Scott was appointed special assistant to the Secretary of War. He was a secretary to Booker T. Washington. He served as an adviser in matters affecting blacks. Scott was assigned to deal with problems of segregation in army camps at home and abroad.

No provisions had been made for the training of black officers. Major Joel E. Spingarn, an NAACP board member, took up this situation with the War Department. A committee of black college men also put pressure on the War Department. A camp for the training of black officers was set up in Des Moines, Iowa. One hundred and six black captains and 533 first and second lieutenants were commissioned from the Iowa officers training school.

Colonel Charles Young was the highest-ranking black officer in the U.S. Army during World War I. He had been retired on the grounds of health. To prove he was not unfit, Young rode a horse alone from Ohio to Washington. He was then assigned to non-combatant service as a military attache but was not permitted to serve in Europe. The NAACP investigated Young's forced retirement. Its investigation revealed that the army was unwilling to promote a black man to the rank of general.

The South objected to black soldiers. Black men in uniform were subjected to even more than the customary Jim Crowisms shown black civilians. At Camp Greene, North Carolina, for example, all the YMCA canteens were marked for the exclusive use of white troops. At Spartanburg, South Carolina, local whites objected to the 15th New York Infantry's training nearby. A race riot was averted by removing the black troops and sending them to Europe to face German armies.

But disorder broke out in Houston, Texas. A number of black soldiers were ganged and beaten by local whites. The black soldiers where disarmed by their superiors. In one particular disturbance, 17 whites were killed. Sixty-four members of the 24th Infantry were court-martialed. Thirteen black soldiers were sentenced to death by hanging. Forty-one were imprisoned for life and a number of others were held in custody pending further investigations.

Medals and Music

Some 200,000 black troops served overseas, 42,000 in combat duty. The entire First Battalion of the 369th Infantry was cited for bravery. Fifty-seven men from the 369th were awarded the Distinguished Service Cross. General Pershing said of the soldiers of the 92nd Division, "You have measured up to every expectation of the Commander-in-Chief."

The 369th Infantry reached France early in 1918. There they attended a divisional training school under French command. They went into action at Bois d'Hauza in April. There they held an entire sector against German fire for two months. They also fought at Minaucourt and took part in the great attack at Maison-en-Champagne, which carried them to the Rhine River.

No man of their number was ever captured and the unit never retreated. Eleven times the 369th Infantry was cited for bravery. The entire regiment received the French Croix de Guerre for gallantry under fire. Individually, 171 of its officers and enlisted men were decorated with the Croix de Guerre and the Legion of Honor.

The 371st Infantry Regiment received its training at Camp Jackson, South Carolina.

Lieutenant James Reese Europe conducting the 369th Regimental Band before the American Red Cross Hospital No. 9 in Paris, France.

Sergeant Henry Johnson.

Needham Roberts.

Returning soldiers of the 369th Infantry.

They also served as part of the 157th French Division under General Goybet. The 371st Infantry remained in the front lines for more than three months. Monthois, a strategically vital point which the Germans had held for almost a year, was captured by this regiment. Its men also took a number of prisoners. They captured a munitions depot and several railroad cars full of supplies. The regiment lost almost half of its 2,384 men. It was praised by General Goybet as having "a most complete contempt for danger." Other black units to serve with distinction in World War I were the Eighth Illinois (renamed the 370th) and the 372nd Infantry, many of whose men were decorated for bravery.

The 369th Regimental Band is credited with being the first group of musicians to introduce jazz to Europe. It was led by Lieutenant James Reese Europe. Its drum major was Sergeant Noble Sissle. Sissle later became well known on Broadway as a singer, conductor and composer. Europe and company played for both American and French troops in camps and hospitals. They also played for civilians behind the lines and in Paris. Once the members of a French military band offered to exchange brasses and woodwinds with the black band. The French musicians didn't believe such strange jazz sounds could be produced by ordinary instruments. The black musicians played just as well on the French instruments. But the puzzled French soldiers could not produce jazz on the American ones.

The first American soldiers in World War I to receive the Croix de Guerre were Privates Henry Johnson of Albany, New York and Needham Roberts of Trenton, New Jersey. Both were members of the 369th Infantry. Before dawn on May 14, 1918, a raiding party of about 20 Germans swooped down on Johnson and Roberts. They were both wounded. After Johnson had fired his last bullets, the Germans began to drag Roberts away as a prisoner. Using the butt of his rifle and a bolo knife, Johnson freed Roberts. Both men then killed four Germans, wounded several others and held their post as the rest fled. Johnson and Roberts were decorated by the French government and their exploit was headlined in newspapers back home.

Not-so-welcome Homecoming

"We return. We return from fighting. We return fighting. Make way for Democracy! We saved it in France, and by the Great Jehovah, we will save it in the U.S.A., or know the reason why!" In the name of the returning black soldiers, so spoke Du Bois in the *Crisis* in the spring of 1919. That summer, race riots became race wars. There was so much violence that it was called "red summer!" Blacks fought back. After having fought "to make the world safe for democracy," some were at least determined to protect their own lives on home soil.

In 1919, there were 83 lynchings. Several were of black veterans in uniform. Some black veterans were burned alive. The Ku Klux Klan held more than 200 public meetings from Indiana and New England to Florida. There were 25 major race riots within seven months.

In Long View, Texas, a mob searching for a teacher accused of writing for the Chicago *Defender,* burned homes, flogged a school principal and ran many blacks out of town.

In Washington, mobs roamed the city for three days in July. A number of blacks and whites were killed and scores were injured.

The Silent Protest Parade, July 28, 1917, in which thousands of New Yorkers carried banners asking, "Mr. President, Why Not Make America Safe for Democracy?", "Give Me a Chance to Live" and "Thou Shalt Not Kill."

That same month in Chicago, 15 whites and 23 blacks were killed. Almost 350 blacks were wounded and 1,000 families burned out. Similar riots occurred in Knoxville, Tennessee, and Omaha, Nebraska. In Omaha, a black was dragged through the streets, shot more than a thousand times and hanged on the main street.

Two summers before in New York City, the NAACP led 10,000 blacks on a silent march down Fifth Avenue. They carried banners protesting racial violence in America. But their message had not been heard.

CHAPTER CHECK

1. Why do you think the War Department was at first hesitant to accept black volunteers during World War I?

2. What were some of the functions performed by black soldiers during World War I?

3. Why do you think there were so many race riots immediately after the war?

4. Imagine . . . you are a young black man in 1917. Would you volunteer for service in the United States Army? Why or why not?

CHAPTER 31

Nationalism in the Black Community

Marcus Garvey.

n the early 1920s thousands of African
Americans were attracted by a rising tide
of black nationalism. Black nationalism
is, according to Howard University Professor
Mary F. Berry, "the belief that black people
share a common culture and world view,

have a common destiny, and have had a common experience." **Pan Africanism** is another
term for black nationalism.

Marcus Garvey's "Back to Africa" movement expressed black nationalism. Many
blacks were discouraged by the slowness

with which organizations like the NAACP were making headway. And many blacks were disappointed with the nation's laxity in enforcing provisions for civil rights. Garvey felt that blacks could not prosper in a "white land" where "poverty is no virtue; it is a crime." He urged blacks to build a civilization in Africa and make a homeland for 400 million black people. For a few years, Garvey was the most famous black leader in the world.

Born, as he liked to boast, "a full-blooded black man" in 1887, on the Caribbean island of Jamaica, Marcus Moziah Garvey was the son of a stonemason. At 16, he was apprenticed to a printer in Kingston. He became a foreman at 20. During a printers' strike, Garvey was the only foreman to join the workers. When the strike failed, Garvey was barred for employment with privately owned printers. He then took a job with the government printing office. He also worked at organizing and improving the lives of workers. Growing restless, Garvey spent two years working in several Central and South American countries.

In 1912, with the help of his sister, Indiana, Garvey went to England. There he worked on the docks and met and traded stories with fellow African and Caribbean dock workers. "All concluded," writes Amy Jacques Garvey, "that suffering was the common lot of the race, no matter where they lived." Through his co-workers, he was introduced to the Egyptian nationalist publisher Duse Mohammed Ali. Ali published *The African Times and Orient Review* and operated an informal center in his home in London for Africans and Asians. The association with Ali and his regular contributions to the review prompted Garvey to spend hours studying in London's Trinity College library. He also attended lectures at Trinity. Garvey became more and more aware of the problems and the oppression of colonialism. (**Colonialism** is the control of one nation by the people of another nation.)

In 1914, when Garvey returned to Ja-

A group of women from Garvey's African Motor Corps on parade in New York City during the 1925 convention.

The Indispensable Weekly
The Voice of the Awakened Negro

The Negro World

Reaching the Mass of Negroes
The Best Advertising Medium

A Newspaper Devoted Solely to the Interests of the Negro Race

VOL. XIV. No. 16   NEW YORK, SATURDAY, JUNE 2, 1923   PRICE: FIVE CENTS IN GREATER NEW YORK
SEVEN CENTS ELSEWHERE IN THE U.S.A.
TEN CENTS IN FOREIGN COUNTRIES

GREATEST NEGRO MOVEMENT IN THE WORLD NOW ON TRIAL

FELLOW MEN OF THE NEGRO RACE, *Greeting*:

The Universal Negro Improvement Association has reached the stage of organization where it is causing the whole world to talk seriously of its aims and objects. There is no one truth that is correctly understood and represented. Men have always differed in their interpretation of human

MARCUS GARVEY THE STORM CENTER OF
TRAITOROUS AND WICKED NEGROES

individual of the race to the fellow and creature of education, of position, of refinement; we find him, even though he suffers from the same prejudices, the same social disadvantages as the other, quite satisfied, quite contented to be a part of an alien race, part of an alien civilization, hoping that one day he will be elevated to the pinnacle and be honored and respected as the members of the ruling race.

Masthead of the *Negro World*.

maica, he organized the Universal Negro Improvement Association. Its objective was to take Africa from the European nations that had colonies there and make it "the defender of Negroes the world over."

Meanwhile, the young man dreamed of establishing in Jamaica a school like Tuskegee. But blacks in Jamaica were at best indifferent. Garvey began a correspondence with Booker T. Washington. Washington invited Garvey to come to the United States. But by the time Garvey arrived, Washington had died. Garvey visited 38 states and talked to many black leaders.

Universal Negro Improvement Association

Harlem, where there were many Caribbean people, attracted Garvey. There, in 1917, he reorganized the Universal Negro Improvement Association. His expanded objectives were the creation of a strong black nation in Africa, the co-fraternity of blacks the world over and the setting up of branches and schools in all lands having black populations. He founded a newspaper,

the *Negro World*. "Africa for the Africans" was its slogan.

As with previous colonization movements in the United States, those whites who wanted to get rid of blacks and their problems hailed the Garvey movement. Even the Ku Klux Klan approved. But no whites were admitted to membership. Garvey denounced white philanthropy and the interracial NAACP. He directed his appeal to the ordinary black man and woman. Much as Booker T. Washington had done, he urged them to do something for themselves.

"Up, you mighty race!" Garvey cried in hundreds of speeches. "You can accomplish what you will. . . . No one knows when the hour of Africa's redemption cometh. . . . One day, like a storm, it will be here!"

Within a few years black workers poured some $10 million into the Garvey movement. Almost unanimously, black intellectuals denounced the Garvey movement. They opposed his stand on integration, his call for a return to Africa, and his acceptance of support from white segregationists. But attending the first UNIA convention in New York in 1920 were 25,000 blacks from all over the United States, the Caribbean, Africa and South America. They elected Garvey "provisional president" of Africa, and listened to the prayers of the former Episcopal priest, George Alexander McGuire. The following year, McGuire founded the African Orthodox Church and became its first bishop.

The Garveyites paraded down Lenox Avenue to trumpets and drums. They held a mammoth meeting in Madison Square Garden. And then they sent a resolution to the League of Nations affirming "the right of Europe for the Europeans, Asia for the Asiatics and Africa for the Africans . . . at this time when . . . 400 million Negroes demand a place in the sun of the world."

Garvey wore a uniform of purple and gold with a helmet of feathers as "tall as Guinea grass." He walked into his crowded meetings at Liberty Hall in Harlem surrounded by his African Legion. The Black Cross nurses were all in white. The African Motor Corps, the African Legion and the Black Eagle Flying Corps wore uniforms of black, red and green. "Black for our race, red for our blood and green for our hope," said Garvey. But hope, at least in its material form, soon went on the rocks. The ships of the Black Star Line, which Garvey had founded to transport blacks from the United States and the Caribbean to Africa, were unseaworthy.

In 1923, Garvey was tried in federal court for using the mails for fraud. He was convicted and sentenced to five years in prison, with a $1,000 fine. He appealed, lost and was sent to the Atlanta Penitentiary. In 1927, after serving two and a half years, Garvey was released and deported to Jamaica. He died in 1940 in London.

Headquarters of the Black Star Line Corporation.

The black attorney Henry Lincoln Johnson remarked at Garvey's trial, "If every Negro could put every dime, every penny. . . into the sea, and if he might get in exchange the knowledge that he was somebody, that he meant something in the world . . . he would gladly do it. . . . The Black Star Line was a loss in money, but it was a gain in soul."

The Roots of Black Nationalism in America

The move to return to Africa did not start with Marcus Garvey. By the time of Garvey's prominence, the Back to Africa idea had been a part of black life and thought for more than a hundred years.

You will recall from Chapter 12 that one of the first signs of black nationalism came from the black sea captain, Paul Cuffee. In 1815, at

Martin Delany.

church. Delany attended the school in the evening until Woodson was forced by money problems to shut down. Delany then entered into a private tutorial arrangement with a man named Molliston Clark. Clark was a student at a nearby college. Through his associations with Woodson and Clark, Delany had been exposed to abolitionist thought. He was also exposed to African history.

In 1843, Delany established a newspaper called *Mystery*. Four years later, he joined Frederick Douglass and was a founding co-editor of *The North Star*. Delany traveled extensively throughout the East and Midwest, speaking and raising money for the publication. After two years, Delany resigned from *The North Star*. He and Douglass had grown apart in their views regarding the plight of blacks. Douglass welcomed the support of white abolitionists, while Delany criticized them for racial prejudice and preferred that blacks help themselves.

With the passage of the Fugitive Slave Act of 1850, it appeared that the people of the United States did not intend to protect the rights of blacks. Delany believed the only solution lay in emigration. (**Emigration** is leaving one country to settle in another.) During the 1850s, Delany helped in setting up various emigration conventions.

Delany advocated the leadership of a select group of blacks who would serve to uplift and accustom the African masses to civilization. They would elevate them morally, religiously and educationally and help to make the continent prosper. Such attitudes took for granted the desires of African masses. Delany felt they would welcome European civilization and all its alleged virtues.

Delany and other emigrationist blacks signed a treaty with the King of Abeokuta,

his own expense, Cuffee transported 38 freed men and women back to Africa. Cuffee's successful return to Africa inspired the controversial American Colonization Society. Led by prominent slaveholders, the Colonization Society came under heavy attack from both free blacks and white abolitionists. They opposed the motive behind the movement. Because of this opposition, less than 15,000 American blacks were settled in Africa.

The first person to use the phrase "Africa for the African race" was Martin Robinson Delany. He is considered by some to be the father of black nationalism. Delany was born free in 1812 in Charles Town, Virginia. By the age of 19, he had moved to Pittsburgh. There he met Lewis Woodson. Woodson operated a school for blacks in the basement of a local

Nigeria, and several African nobles on December 27, 1859. The treaty permitted emigrating blacks to settle on unused tribal lands in exchange for sharing their skills and education with the native Africans. This program was never fully developed because Delany's attention turned to America's Civil War.

Henry McNeal Turner

Another black American leader who supported African repatriation was Henry McNeal Turner. He was born in 1834 in South Carolina. Turner was one of the leaders of the early African Methodist Episcopal Church.

Turner's spiritual beliefs were unique. He rejected the "white-washing" of Christianity. At all levels, things white were perceived as good and virtuous, and things black were perceived as sinister and evil. Turner was offended by these notions. He was especially offended by songs whose lyrics offered the listener the hope of making their souls "white as snow." He believed individuals should perceive God in their own image.

The wholesale abandonment of the Reconstruction programs prompted Turner to advocate a return to Africa for American blacks. He had long believed that God's plan was to Christianize Africa. His African repatriation program linked the Christian's mission with his dream of a strong and proud black nation.

In November 1893, Turner headed a national convention of blacks to discuss the future of the race. He received warm support for his emphasis on fighting against racial injustice. But his plea for emigration fell on deaf ears.

Back to Africa movements have repeat-

Henry McNeal Turner.

edly appeared in African American history. They usually surface during heavy racial violence and oppression. They help to provide racial pride at a time when it is especially needed. But Back to Africa movements have never received wide popular support in black American communities. Most African Americans have come to think of America as their home.

CHAPTER CHECK

1. What is black nationalism?
2. Why do you think that Back to Africa movements have repeatedly appeared in African American history? Why do you think that most black Americans have not chosen to move to Africa?
3. Imagine . . . you are an African American living in 1920. Would you be a supporter of Marcus Garvey? Why or why not?

CHAPTER 32

A Brilliant Season in the Arts and Sciences

Writers Jessie Fauset, Langston Hughes and Zora Neale Hurston at Tuskegee.

By the end of World War I, New York City's Harlem had become the largest black urban community in the country. Beginning in the early twentieth century, thousands of Southern blacks began migrating to Northern cities. Blacks had more economic opportunities there and living conditions were less harsh. This migration greatly increased during World War I. Workers were needed in Northern factories and blacks eagerly filled those positions. It has been estimated that 350,000 Southern blacks migrated to Northern cities between the years 1915 and 1918 alone.

Southern blacks moved to all Northern cities. But the city which attracted blacks the most was New York. Between 1910 and 1920, New York City's black population increased by 66 percent. Its growth was even greater in the next decade, more than doubling in size. By 1930, New York City had more African Americans than Birmingham, Memphis and St. Louis combined.

New York also attracted many foreign-born blacks. British West Indians, Cubans, Puerto Ricans and Haitians contributed colorful elements. Harlem's crowded streets were alive with a variety of accents and languages. Its music ranged from jazz to rumbas, hymns to parlor ragtime, spirituals to chamber quartets.

The excitement and energy of Harlem drew black intellectuals and artists from all over the world. For many it felt like coming home. In 1921, a young Langston Hughes first arrived there after living in a number of states and countries. He later recalled, "I can never put on paper the thrill of the underground ride to Harlem. I went up the steps and out into the bright September sunlight. Harlem! I stood there, dropped my bags, took a deep breath and felt happy again."

During the 1920s, there was a celebration of black literature, art, music and theater. This upsurge of creativity was stimulated by the cosmopolitan atmosphere of cities. There was also a new determination to resist oppression. Finally, changes in American society brought an interest in things new. A vogue for black artists developed among white New Yorkers and spread across the country. White Americans became more aware of black writers and artists. The 1920s were, in a way, a Black Renaissance. And since most of this activity occurred in New York, this movement has often been called the Harlem Renaissance.

Harlem as a Literary Mecca

More books were published by black authors during the 1920s than during any previous decade in American history. Most protested the social and economic wrongs of American society. The majority of these books were by younger writers living in Harlem. But older blacks also continued their literary output. W. E. B. Du Bois published two collections of essays: *Darkwater* in 1920, and *The Gift of Black Folks* in 1924.

Poet Claude McKay.

The first significant writer of the Harlem Renaissance was the Jamaican, Claude McKay. Many people believe that the movement really began with the publication of his book of poems *Harlem Shadows*, in 1922. It contains his sonnets "If We Must Die," "The White House" and "The Lynching." Later in the decade, McKay published two novels: *Home to Harlem* in 1928, and *Banjo* in 1929.

James Weldon Johnson was a well-known writer before the 1920s. During that decade

Johnson produced a number of works promoting black art. In 1922, Johnson published his *Book of Negro Poetry*, which showcased many of the new young poets. Johnson also edited two books of black spirituals and one on black sermons. In 1927, his *Autobiography of an Ex-Coloured Man* was reissued. Johnson later became one of the leading historians of the Harlem Renaissance.

Another chronicler of black artists was the scholar and critic, Alain Locke. In 1925, he published an anthology, *The New Negro*. This work helped to convey the artistic and social goals of the movement.

The most prolific and best known writer of the Harlem Renaissance was the poet and author, Langston Hughes. His first book of poetry, *Weary Blues*, appeared in 1926. Hughes spent the next 40 years writing numerous poems, plays, short stories, novels, and television scripts about black life in America.

Some of the many other talented writers of this time were Jean Toomer, Walter White, Countee Cullen, Jessie Fauset, Eric Waldron, Rudolph Fisher, Nella Larsen, Wallace Thurman, and Georgia Douglass Johnson. *Opportunity* and the *Crisis* conducted literary contests during the 1920s. Among those who received awards from these magazines were Arna Bontemps, Waring Cuney, Lucy Ariel Williams, Frank Horne, Cecil Blue and Zora Neale Hurston.

In 1926, the Carnegie Foundation purchased from Arthur Schomburg his vast accumulation of black books, manuscripts, etchings and pamphlets and presented them to the New York Public Library. Now housed in Harlem, the Schomburg Collection is an important research center, open to students of black life and letters.

Visual Artists

During the 1920s, the work of black painters and sculptors attracted wide attention. Locke brought from Europe a priceless collection of ancient African art for exhibition in America.

The most popular black American painter of the decade was Aaron Douglas. Using African subjects, he painted large wall paintings, or murals. In New York, he painted murals for the Harlem Branch YMCA and the 135th Street Branch of the New York Public Library. His murals also hung at the Hotel Sherman in Chicago and the Fisk University Library, where he headed the fine arts department.

Award-winning black painters of the 1920s include William H. Johnson, Hale Woodruff, Palmer Hayden, and Malvin Gray Johnson. Among the other well-known visual artists were the cartoonist E. Simms Campbell, and the sculptors Richmond Barthe, Augusta Savage and Sargent Johnson.

Performing Artists

Early in the 1920s, Hall Johnson formed a group of young Harlem singers. They presented folk songs in simple musical settings. The Hall Johnson Choir became famous in concerts and films. Other famous singers of folk music and spirituals include J. Rosamond Johnson, Taylor Gordon and the actor/singer Paul Robeson.

Two of the most well-known classical concert singers were Roland Hayes and Marian Anderson. In their performances, they included music by Mozart, Bach and Beethoven, as well as great operatic arias.

Georgia-born Roland Hayes broke the color bar in the concert halls for black singers of classical selections. After a command

An Aaron Douglas drawing entitled "Rise, shine for thy light has come."

Singer Marian Anderson.

Composer R. Nathaniel Dett.

Actor Richard B. Harrison.

performance before King George V at Buckingham Palace, Hayes returned to America in 1923 to become one of the most popular concert artists.

Marian Anderson went to Europe on a Rosenwald Fellowship in 1930. She returned with medals from the King of Denmark and the King of Sweden. Nine years later, Anderson would focus national attention on lingering discrimination. At Constitution Hall in Washington, the Daughters of the American Revolution refused to let her perform. The public outcry was so loud that Secretary of the Interior Harold Ickes offered an alternative. He invited Anderson to sing on Easter Sunday from the steps of the Lincoln Memorial. She sang at the feet of the Great Emancipator before a vast, unsegregated audience.

One of the most popular black composers in the 1920s was R. Nathaniel Dett. Other young black composers who emerged during the decade were William Grant Still, William L. Dawson and John W. Work, Jr.

Popular Music

In the field of popular music, the pianist Jelly Roll Morton, W. C. Handy, called the 'Father of the Blues", J. P. Johnson, famous for the Charleston, Thomas "Fats" Waller, Clarence Williams and Spencer Williams all added to America's rich music. Fletcher Henderson, for many years had his own band and also did arrangements for other famous bands, such as Benny Goodman's.

In 1922, Duke Ellington brought his first orchestra, the Washingtonians, and his great talent for popular composition to Harlem and Broadway. From then on, jazz was on the upswing. Combining American blues and black spirituals with African rhythms, jazz has become a unique American contribution to Western culture. Eventually, the government sent jazz bands on world tours to make friends for democracy. Among these musical ambassadors were Louis Armstrong, Lionel Hampton and Dizzy Gillespie. Air waves and records carried their rhythms to listeners here and abroad.

Black Theater

In 1921, a musical, "Shuffle Along," filled a theater for almost two years. It was written, directed, performed and originally produced by blacks—Noble Sissle, Eubie Blake, Flournoy Miller and Aubrey Lyles. And it brought to fame a new singing and dancing star, Florence Mills.

After the production of "Shuffle Along", a

series of lively all-black musical shows came to Broadway. Among the more popular black musical reviews of the 1920s were "Liza," "Running Wild," "Chocolate Dandies," "Dixie to Broadway," "Blackbirds," "Rang Tang," "Africana," "Blackbirds of 1928" and "Hot Chocolates."

When Eugene O'Neill's play "The Emperor Jones" opened in Greenwich Village, black actor Charles Gilpin played the lead role. Gilpin was voted by the Drama League as one of the 10 persons of 1920 who had most greatly advanced the American theater.

Jazz composer, bandleader and pianist Duke Ellington.

In 1923, the Ethiopian Art Players presented "Salome." That same year, the decade's foremost black stage star, Paul Robeson, made his debut as a voodoo king in "Taboo." The following year, Robeson played the male lead opposite a white actress, Mary Blair, in Eugene O'Neill's "All God's Chillun Got Wings." Other famous black dramas of the 1920s included "Lulu Belle," "In Abraham's Bosom" and "Porgy." This decade of

almost continuous brilliant black entertainment closed with Marc Connelly's fantasy "The Green Pastures."

Scholars and Scientists

Less highly publicized than black achievements in the arts, but of no less importance, were the contributions by scientists and scholars. Most of them were educated at leading Northern universities. The historians Carter Woodson and Rayford Logan received their doctorates at Harvard. The economist Abram Harris received his at

Paul Robeson with Mary Blair in "All God's Chillun Got Wings."

Columbia. The biologist Ernest Just and the sociologists Charles Johnson and E. Franklin Frazier each received their doctorates from the University of Chicago.

The most famous black scientist was George Washington Carver, who received degrees from Iowa State College during the 1890s. Carver later taught at Tuskegee and worked on experiments with the peanut, sweet potato and soybean. He is also credited with helping Southern farmers move away from dependency on cotton by diversifying their crops. By the time of his death in 1943, Carver was widely honored as one of the nation's most influential agronomists.

Dr. Percy Julian graduated from De Pauw University in Indiana in 1920. He received his doctorate in chemistry at the University of Vienna, Austria, in 1931. As director of research on soya products for the Glidden

Historian Carter G. Woodson.

Company of Chicago, he perfected a method of extracting steroids from soybean oil for the manufacture of sex hormones.

Dr. Charles R. Drew graduated from Amherst College in Massachusetts in 1926. He received his medical degree in 1933 from McGill Medical College in Canada. Drew be-

came a leading authority on the preservation of blood plasma. And, during World War II, he aided the American Red Cross and was surgical consultant for the U.S. Army.

Other distinguished blacks in scientific fields included Dr. William A. Hinton, a clinical professor at the Harvard Medical School and originator of the Hinton test for syphilis; James A. Parsons, a metallurgical chemist; Julian H. Lewis, a pathologist, and Elmer S. Imes, a physicist. In 1921, the first black women to receive doctors' degrees in the United States were Georgiana Rosa Simpson, at the University of Chicago; Sadie T. Mosell, at the University of Pennsylvania, and Eva B. Dykes, at Radcliffe College.

In 1923, Charles S. Johnson founded the magazine *Opportunity* in which many young black writers and artists achieved first publication. Dr. Johnson became one of America's leading sociologists, the author of numerous books, a member of the United States National Commission to UNESCO in Paris and the recipient of six honorary degrees from leading universities at home and abroad.

CHAPTER CHECK

1. What was the Harlem Renaissance?
2. Why do you think the Harlem Renaissance occurred when it did?
3. Imagine . . . you are a young Southern black person who just moved to Harlem in the 1920s. How would your life be different from what it was before? Explain.

Children in Washington, D.C. during the Depression.

CHAPTER 33

Black America and the Great Depression

"Something is happening in Chicago," declared the Chicago *Defender* early in 1929, "and it should no longer go unnoticed. During the past three weeks, hardly a day has ended that there has not been a report of another firm discharging its employees."

Later that year the Urban League stated, "Every week we receive information regarding the discharge of additional race workers." But the ordinary black did not need to read such statements to sense the coming slump in employment. In October 1929, the stock market crashed. In its wake began the longest and most severe depression in American history.

At the height of the Great Depression decade there were 15 million unemployed, including many blacks. Black colleges, heavily dependent on contributions from the wealthy, fared badly. Hard-pressed Southern communities were forced to slice public school budgets. The first cuts they made were in the already poorly supported black schools. Many teachers lost their jobs and some schools closed. Cotton prices slumped and foundries shut down. By the mid-30s, twice as many blacks needed public assistance as whites. In some cities, 70 to 80 percent of the people on relief were black. Housing became more rundown than ever. On Chicago's South Side, almost 250,000 blacks were crowded into eight square miles of tenement housing.

Father Divine

"The depression, with a devastating impact," recorded an Illinois State Commission, "reversed the trend of the Twenties and turned black people from a group with more than its share of gainfully employed into a population predominantly dependent upon government relief." National and local leaders, black and white, were at first powerless to cope with the problems. But one black leader would permit none of his followers to accept public relief, and none went hungry. Everyone who came to his restaurants received full meals for 15 cents. If one had no money, one received a free meal. He sold coal at cost from his coal yards. And he offered haircuts in his shops at a quarter of what other barbers charged. He was called Father Divine.

He was born George Baker sometime around 1880. He was the son of a sharecropping family from Hutchinson's Island, Georgia. His spiritual father was Samuel Morris, who called himself Father Jehoviah. In 1899, as the messenger and son of Father Jehoviah, Baker opened his first mission in Baltimore, Maryland. Its purpose was to distribute aid to the needy.

In 1912, Baker proclaimed his own divinity and moved to Georgia. He was soon prosecuted by the law there. In 1915, Baker moved his flock to New York City. In 1919, he adopted the name of Major Morgan J. Devine and moved to Sayville, Long Island. There his followers lived in **communes** where everyone shared their earnings and duties. In 1930, Baker changed his name to Father Divine. He became one of the best known religious leaders in the United States.

Divine thought of himself as God. His followers were called angels, and his communes were called heavens. His followers included several thousand lower-income blacks, a much smaller number of whites, and countless well-wishers.

Father Divine established throughout the East, and in various cities across the country, a chain of religious cooperatives. His followers gave of labor and income according to their abilities and received according to their needs, without distinction as to color. Father Divine ordered followers who were illiterate

Father Divine and followers at his Krum Elbow estate on the Hudson in New York.

A Father Divine shop in Harlem which sold food at cost to the public.

Father Divine.

Father Divine Shoeshine Parlor.

to attend night school. Any followers who had been dishonest were ordered to return whatever they had taken. He taught rigid principles of decency, hygiene and self-reliance. In fact, he prohibited alcohol, sexual relations, family living arrangements, sickness and death. If someone in his group died, they were judged not true believers. His religious meetings were combined with abundant feasting in the very midst of the Great Depression. By the 1960s, Father Divine's movement controlled property estimated to have a value of $10 million.

Father Divine didn't train anyone to take over his organization. When he died in 1965, his movement waned.

A Shift to the Democratic Party

In his 1932 reelection bid, President Herbert Hoover had to face the Great Depression as a campaign issue. His Democratic opponent was Franklin D. Roosevelt. Roosevelt promised to take drastic steps to rescue America from the clutches of the Great Depression. He was elected. The programs Roosevelt sponsored were part of what he called the New Deal.

Several governmental agencies were set up to cope with the problems brought by the Great Depression. These agencies aided blacks culturally and financially. The Roosevelt administration appointed many black advisers to various government agencies. They included the National Youth Administration (NYA), the Civilian Conservation Corps (CCC) camps and the Work Projects Administration (WPA). The last employed many artists, actors and writers. New Deal programs gave hundreds of thousands of blacks industrial training, theatrical experience and opportunities to paint and write.

A worker at the Tennessee Valley Authority
project in the 1930s.

The programs opened up jobs to blacks from which private industry had excluded them. When he ran again in 1936, blacks voted overwhelmingly Democratic.

Federal Projects

Sterling Brown served as editor in black affairs for the Federal Writers Project (part of the WPA). In Chicago, Arna Bontemps was in charge of a unit. Writers who were given employment by the project included Claude McKay, Richard Wright, Roi Ottley, Zora Neale Hurston, Frank Yerby, Margaret Walker, Marcus Christian, Robert Hayden, Ralph Ellison and John H. Johnson. Johnson went on to become the publisher of the leading black magazines *Ebony* and *Jet*.

In New York, Dean Dixon conducted the National Youth Administration Orchestra. It was made up of young people of all racial backgrounds. In the Federal Theater, black actors in Northern cities performed in inter-

racial units. They also performed with all-black companies in Harlem, Chicago, Birmingham and Los Angeles. In Los Angeles, Clarence Muse produced Hall Johnson's "Run, Little Chillun." It had the longest run of any Federal Theater group production.

At the Lafayette Theater in Harlem, plays by blacks were done. Frank Wilson's "Walk Together, Children," Rudolph Fisher's "Conjure Man Dies," and "Turpentine," by J.A. Smith and Peter Morrell were produced there. Canada Lee, Edna Thomas and Jack Carter appeared in a stunning tropical "Macbeth," staged by Orson Welles and John Houseman. And in Chicago, the black "Swing Mikado" was a jazz success.

Mary McLeod Bethune

In 1935, Mary McLeod Bethune became director of Negro Affairs of the National Youth Administration. She was a friend of the Roosevelts and a powerful figure in New

Deal policies relating to blacks. Bethune organized all of the high-level black advisors to the New Deal programs. The group was called the Federal Council on Negro Affairs. It was informally known as the Black Cabinet.

Bethune was born near Mayesville, South Carolina, in 1875, to parents who had been slaves. She worked as a child in the cotton fields and walked five miles a day to a mission school. She received her higher education at Scotia Seminary in North Carolina and Moody Bible Institute in Chicago. After completing her formal education, Bethune dedicated her life to improving the lot of black Americans through education. In 1904, she established a school in Florida. It was called the Daytona Normal and Industrial Institute for Negro Girls. In 1923, it merged with the Cookman Institute of Jacksonville and became co-educational. This school became known as Bethune-Cookman College. Bethune served as its president until 1942.

Members of Roosevelt's Black Cabinet were competent specialists in various fields. In 1938, the group included *(front row, left to right)* Dr. Roscoe E. Brown, *Public Health Service;* Dr. Robert C. Weaver, *Housing Authority;* Joseph H. Evans, *Farm Security Administration;* Dr. Frank Horne, *Housing Authority;* Mary McLeod Bethune, *National Youth Administration;* Lt. Lawrence A. Oxley, *Department of Labor;* Dr. William J. Thompkins, *Recorder of Deeds;* Charles E. Hall, *Department of Commerce;* William I. Houston, *Department of Justice.* In the back row, *(left to right)* are Dewey R. Jones, *Department of the Interior;* Edgar Brown, *the Civilian Conservation Corps;* J. Parker Prescott, *Housing Authority;* Edward H. Lawson, Jr., *Works Projects Administration;* Arthur Weiseger, *Department of Labor;* Alfred Edgar Smith, *Works Projects Administration;* Henry A. Hunt, *Farm Credit Administration;* John W. Whitten, *Works Projects Administration;* and Joseph R. Houchins, *Department of Commerce.*

Additional Benefits

The educational program of the National Youth Administration enrolled more than 400,000 blacks in its classes. Many of the state and local supervisors, as well as teachers, were black. In its student work program, more than 64,000 young black men and women learned skilled trades. Older people were given opportunities for education through the Adult Education Projects, and jobs were provided for unemployed teachers. In the camps of the Civilian Conservation Corps, some 250,000 black boys received practical training in the conservation of natural resources.

By 1939, more than a million unemployed blacks owed their livelihood to the Works Progress Administration. Other benefits came through the construction projects of the Public Works Administration. Buildings on black college campuses, new black hospitals, community centers and playgrounds were constructed through the PWA. Black artisans were employed in their construction except where white union locals prohibited them.

Pickets and Protests

In many Northern cities during the Great Depression, blacks picketed and boycotted white-staffed businesses in black neighborhoods, demanding jobs. "Don't Buy Where You Can't Work" was their slogan. A number of businesses, including the Woolworth chain on the South Side of Chicago, gave in and hired black clerks. In New York, 125th Street is the heart of Harlem. There were many flourishing white-owned businesses which depended on black customers. But these same businesses had no black employees. Adam Clayton Powell, Jr. of the Abyssinian Baptist Church, led protest marches in front of such shops.

When World War II broke out in Europe, many plants with government contracts refused to employ black workers. Protests of the NAACP, the Urban League and other groups were to no avail. Labor leader A. Philip Randolph proposed a March on Washington of from 50,000 to 100,000 black people. As large delegations from all across the nation prepared to journey to the nation's capital on July 1, 1941, President Roosevelt called a conference of black leaders. On June 25, the President issued Executive Order 8802. It banned discrimination in industries holding government contracts and set up the Fair Employment Practices Commission.

Marion Anderson singing at the Lincoln Memorial.

A picket line near the Capitol protesting delays in passing Fair Employment Practices laws.

When the long-running Broadway play "The Green Pastures," with an all-black cast, was performed at the National Theater in Washington in 1934, no blacks were allowed to buy tickets. Blacks could not then attend any downtown theater in Washington, D. C. At Constitution Hall, where the Daughters of the American Revolution permitted black patrons to buy segregated seats, no black could appear on the stage.

Fifteen years later, by refusing to permit union actors to appear in Washington's segregated theaters, Actors' Equity broke the audience color bar in the capital.

CHAPTER CHECK

1. What effect did the Great Depression have on African Americans?

2. How did the New Deal change the relationship between the federal government and African Americans? Why do you think this happened?

3. Imagine . . . you are an unemployed black worker during the 1930s. What types of aid would you have available to help you? How would this affect your impression of the federal government and the Democratic Party?

The job of subway conductor was one that opened to blacks in the thirties and forties.

Main Events

1. In 1905, W. E. B. Du Bois and 29 other black leaders began the Niagara Movement in opposition to Booker T. Washington.

2. In 1910, the interracial National Association for the Advancement of Colored People was formed.

3. Some 200,000 black troops served overseas during World War I.

4. The summer of 1919 became "red summer" when race riots turned into race wars.

5. In 1917, Marcus Garvey reorganized his Universal Negro Improvement Association in Harlem, attracting wide support for his Back to Africa movement.

6. In the early twentieth century, hundreds of thousands of Southern blacks migrated to Northern cities.

7. During the 1920s, there was a celebration of black literature, art, music and theater. This has been called the Harlem Renaissance.

8. While the Great Depression of the 1930s had a devastating effect on the entire country, the black community suffered especially hard.

9. Due to the policies of Franklin Roosevelt's New Deal, by 1936 blacks switched their political allegiance from the Republican to the Democratic party.

10. The actions of the Roosevelt administration were only temporary solutions to immediate problems, but they signalled a new commitment on the part of the federal government for enforcing racial equality in America.

Dedication of the Harlem River Housing Project, built by the Public Works Administration in New York.

Words to Know

Match the following words with their correct definitions. Number your paper from 1 to 8, and write the correct word beside each number.

autocracy
colonialism
communes
draft

emigration
Harlem Renaissance
Niagara Movement
stevedore

1. the celebration of black literature and art during the 1920s
2. the opposition against the policies of Booker T. Washington led by W. E. B. Du Bois
3. a person who loads and unloads ships
4. the control of one nation by the people of another nation
5. a government in which one person has all the power
6. leaving one country to settle in another
7. required participation in the military
8. places where people live together, sharing earnings and responsibilities

Thinking and Writing

A. Comparing Two Leaders

Booker T. Washington and W. E. B. Du Bois were both important leaders for African Americans. Review Chapter 28, "A School is Born," in Part 5. Then, reread Chapter 29, "The Liberation Movement." Write down the ways in which the two leaders were similar in their opinions about race relations in America. Write down the ways in which they were different. Which leader do you think had the best policies? What factors do you think influenced their reasoning? Give reasons for your answer.

B. Writing a Letter

Imagine it is 1922 and you are a young African American who has moved from the rural South to New York City. Write a letter back home describing your experiences. Give some *facts* about your life. Tell about some of the things you have seen and done since arriving there. Then discuss your *feelings*. How is your life different from what it was before? Do you think you made the right decision in moving?

PART SEVEN

SEARCHING FOR FREEDOM

1940-1980

A soldier in one of two black tank battalions.

LOOKING AHEAD · PART SEVEN · 1940–1980

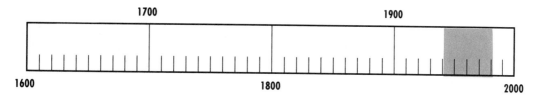

World War II, President Franklin D. Roosevelt declared, was necessary to ensure that freedom was available to everyone. Black Americans eagerly rushed to offer themselves for service. They courageously fought in all fronts of the war. This time, they did not want the nation to forget their contributions and their freedoms. They were determined.

At war and at home, many things did not change for black Americans. Most army units remained segregated, and blacks were excluded from some programs. Also, Jim Crow laws remained in effect at home. And black gains were met with racial violence. Just as during World War I, thousands of Southern blacks moved North and West to work in defense industries. Several race riots broke out due to white resentment.

Still, important changes had occurred for African Americans. The army's officer candidate schools admitted blacks for unsegregated training, and blacks were accepted in every branch of the military. In a way, World War II proved a hidden revolution for American blacks. Fighting a war for freedom helped motivate them to demand the freedoms for which the war was fought.

Beginning in the 1930s, the NAACP initiated an aggressive campaign to chip away at the legal inequalities in American life. The results of many of these cases came in the post-war years. The NAACP filed suits covering a wide range of civil rights. But none were more important than those in education.

The case which revolutionized American education was *Brown v. Board of Education*. In this 1954 case, the Supreme Court declared that separate schools for blacks and whites were unconstitutional. The court ruled that all segregated schools in America would have to be integrated with "all deliberate speed."

Many school boards in the upper South integrated their schools. But whites in the Deep South opposed desegregation and were willing to fight to stop it. In 1957, the governor of Arkansas ordered the state's national guard to surround Little Rock's Central High School. He wanted to prevent nine black teenagers from entering the school. President Dwight Eisenhower was forced to send in federal troops to put down the riot and integrate the school.

The federal government again sent troops to enforce school desegregation in Mississippi in 1962. A riot had broken out when James Meredith, a black man, tried to integrate the state university.

The fall of legal barriers to an equal education rekindled a dream in the heart of black America. That dream was to live in a nation where all people were treated equally

Signs of a segregated America.

and were not judged by the color of their skin. By the 1950s, many blacks began action to make that dream become a reality. The result was the modern civil rights movement. It began in 1955 in Montgomery, Alabama. A black woman, Rosa Parks, refused to give up her seat on a bus to a white man. For this she was arrested. In protest, the blacks of the city led a boycott against the segregated buses. After one year, the protesters won and the buses were desegregated.

The leader of the Montgomery bus boycott was Dr. Martin Luther King, Jr. King emerged from the boycott an international hero. He went on to become the most prominent and influential leader of the civil rights movement. King inspired millions with his courage and belief that social change could be brought about by refusing to meet violence with violence.

Breaking the back of segregation was the number one priority of the movement. American college students played an active part in this movement. Sit-ins were one of their earliest and most successful activities.

Boycotting and picketing of shops that refused to serve blacks were also used to good effect. The most dangerous operation led by students were efforts to desegregate public transportation. Although the students were violently attacked, they succeeded.

In 1963, King and other civil rights leaders led a massive march on Washington demanding equal rights for blacks. The next year, the most far-reaching civil rights act in almost 100 years was passed. In 1965, a voting rights act wiped out all laws restricting voting.

By the mid-1960s, legal segregation had been eliminated. But many blacks still saw basic inequalities in American society. Racism was a national problem, not just a Southern one. Many began to question whether any real change could ever occur without violence. More militant blacks started taking over the movement. Black-white tensions developed in the various civil rights organizations. And violence erupted not only in the South but all over the nation.

A good example of the changes which oc-

Black Panther leaders Huey Newton and David Hilliard.

curred in the civil rights movement can be seen in what happened to the Student Non-violent Coordinating Committee (SNCC). Begun as an offshoot of King's Southern Christian Leadership Conference, SNCC coordinated student sit-ins in the South. Within a few years, SNCC was organizing other activities such as freedom rides and voter registration. The violent resistance of whites which members faced helped convince many that nonviolence was no match for such entrenched opposition and hate. By 1965, SNCC openly called for violence in return for violence and broke with King.

Even more militant in their determination to fight racism during these times were the Black Panthers and the Black Muslims.

As the war against racism picked up, so did another war. This one was in the Southeast Asian country of Vietnam. There, the United States was backing the government of South Vietnam in a civil war with communist-supported North Vietnam. Although the war had been going on since 1957, U.S. ground troops did not take part until 1965.

The services were now integrated. Indeed, blacks took part in greater proportions to their population than did any other group. But often they were at the bottom of the ladder—in the infantry and the artillery. More aware of racism than ever before, black soldiers resented being used as "cannon fodder." Many times, black enlisted men attacked racist white officers. The war in Vietnam divided Americans in many ways. Before American troops were withdrawn in 1973, many blacks had begun to ask if their country was asking too much and giving too little in return.

The frustration of many blacks was expressed by the wave of violence which spread across American cities in the late 1960s. Most tragic were the riots that followed the assassination of King in 1968. By the 1970s, racial violence had decreased. But racial tensions have continued. And the Ku Klux Klan remains a nagging presence in American life.

CHAPTER 34

Patriotism and Prejudice

Air Force hero Benjamin O. Davis, Jr., later became a lieutenant general.

Troops of the 92nd Division in Italy.

Machine-gunners at Bougainville.

Removing the Bougainville wounded.

The first World War was fought, it was said, "to make the world safe for democracy." Millions of black Americans dedicated their lives, their fortunes, and their honor to achieve that goal. It was not realized. Blacks were denied equality in America, and another war was needed to stop oppression abroad.

World War II, President Franklin D. Roosevelt declared, was necessary to ensure that four basic freedoms were available to everyone. They were freedom of speech, freedom of religion, freedom from want, and freedom from fear. Again, black Americans rushed to offer themselves as unreserved patriots. But black soldiers were also determined that the **Four Freedoms** would be available to them and to their families. This time they did not want the nation to forget their contributions and their freedoms.

Even before the war, when defense preparations began and the draft act was passed, a group of black leaders presented a memorandum to President Roosevelt. It urged that discrimination be abolished in the navy and the air corps. It asked that black recruits be given the same training as whites. It asked that blacks be accepted on the basis of ability for assignments and commissions. And it asked that black doctors and nurses be integrated into the services.

Still, strict segregation continued. Black recruits were segregated in the army, and denied entrance to some training programs. The American Red Cross even segregated the blood in its blood banks. The black press protested vigorously. And in January 1943, as a protest at the continuing racist policy in military administration, William H. Hastie resigned. Hastie had been the civilian aide to the Secretary of War. His place was filled by another black, Truman Gibson, Jr.

Although discrimination continued throughout the war, many changes did occur. During World War II, blacks had more opportunities than in any previous war. The army's newly established officer candidate schools began to admit blacks for unsegregated training in 1941. In 1942, the navy agreed to accept blacks for general service, as did the marines. The air force opened a post for the training of black pilots at Tuskegee. More than 4,000 black women served as **WACS** (Women's Army Corps) and **WAVES** (U.S. Navy—it stands for Women Accepted for Volunteer Emergency Service).

Before the end of the war there were more than a million black men and women in uniform. About 6,000 of them were officers. Integration in the ground troops of the army finally began in 1945. Volunteer black infantrymen saw action alongside white soldiers in the First Army's invasion of Germany. They established themselves, according to a War Department communique, "as fighting men no less courageous or aggressive than their white comrades."

Action in World War II

Dorie Miller became one of the first heroes of World War II. Miller, a navy messman on the battleship *Arizona* at Pearl Harbor, shot down four Japanese planes over his ship. Colonel Benjamin O. Davis, Jr., after taking the 99th Pursuit Squadron to Tunisia, returned to organize the 332nd Fighter Group. The 332nd was instrumental in battles in the Mediterranean and Eastern Europe. Eighty-eight of its pilots, including Colonel Davis, received the Distinguished Flying Cross.

In ground action, the 761st Tank Battalion won distinction, as did the 614th Tank De-

WAVE Ensign Frances Wills.

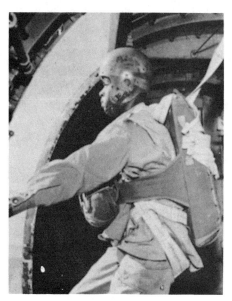

An army air force paratrooper.

stroyer Battalion. The black soldiers of the 92nd Division saw hard fighting and were heavily decorated. The black soldiers of the famous Red Ball Express maintained the supply lines for the Normandy offensive under extraordinary enemy fire.

In the Pacific, the 93rd Division saw action at numerous South Sea islands, including parts of the Solomons, Indonesia, and the Philippines. The 24th Infantry routed the Japanese from the New Georgia Islands. And some 10,000 black soldiers helped to build the 478-mile Ledo Road through the Himalayan Mountains, while fighting the enemy at the same time. Black members of the coast guard were among the first to land at Okinawa. Black marines were scattered throughout the Pacific. Black sailors served on most American battleships. In the mer-

chant marine, 24,000 black seamen served in mixed crews. Eighteen Liberty ships were named for black Americans. And some, like the *S.S. Booker T. Washington*, under Captain Hugh H. Mulzac, were staffed by black officers with mixed crews.

Jim Crow on the Home Front

America was at war, and its national existence was at stake. Yet on the home front, if Americans were united in spirit and effort, they were separated and segregated in all else. Blacks eagerly contributed to the war effort, and fought for freedom abroad. But they still faced strong racist oppression at home. Jim Crow laws remained in effect, and black gains were met with racial violence. This proved especially bitter to those participating in the war effort.

Just as during the first World War, thousands of Southern black workers poured into Northern and Western cities. More than 50,000 blacks moved to Detroit alone, seeking work in the many defense industries centered there. Everywhere housing presented a problem. White workers often violently resented black families moving anywhere near them. Bombings, arson and forced evictions were frequent. Serious race riots broke out in Detroit, New York, Mobile, Beaumont (Texas) and other communities.

There were riots at some military centers, too. Sometimes local customs clashed with military attempts to provide decent treatment for black soldiers. German prisoners in transit could dine in Southern railway-station restaurants, while their black American guards could not. Recreational facilities for black soldiers were often lacking. USO centers were segregated, although the Stage Door Canteens were open to all.

MONDAY, MAY 10, 1948.

GOV. WRIGHT BIDS NEGROES BE QUIET

Any Wanting Social Equality Had Better Quit Mississippi, He Says on Radio to Race

By JOHN N. POPHAM
Special to THE NEW YORK TIMES.

JACKSON, Miss., May 9—In an action believed to be unprecedented in Southern history, Governor Fielding L. Wright "advised" the Negroes of this state today that if they contemplated eventual social equality and the sharing of school, hotel and restaurant facilities with white persons to "make your home in some state other than Mississippi."

Although racial   ation

Los Angeles veterans in the ruins of their home bombed by racists.

For civilians, most unions welcomed black members, and even in the South some locals were mixed. But limited transportation facilities created grave problems. It was hard for some black travelers standing on the railway platforms if the lone Jim Crow coach was filled. Buses packed with whites often would not even stop for black passengers. Black soldiers on **furlough** (leave) sometimes could not get home. If they did get there, they were not always able to return to camp on time.

Despite fighting a war for freedom, many things had not changed for black Americans. Segregation and racist oppression continued. Still, important changes had occurred. The war opened up new opportunities for blacks in the military and in the workplace. It also renewed the national commitment to freedom and equality. Just as after World War I, blacks refused to accept the restrictions placed on their lives before the war. And the experience of World War II helped provide the motivation to demand the freedoms for which the war was fought.

CHAPTER CHECK

1. How did World War II provide new opportunities for blacks?

2. In what ways did nothing change for blacks after World War II? In what ways were things different?

3. Imagine . . . you are a young black man or woman who has just served in the United States Army during World War II. How would your reaction to Jim Crow laws and other racial restrictions be different than before the war? Why?

George W. McLaurin, who entered the University of Oklahoma in 1948 as its first black student, with his wife. Mrs. McLaurin had applied unsuccessfully in 1923.

CHAPTER 35

Rights Reaffirmed

Beginning in the 1930s, the NAACP began aggressively chipping away at the legal inequalities in American society. Numerous suits were filed in the nation's courts. These suits covered a wide range of civil rights. But none more important than the right to an equal education.

Many Southern state-supported universities would not admit the sons and daughters of black taxpayers. In 1936, the NAACP won a suit against the University of Maryland law school, and blacks were admitted. Two years later another major victory was won. The Supreme Court declared that it was unconstitutional for Missouri to refuse to allow blacks to attend the state university when there was no equal school available to them.

One of the leading lawyers for the NAACP

was Thurgood Marshall. Marshall argued many of the NAACP's most important cases, and later became the first black member of the U. S. Supreme Court. One case which he helped win revolutionized American education.

Brown v. Board of Education

On May 17, 1954, the U. S. Supreme Court ruled in *Brown v. Board of Education* that persons who were required on the basis of race to attend separate schools, were "deprived of the equal protection of the laws guaranteed by the Fourteenth Amendment." In a unanimous decision, the court set aside the "separate but equal" doctrine of the *Plessy v. Ferguson* decision of 1896.

This decision dramatically altered the educational system of the South. It affected the District of Columbia and 17 other states. Race relations in America would be forever changed.

Washington, D.C. began at once to set a positive example by quickly integrating its schools. By 1956, Baltimore had integrated 11,000 of its 51,000 black pupils. But in the rest of Maryland, efforts were half-hearted.

In West Virginia, only a few areas hung back. The formerly all-black West Virginia State College (with a black faculty) soon had more than 400 white students, more than a third of its student body. In Kentucky, some black teachers were assigned to integrated classes. The University of Louisville was opened to all races. And Berea College, which had been forbidden by Kentucky law in 1904 to continue admitting blacks, again accepted them. Oklahoma and Missouri officially began desegregation. Schools on federal military posts throughout the South were integrated.

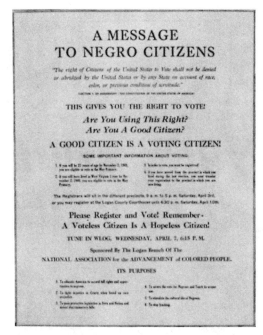

Flyer urging blacks to vote.

Black voters in the 1946 Georgia Democratic primary.

Blacks voting in the 1948 Charleston primary for the first time since Reconstruction.

The New York

Copyright, 1954, by The New York Times Company.

VOL. CIII...No. 35,178.

Entered as Second-Class Matter.
Post Office, New York, N. Y.

NEW YORK, TUESDAY, MAY 18, 1954

HIGH COURT BANS SCHOO
9-TO-0 DECISION GRANTS

Desegregating America: The Law Defied

But there is another story. In 1954, school desegregation in America became front-page news in papers throughout the world. Clinton and Oxford, Mississippi, Nashville, Atlanta, and Little Rock were particularly bitter in their opposition to the court's ruling.

Within months of the Brown decision, hundreds of school boards in the upper South desegregated their schools. But in the Deep South, opposition was bitter and no action was taken. Public opinion polls showed that over 80 percent of white Southerners opposed desegregation.

One problem with the Brown decision was that it set no deadline for desegregating schools. One year later, on May 31, 1955, the court responded to this problem by directing that educational integration be achieved with "all deliberate speed," based on equitable principles and a "practical flexibility." This angered many blacks and civil rights

supporters, because without a fixed date, little, if any, action would be taken. This appeared to be a concession to white segregationists.

Powerful forces opposing desegration were gathering throughout the South. On March 12, 1956, 101 Southern members of Congress issued a Southern Manifesto opposing public school integration. They asked their states to refuse to obey the Supreme Court's order. They termed the court decisions "unwarranted" and a "clear abuse of judicial power." The court had trespassed on the rights reserved to the states. "We pledge ourselves," they announced, "to use all lawful means to bring about a reversal of this decision ... and to prevent the use of force in its implementation."

Encouraged by the stand, the Ku Klux Klan and the White Citizen's Council came out of hiding. They turned to open intimidation of black citizens. Often the actions of these terrorist groups had no relation to

LATE CITY EDITION

Fair and cool today. Mostly sunny,
continued cool tomorrow.
Temperature Range Today-Max., 68; Min., 52
Temperatures Yesterday—Max., 69; Min., 61
Full U. S. Weather Bureau Report, Page 51

Times Square, New York 36, N. Y.
Telephone LAckawanna 4-1000

FIVE CENTS

EGREGATION;
E TO COMPLY

school desegregation. In Mississippi, for example, Emmett Till, a Chicago schoolboy,
was spending a summer vacation on his
uncle's farm. In the middle of the night white
terrorists seized him and spirited him away.
Later, his body was found tied to an iron cot-
ton-gin wheel at the bottom of the Tal-
lahatchie River. He had been brutally beaten
and shot through the head. The two white
men accused of the crime were acquitted.
And what was Till's crime? He was said to
have whistled at a white woman in a country
store.

Symbolic of the Deep South's defiance of
the Supreme Court's desegregation decision
was an outbreak in Tuscaloosa, Alabama. For
three years a black woman named Autherine
Lucy had been trying to enroll as a student in
library science at the tax-supported University of Alabama. By federal district court order, she was finally admitted to the university
as its first black student. She attended her
first class on Friday, February 3, 1956.

When she returned on Monday, riots
broke out on the campus. A mob of more
than a thousand men pelted the car in which
the dean of women drove Lucy to and from
classes. Threats were made against her life,
and the school president's home was stoned.
Lucy was suspended. When she was rein-
stated a few weeks later, by order of the Birmingham federal court, university trustees
met and expelled her permanently on a
quickly invented technicality. Seven years
were to pass before a black applicant was
permitted to attend the university.

Little Rock to Ole Miss

In September 1957, nine black teenagers
sought admission to Little Rock's Central
High School. At first, little opposition was
foreseen. Little Rock was considered a moderate southern city, outside of the Deep
South. It had also proposed a desegregation
plan that had been approved by federal
courts.

On the day before school was to begin,
Governor Orval Faubus decided to oppose
desegregation. He posted the Arkansas National Guard in front of the building to bar
the students' way. Mobs outside the school
surged around the black students and men-
aced everyone who appeared to be sympathetic to them. Reporters were kicked and
beaten while policemen stood by.

This was the first time a Southern state
used state troops to defy federal law in opposing the Brown decision. President Dwight
Eisenhower was forced to send in federal
troops to enforce the law. One thousand
paratroopers from the 101st Airborne Division of the United States Army arrived to ensure the safety of black students. Eisenhower also placed 10,000 members of the

Daisy Bates picketing in Little Rock.

Rioters at the University of Mississippi.

Arkansas National Guard on special federal service. After two months, the paratroopers and most of the guardsmen were removed. But a small number of the federalized troops remained on duty until the end of the school year.

Mrs. Daisy Bates spearheaded the admission of the nine young people. She was the state president of the NAACP. She was also co-owner with her husband of a black weekly, the Arkansas *State Press*. The Bates' home was bombed more than once. It was sprayed with bullets at night. Front windows were smashed by rock-throwing mobs and crosses were burned on the lawn. Newsboys selling the paper, and its black and white advertisers, were intimidated. The paper, the family's sole source of income, was forced to close.

The school board's rooms and the mayor's office were bombed. Forty-four teachers who refused to side with the segregationists were discharged. The superintendent of schools was removed. Anti-integrationists kept violence and disorder alive in Little Rock for three years.

By 1962, all the formerly all-white high schools in Little Rock were desegregated (although elementary schools remained separated by races). But in other, deeper Southern states, segregation was still supreme.

Mississippi faced its test in 1962 when James Meredith sought to enroll at the state university. Meredith was a 29 year-old black air force veteran. Governor Ross Barnett, physically barring his way, said to the television cameras and the world that he would go to jail before permitting a black student to attend "Ole Miss." Barnett was found guilty of contempt of federal court and ordered to leave. Meredith was escorted to school by

U.S. marshals. When the governor himself failed to bar Meredith, a mob of students and others took over.

During the riots that shook the university campus and the town of Oxford, two men were killed, one of them a French correspondent. Over 100 people were wounded, and property was destroyed. Once again, 12,000 federal troops and nationalized guardsmen were sent to restore order and enforce federal law. White coeds shouted, "Kill the nigger," but James Meredith registered and attended classes—with 300 soldiers to escort him. "It's more for America than for me," he said.

Mobs were rarely punished, even when federal troops were used against them. Although police were on the scene and hundreds of rioters could be clearly identified from the television films, almost no arrests were made.

"During the school year," Daisy Bates stated, "the FBI interviewed hundreds of persons. Many of those who had been part of the mob in Little Rock could easily have been identified from photographs taken in front of the school. Yet no action was taken against anyone by the U.S. Attorney or the Department of Justice."

This was the pattern almost everywhere—terrorists literally got away with murder, as well as widespread property destruction. Violence spread from the schoolyard to the churchyard, from the lunch counter to public transportation, and to the ballot box.

CHAPTER CHECK

1. Why do you think many whites were opposed to equal education for blacks?
2. What were some of the tactics used by blacks to obtain desegregation in the classroom?
3. Imagine . . . you are one of the black teenagers at Little Rock Central High School in 1957. Describe both the events of that fall, and also your thoughts and impressions of those events.

Federal troops accompanied black students home from Little Rock Central High School.

CHAPTER 36

The Struggle for a Dream

The law had finally spoken. But opposition to the letter, the spirit and the intent of the law was formidable. On every hand there was resistance, delay and attempts to get around it. But the law, as expressed by the order to desegregate, rekindled a dream in the heart of black America. That dream was perhaps best expressed for most by Martin Luther King, Jr., a young Baptist minister who grew up in Atlanta.

Dr. King delivered his "I Have A Dream" address at the Lincoln Memorial on August 28, 1963. The occasion was part of the massive March on Washington organized by King and other black leaders. They wanted to encourage passage of a new civil rights act. More than 200,000 people attended the day-long rally. As the giant crowd seated on the grass before the memorial cheered and applauded, and other millions watched via television, King declared:

> "I have a dream that one day this nation will rise up, live out the true meaning of its creed: 'We hold these truths to be self-evident that all men are created equal.'
>
> "I have a dream that one day . . . sons of former slaves and sons of former slave-owners will be able to sit down together at the table of brotherhood . . . .
>
> "I have a dream that . . . little children will one day live in a nation where they will not be judged by the color of their skin but by the content of their character.
>
> "I have a dream that one day . . . little black boys and black girls will be able to join hands with little white boys and white girls as sisters and brothers . . . ."

Such a dream would require more than the law to make it viable. The people would have to get involved if King's dream were ever to be more than a passing fancy. They did. King became their leader and the sym-

Baptist ministers Ralph D. Abernathy (left) and Martin Luther King, Jr., leave the Montgomery courthouse.

The Lincoln Memorial surrounded by the March on Washington.

Rosa Parks was fingerprinted after being indicted on a rarely enforced anti-boycott law.

One of the buses boycotted in Montgomery. The boycott forced fares up for white riders.

bol of nonviolent protest in America.

It had begun in 1955, in Montgomery, Alabama, when a black NAACP official named Rosa Parks refused to relinquish her seat on a bus to a white man. For this she was arrested. In protest, black citizens led by King, the 26 year-old pastor of Dexter Avenue Baptist Church, refused to ride the segregated buses. Hundreds of blacks were arrested and otherwise intimidated. King's home was bombed. The resistance held firm, with thousands of blacks walking to their jobs by day and gathering for prayer and spiritual reinforcement at night. After a year, the buses were desegregated. King emerged as an international hero.

The stage was set for an unbelievable saga that brought King the Nobel Peace Prize, and eventually cost him his life. For 12 years, King preached his dream in the streets, the jails and the churches of America. He was assassinated in Memphis in 1968.

Martin Luther King, Jr. was one of the most prominent social leaders America has produced. He inspired millions all over the world. More than that, he exposed the deep-seated hypocrisy that compromised American democracy. Perhaps he gave America back its conscience, if only for a fleeting interlude. The Center for Non-Violent Social Change in Atlanta is a memorial to King and his work. And his birthday, January 15, is now celebrated as a national holiday.

Other Dreamers, Other Dreams

Other blacks shared King's dream. Some shared it only in part, others shared it hardly at all. Still others had dreams of their own. One of the many prominent black leaders was the Reverend Ralph Abernathy. Abernathy took over the Southern Christian Lead-

A sit-in at a Chattanooga variety store lunch counter, 1960.

ership Conference (SCLC), after King's death. Another was A. Philip Randolph, a long-time activist in both the civil rights and labor movements. He was a leading organizer of the March on Washington.

Among the older civil rights leaders, Roy Wilkins proved extremely influential as the executive secretary of the NAACP. Wilkins' intense lobbying helped bring about passage of the various civil rights acts of the 1960s. During that decade, Whitney Young was the dynamic and effective leader of the Urban League. James Farmer helped establish the Congress of Racial Equality (CORE) in 1947 and turned the organization into a powerful force in the 1960s.

All these leaders were determined that blacks should be able to participate fully in the whole range of activities available to other Americans. Together they created the Civil Rights Movement, or the Black Revolution.

Student Sit-Ins

Breaking the back of segregation was the number one priority of the movement. One of the earliest and most successful developments in this area were the student sit-ins. During a **sit-in**, blacks peacefully occupied "white" sections of public facilities and demanded equal service. Often they were met with harassment and violence.

"Education without freedom is useless," said Bernard Lee, one of the students expelled from all-black Alabama State College at the insistence of the governor. They were expelled for waiting for service at a lunch counter in the Montgomery Courthouse.

It seemed that all over the South, thousands of students had the same idea about education without freedom. Sit-ins starting first with lunch counters, began in early 1960 in dozens of cities. A new social awareness had come to the campuses of America. The sit-ins often had the support of sympathetic

Northern white students who went South to help their black counterparts. Established civil rights organizations such as the NAACP, CORE and King's SCLC also gave their support.

Dime stores, department stores and other facilities such as train and bus terminals, first felt the effect of the student sit-ins. But soon they spread to become read-ins in public libraries, wade-ins in municipal swimming pools, kneel-ins at churches and stand-ins at motion picture theaters that barred blacks.

Boycotting and picketing of restaurants and shops refusing service to blacks followed the student sit-ins. Selective buying—trading only with establishments that did not practice segregation—was used to good effect. And, in the South, some shops dependent on black patronage went out of business when they refused to abolish their separate "colored" and "white" drinking fountains or lunch counters. Northern branches of chain

stores that discriminated against blacks in the South were also boycotted. Sometimes they found picket lines before their doors.

Color bars began to fall at local lunch counters, on buses and in city parks by the summer of 1960. Boycotts, combined with sit-ins, speeded integration of public facilities in Atlanta, Nashville, Dallas, and other Southern cities—but not without violence.

Conventional sentiments and customs were disrupted by this sudden movement on the part of black and white youth for the right to buy a hotdog or a hamburger at the same lunch counter. The result was broken arms and broken heads for both men and women. Police dogs were also set upon students.

In Jacksonville, the New York *Times* reported, "Whites armed with ax handles, baseball bats and other weapons set upon black youth. Intermittent rioting followed. Other riots have taken place in Portsmouth,

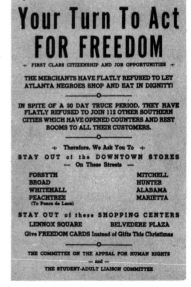

University of Chicago students (left) marched in support of Southern sit-ins. Leaflet circulated in Southern cities.

Freedom Riders in the "whites only" section of the Montgomery bus station.

Virginia, and Chattanooga, Tennessee. . . . There have been mass arrests in many Southern cities."

There were hundreds of long, drawn-out and expensive trials, unreasonably high fines and heavy prison sentences. In 1960, more than 40 percent of the annual budget of the NAACP went toward defending 1,700 student demonstrators standing trial. A victory came with a Supreme Court decision in 1961. In it, the court reversed the conviction of 16 sit-in demonstrators arrested in Baton Rouge, Louisiana.

Freedom Riders

The public bus had long been the chief means of transportation for blacks and poor whites alike in the South. Seating was segregated, with blacks required to ride in the back. Until 1961-62, most Southern bus stations had separate waiting rooms, ticket windows and separate toilets (if any) for black passengers. Sometimes a single "colored" toilet was required to serve both men and women.

The lunch counters at rest stops did not serve blacks, even **interstate** (between states) passengers, including servicemen in uniform. Protests over the years did no good. The Interstate Commerce Commission's ruling that segregation was illegal went unobserved. Finally, black students in the South, inspired by the success of the sit-in campaign, began a series of "freedom rides" to test bus, rail and air facilities. They were joined by Northern white students and members of CORE. All were pledged to nonviolence.

The riders were met by mobs and police brutality almost everywhere along the routes between Atlanta or Nashville to Birmingham, Montgomery, Jackson and New Orleans. This violence was unrestrained and often seemed to have the tacit approval, if not the

A bombed-out bus on which Freedom Riders crossed the Alabama state line.

outright support, of national guard units and local police.

Federal agents sent by Washington to protect civil rights were actually threatened with arrest by Alabama's Governor John Patterson. He said, "We do not recognize the federal marshals as law-enforcement officers in this matter." In Mississippi, Governor Ross Barnett declared: "Integration will ruin civilization." And at Jackson, officers with police dogs arrested Freedom Riders as soon as they stepped off buses or trains. On a single day in Jackson, 150 Freedom Riders were brought to trial at the Hinds County Courthouse. Many were illegally incarcerated in Parchman Penitentiary, designed for hardened criminals. High bails were set and fines imposed to the limit.

In Albany, Georgia, 400 hymn-singing youth were arrested for protesting the treatment of Freedom Riders. Outside Anniston, Alabama, a fire bomb was tossed into a crowded bus. The bus was destroyed and a number of its passengers badly injured. In Montgomery, a black church was surrounded by a stone-throwing mob and the congregation held captive inside all night.

The Freedom Riders won. A number of

bus and railroad stations in the South integrated their facilities. And, in 1962, the Interstate Commerce Commission ordered separate "white" and "colored" signs taken down. Seats anywhere in a public bus were available to everyone. Four hundred federal marshals and a federal court injunction were required to enforce the order. But most important was the incredible courage of the young people who risked their lives for freedom.

The actions of the Civil Rights Movement had a profound effect on the nation. One result of the sit-ins, the Freedom Rides, and the March on Washington was the passage of the Civil Rights Act of 1964. This was the most far-reaching civil rights law since the 1870s. It outlawed racial discrimination in all public accommodations and provided more federal authority in voting and school matters. It also contained an equal opportunity provision which prohibited discriminatory hiring based on race or other grounds.

One year later, Congress passed the Voting Rights Act of 1965. Beginning in the 1940s, the Supreme Court had been slowly overturning Southern voting restrictions. It singled out the South for its restrictive practices, and it authorized federal examiners to register voters and monitor elections in the Deep South. Within three years, more than a million blacks in the Deep South had registered to vote.

By the mid-1960s, at least part of the dream shared by many had been obtained.

CHAPTER CHECK

1. Why do you think the Civil Rights Movement started when it did?
2. What made the sit-ins and freedom rides so effective in obtaining support for civil rights?
3. How did the Civil Rights Act of 1964 and the Voting Rights Act of 1965 change American society? Why did they only fulfill part of the dream shared by many with Dr. King?
4. Imagine . . . you are a young person living in the Deep South during the early 1960s. How would you react to the sit-ins, Freedom Rides, and the March on Washington? Would you participate in them? Why or why not?

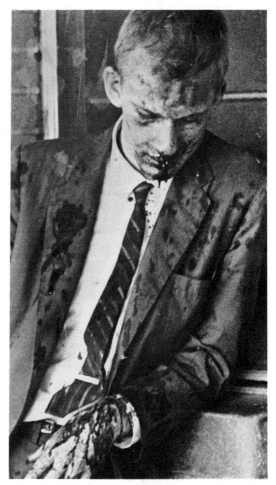

James Zerg, a white Freedom Rider, was attacked at the Montgomery bus terminal.

A demonstration for open housing in Louisville, Kentucky.

CHAPTER 37

Styles of Dissent

The gains of the civil rights movement helped to remove the legal inequalities in American society. But many blacks still saw fundamental inequalities in American life. Racism was not just a Southern problem but a national one.

By the mid-1960s, many blacks began to question Martin Luther King, Jr.'s theory of nonviolence and interracial cooperation. They wondered if real change could ever occur without violent action. More militant blacks began arguing for change in tones which often shocked white liberals. Black-white tensions appeared within the various civil rights organizations, and now, more radical ones developed.

SNCC

The Student Nonviolent Coordinating Committee (SNCC) was founded in April 1960 at Shaw University in Raleigh, North Carolina. More than 200 students from all over the country met for a conference suggested by Ella Baker, then executive secretary of King's SCLC. SNCC's role was to coordinate student sit-ins in the South.

John Lewis was elected the first chairman in 1963. Under his leadership, SNCC's objective was broadened to include other activities promoting integration. It organized sit-ins, freedom rides and voter registrations.

All of these activities were part of the Mississippi Freedom Summer Project launched in 1964. Project members hoped to bring about change in that state through voter registration and education. SNCC members, including almost 1,000 Northern white students from all over the country, traveled to Mississippi.

Fifty Freedom Schools were organized, and another 50 community centers were established. SNCC organized a new political party open to all, the Mississippi Freedom Democratic Party (MFDP). Nearly 60,000 blacks enrolled. The MFDP challenged the regular, all-white Mississippi delegation for seating at the 1964 Democratic National Convention, but failed to win recognized admission.

That summer in Mississippi, the unprovoked killing of blacks and unpunished crimes against them multiplied. The students incurred 1,000 arrests, 30 shootings and three murders. A trio of student organizers—James Chaney, Andrew Goodman and Michael Schwerner—were shot by white terrorists. Their bodies were then buried in an earthen dam. This had a strong influence upon many SNCC members. They began to question the effectiveness of nonviolence. By the middle of the summer most SNCC members in Mississippi carried guns.

In 1965, SNCC publicly opposed the war in Vietnam and the military draft. Following this, contributions fell off drastically. And Julian Bond, SNCC's communications director was refused a seat in the Georgia legislature after being elected.

About the same time, SNCC also encouraged pride in a black identity and discouraged white participation. In 1966, Lewis was replaced as chairman by Stokely Carmichael, who popularized the "Black Power" and "Black is Beautiful" slogans. Carmichael also embraced the idea of violence in retaliation for violence. Northern white activists were expelled, and the group broke with Dr. King.

The next year Carmichael was suceeded by H. Rap Brown as president. Brown pushed for an even more radical stance. He became known for his statement that "vio-

SCLC officer Ella Baker.

249

Black Panthers Bobby Seale and Eldridge Cleaver.

Black Panther members at a party office
in Seattle, Washington.

lence is as American as cherry pie." The name of the organization was changed to Student National Coordinating Committee in 1969, and faded from public consciousness. Its credibility was seriously eroded by increasingly controversial policies. Yet its contributions were substantial, and they are a reminder of the power in coalitions for a common cause.

The Black Panthers

The Black Panthers were organized in 1966 as the Black Panther Party for Self-Defense. The founders were Bobby Seale and Huey Newton. They were two young blacks who gave vent to their anger at the hopelessness of ghetto life.

What was their dream? Said Newton, "We stand for the transformation of the decadent, reactionary, racist system that exists at this time." They called for full employment, decent housing, black control of the black community and an end to every form of repression and brutality.

The Panthers ran their own community-oriented projects. These included free breakfasts for ghetto children, free health clinics and testing for **sickle-cell anemia** (a disease genetically linked to blacks) and free food distribution. They also ran "liberation schools" and "survival conferences" where they spoke of their beliefs.

At the height of the movement, the Panthers had a membership of about 2,000 in 40 chapters across the United States. The early days of the movement were symbolized by news pictures of tight-lipped young blacks in confrontation with some element of the white establishment. In these pictures they wore leather jackets and black berets and were armed with shotguns and rifles. Their

Members of the Black Panther chapter in Kansas City, Missouri, serve free breakfasts to children before school.

public statements were also confrontational. Newton called electoral politics "bankrupt," and proclaimed that "political power comes from the barrel of a gun." Eldridge Cleaver, the party's most articulate spokesman, declared that the choice for the country was either "total liberty for black people or total destruction for America."

Because of their radical stance and insistence on the right to arm themselves, FBI director J. Edgar Hoover called the Black Panthers "the most dangerous group of militants in the country." Across the nation, police raids on Black Panther headquarters were frequent and bloody. The ranks of the party were soon decimated by police bullets or imprisonment. Some Panthers fled the country.

The Black Panthers were a tragic and bloody footnote to American social history. They died in numbers for what they believed in most—themselves as persons of value.

The Nation of Islam

The Nation of Islam, popularly known as the Black Muslims, grew out of the poverty and frustrations of working-class black migrants living in Detroit in the 1930s. Their dream was the restoration of blacks in America to their rightful heritage of dignity and prominence in the world and favor in the eyes of Allah, or God.

Islam was founded in the 7th century by Muhammad, an Arabian. In the 1930s, a man named Wallace Fard Muhammad came to the U.S., supposedly from Mecca, the Muslim holy city. He started an Islamic mosque, or temple, in Detroit, and encouraged blacks to worship with him. He had also come to deliver them from racial oppression and economic want. His program was a mixture of pride of race, self-help and black unity blended with a racial interpretation of Islam. He told his followers to give up Christianity, calling it a tool whites used to oppress blacks.

In 1934, Wallace Fard Muhammad mysteriously disappeared. Leadership of black American Muslims was taken over by one of his followers, Elijah Poole, who took the name Elijah Muhammad. He established a second mosque in Chicago. Under him the religion spread far.

Malcolm X was Elijah's most visible follower. In the 1960s, he carried the nation's message of black unity and separation from whites and Christianity. Malcolm had little use for the moderate civil rights movement. He urged blacks to fight racism "by any means necessary," and justified violent self-defense. Many followed his call.

The Muslims demonstrated that hard work, efficiency and self-sacrifice can mean a better life. In a few years they had developed successful farming operations in Michigan, Alabama and Mississippi. The Muslims developed their own schools, and established numerous business enterprises in the black ghettos of large U.S. cities. They became a major symbol of black pride.

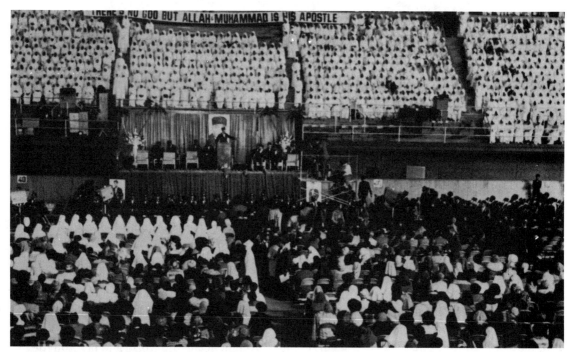

A convention of thousands of members of the Nation of Islam in Chicago on Saviour's Day, February 26, 1963.

After some serious disagreements with Elijah, Malcolm left the Nation of Islam. He began forming the Muslim Mosque, Inc. However, in 1965, before organization could get very far, Malcolm was assassinated in New York City.

In 1975, Elijah was succeeded by his fifth son, Wallace D. Muhammad. Under him, the movement changed. Wallace opened the movement to people of all colors. The teachings of Elijah Muhammad were deemphasized in favor of a more orthodox approach to Islam. He changed its name from the Nation of Islam to the World Community of al-Islam in the West, and then to the American Muslim Mission.

Louis Farrakhan, a long time follower of Elijah Muhammad, initially cooperated with Wallace D. Muhammad. But in 1976, a group of dissatisfied members, led by Farrakhan split from the main group. They revived the name Nation of Islam. And they reestablished the separatist principles.

The Sound is Diminished,
The Fury Subsides . . . Somewhat

The riot that erupted in Harlem in the summer of 1964 suggested a pattern of racial explosions that came to be referred to as the "long, hot summers." In Watts, a black community of Los Angeles, the long, hot summer of 1965 carried a death toll of 34, with 1,032 injured, and 4,000 arrested. Property damage exceeded $40 million. The Watts riot, like the one occurring in Harlem a year earlier, was ignited by black resentment of what was felt to be the gross mistreatment of black citizens by white policemen.

There were major riots in Chicago and Cleveland in 1966, Newark and Detroit in 1967. In April 1968, Martin Luther King, Jr.

Malcolm X, 1963.

was assassinated in Memphis. Rioting broke out in 125 cities. The biggest were in Washington, D.C., Baltimore, Chicago and Pittsburgh. At least 46 people died, and more than 3,500 were injured. Property damage was set at $45 million. Many black communities suffered damage from which they would never recover. Saddest of all was the violence triggered by the senseless death of a hero of peace.

A commission of distinguished Americans appointed by President Lyndon Johnson investigated the causes of the riots. It became known as the Kerner Commission after its head, Illinois Governor Otto Kerner. Its report placed the blame on "white racism." The document, sometimes called *The Kerner Report*, officially confronted America

A Chicago street in April 1968 after a riot.

Riot-torn Newark, New Jersey, in July 1967.

with its most dangerous and disruptive social force.

Since the 1970s, the Ku Klux Klan has publicly organized across the nation in schools, colleges and even the military. There have been cross burnings, desecration of buildings, and demonstrations. KKK membership is estimated at 17,000—nearly four times the membership in 1961. In Greensboro, North Carolina, in 1979, five people were killed in a KKK attack. Members of the Klan and American Nazi Party brought to trial were all acquitted. This sparked a prolonged protest movement in which law enforcement officers were accused of participating in the assaults.

But white supremacists lost some battles, too. In Mobile, Alabama, all-white juries convicted three Klansmen in the 1981 death of 19 year-old Michael Donald. Donald, a black, was strangled and hanged in random revenge for another trial in which a black man was acquitted of killing a white policeman.

Donald's mother also won a civil suit against the United Klans of America. A jury awarded her a $7 million verdict which included a Klan headquarters in Tuscaloosa, Alabama.

CHAPTER CHECK

1. Why do you think that the Civil Rights Movement became increasingly separatist and violent?

2. Which group do you think was more effective, the Black Panthers or the Southern Christian Leadership Conference? Why?

3. Imagine . . . you are a young student participating in the Mississippi Freedom Summer Project. How would you react to the deaths of the three SNCC members?

Members of an armored tank division going into combat in Vietnam.

CHAPTER 38

Struggles in Asia

Since World War II, the United States has been involved in two civil wars in Asia. One was in Korea, and the other in Vietnam. In both cases, the United States wanted to stop communist-backed governments from taking control. Black soldiers served with distinction in both conflicts.

The order to integrate the armed services was handed down by President Harry Truman in 1948. The United States was not at war, but there was a draft. A. Philip Randolph warned the Senate that he would urge blacks not to register if the services remained segregated.

By 1950, the United States was involved in helping the government in South Korea fight off its communist neighbors in North Korea.

Planning combat strategy in Vietnam.

Vietnam Heats Up

The United States began sending military aid to Vietnam in 1950. In this Southeast Asian country, French colonial rulers were battling a communist Vietnamese leader, Ho Chi Minh. The United States was opposed to colonial rule. But it was more opposed to the growing communist power in Asia. By 1954, U.S. aid paid for 78 percent of the French effort. Nevertheless, the French were defeated. That year, Vietnam was divided into two countries, North and South.

The United States continued to back the government in South Vietnam against communist troops, called Viet Cong. The Viet Cong wanted to unite with North Vietnam and kick out the Americans. China and the Soviet Union backed the government of North Vietnam.

American aid continued to pour into Vietnam, but it wasn't until 1965 that the first fighting troops were sent. In 1965, blacks were about 11 percent of the U.S. population. However, blacks comprised 12.8 percent of the army's personnel and 14.9 percent of its combat troops. The next year, they formed 11.3 percent of the army but 17.2 percent of combat troops. Black casualties were even higher. In 1965, more than one in five Americans killed were black.

Why were blacks killed in such high proportion to whites? For one thing, they were often on the firing lines in infantry and artillery. The military paid more for hazardous duty. Many blacks needed the money. They also hoped to gain promotion for their daring.

The government offered **deferments** (postponements) of military service to college students. Since many more college students were white than black, they got more

The country had been divided since World War II. Now the North Koreans, whose northern frontier bordered on the People's Republic of China, wanted to unite Korea under a communist government. President Truman was pledged to stop them.

The war increased the need for recruits. That, in turn, led to more black participation. In 1951, black United States field troops were about nine percent of the total. That summer, the percentage jumped to 30 percent. When U.S. troops were withdrawn in 1953, 90 percent of black soldiers served in integrated units. There had been lots of resistance to integration. But the pressures of war had made it clear that the United States needed its black soldiers. If it intended to keep them, they were going to have to be treated more equally.

deferments. By the time many finished college, the war was over. Other young men were released from military service as **conscientious objectors (COs)**. In other words, they were opposed to war on moral and religious grounds. Most of these objectors were white, because whites were more likely to have counseling to help them get CO status. A third way of avoiding the draft during the Vietnam war was to leave the country. Thousands of young men fled to Canada or other countries who agreed to give them refuge. Most blacks felt it unpatriotic to avoid combat.

The war in Vietnam increasingly was fought by the poor and the less educated. And blacks were often both because they had been denied so many opportunities.

Wallace Terry, a black journalist, wrote an oral history of black participation in Vietnam. His book was titled *Bloods* for the name by which black soldiers referred to each other. In his introduction, Terry noted that in 1967, most black soldiers in Vietnam supported the war. They believed in the government of South Vietnam, and they wanted to stop the spread of communism. By 1969, when combat fatalities had dropped to 14 percent, blacks had a different attitude. Many soldiers had taken part in civil rights demonstrations. Still others had been caught up in urban riots. They would speak out when they were discriminated against in receiving decorations, promotions and assignments.

"Bloods" would not overlook racial insults. They were not only at war with the Viet Cong. Many were at war with white America. Some black soldiers gave vent to their rage by attacking their officers. There were 100 **fraggings**, or grenade attacks, on

An honor guard, part of the air strip's welcoming committee.

army officers during the summer of 1969.

A favorite tactic of white racists was to flaunt the Confederate flag. At An Loc, whites raised one over the camp. Later, a gas grenade was hurled into an all-black barracks. When Private James Taylor, a black, asked the new company commander to tell the Inspector General the racial situation was out of hand, the captain refused. Taylor was so enraged that he killed his commander before several witnesses. He was sentenced to 15 years in a federal penitentiary.

Unrest at Home

Not since the Civil War had America been so divided. There were demonstrations against the war. Others insisted the United States was being held back from winning the war out of fear of provoking the Chinese.

Arrival of an aircraft carrier supply unit to a combat zone.

While most demonstrators against the war were white, important blacks raised their voices in protest. Martin Luther King, Jr. demanded in 1965, "The long night of war must be stopped." Later he preached, "The bombs in Vietnam explode at home. They destroy the hopes and possibilities of a decent America."

Not all blacks agreed with King. Many, like U.S. Senator Edward Brooke, Ralph Bunche and Jackie Robinson, lambasted him for urging young men to become conscientious objectors. President Lyndon Johnson did all he could to destroy King's reputation when he turned against the war.

It took a Supreme Court order to put SNCC leader Julian Bond in the Georgia legislature. He had praised young men who burned their draft cards.

Perhaps most controversial was the case of boxer Muhammad Ali. As Cassius Clay, he won the light-heavyweight title at the 1960 summer Olympic Games. In 1964, he won the heavyweight boxing championship by knocking out Sonny Liston. That same year, he became a follower of Elijah Muhammad and changed his name to Muhammad Ali. He also sought status as a conscientious objector. Ali won the heavyweight title again in 1967, but it was taken from him after he refused to enter the army. He was sentenced to five years in prison and fined $10,000. The Supreme Court reversed Ali's conviction in 1971. He won the title two more times.

The War Winds Down

In 1968, President Johnson announced he would not seek re-election. The conflict at home between the war's advocates and its foes had made it almost impossible to govern. Peace talks started in Paris that year, and the U.S. slowly began to withdraw its forces the next. Not until January 1973, was there a cease-fire. American ground troops left in March. The war ended April 30, 1975, when the South Vietnamese surrendered to the North. Today the country is united under communist rule.

At home, it would take years for the scars of war to heal. The American public did not welcome Vietnam veterans as heroes. Many had serious problems. Jobs were hard to find, and veterans often had trouble fitting into civilian life. Many had been brutalized by combat, drugs and racial experiences.

Wallace Terry wrote of black veterans, "There were no flags waving or drums beating upon the return of any Vietnam veterans, who were blamed by the right in our society for losing the war, and by the left for being the killers of the innocent. But what can be said about . . . Vietnam veterans in general can be doubled in its impact upon most blacks; they hoped to come home to more than they had before; they came home to less. Black unemployment among black veterans is more than double the rate for white veterans."

Blacks, however, continue to serve in great numbers in the military. Some say this reflects the limited opportunities open to them elsewhere. Of enlisted personnel, 21.7 percent are black. The army has the highest percentage of blacks—about 28 percent in 1987. The navy has the lowest. Only about 11 percent of navy personnel in 1987 were black. That makes the navy less integrated than society in general.

During the Vietnam war, there were few black officers. In 1967, there were only two black generals among 1,346 generals and admirals—one each in the army and air force. The marines had no black colonels. Only two batallion commanders out of 380 on the battlefield were black. Blacks are still underrepresented among officers. In 1988, only 6.6 percent were black.

CHAPTER CHECK

1. What event in 1951 increased the demand for recruits in the armed forces? What was the impact on black troops?
2. More than one in five American soldiers killed in Vietnam were black. Why is this number disproportionate? Give three reasons why.
3. How did Martin Luther King, Jr. show his opposition to the Vietnam war? Who were some of the black leaders who disagreed with him? Was Muhammad Ali's objection to military service a protest against the Vietnam war? Explain.
4. Imagine . . . you are a black Vietnam war veteran. How would you respond to the public treatment of you?

Muhammad Ali, 1965.

Jesse Jackson, Martin Luther King, Jr. and Ralph Abernathy on the balcony of the Lorraine Motel in Memphis, Tennessee, one day before the King assassination.

Main Events

1. In 1936, the NAACP won a suit against the University of Maryland law school, and black students were admitted.

2. In 1941, the United States entered World War II with mostly segregated forces. The army's officer candidate schools admitted blacks, but other services were not integrated.

3. During the war, thousands of Southern black workers poured into Northern and Western cities.

4. On May 17, 1954, the U. S. Supreme Court ruled in *Brown v. Board of Education* that racially segregated schools were unconstitutional and must be integrated.

5. On March 12, 1956, 101 Southern members of Congress issued a Southern Manifesto opposing school integration.

6. In 1956, a black woman, Autherine Lucy, attended classes at the University of Alabama. This caused rioting, and she was expelled.

7. In 1957, President Dwight Eisenhower sent 1,000 army paratroopers to Little Rock, Arkansas, to ensure the safety of nine black students integrating Central High School.

8. In the early 1960s, a series of sit-ins and freedom rides forced integration of public facilities across the South.

9. In 1962, 29 year-old James Meredith integrated the University of Mississippi, escorted by U.S. marshals.
10. Also in 1962, the Interstate Commerce Commission ordered separate "white" and "colored" signs taken down in public transportation facilities. Seats anywhere on a public bus were available to all.
11. In August 1963, more than 200,000 people attended the March on Washington to support civil rights for blacks. King's "I Have a Dream" was the main address.
12. The Civil Rights Act of 1964 outlawed racial discrimination in all public accommodations.
13. The Voting Rights Act of 1965 wiped out all prohibitory voting restrictions.
14. In 1965, the U.S. sent its first troops to Vietnam. One in five Americans killed that year were black.
15. On April 4, 1968, Martin Luther King, Jr., was assassinated at a Memphis motel. Riots broke out in 125 cities.

1. between states
2. grenade attacks often by black enlisted men against white officers
3. civil rights group headed by Dr. Martin Luther King, Jr.
4. organized, peaceful civil disobedience
5. denounced the Supreme Court's order to desegregate public schools
6. peaceful occupation of segregated sections of public facilities
7. series of actions designed to test segregation on buses, trains and airplanes
8. people who refuse to fight on moral or religious grounds
9. an order or command by a court forbidding something or demanding something to be done
10. a leave from military service
11. religious group formed in Detroit in the 1930s
12. placed the blame for riots in black communities on white racism

Words to Know

Match the following words with their correct definitions. Number your paper from 1 to 12, and write the correct word beside each number.

conscientious objectors
fraggings
freedom rides
furlough
injunction
interstate
Kerner Report
Nation of Islam
nonviolent protest
sit-in
Southern Christian Leadership Conference
Southern Manifesto

Thinking and Writing

A. Keeping a Journal:
It's the summer of 1961. You are a student from the North and you are going to participate in the freedom rides. You decide to keep a journal of your experiences. What would you see? Where would you go? What do you think would happen to you and your fellow freedom riders?

B. Working with Outlines:
For each subject, list at least three important details you would include if you were writing a paragraph on the topic.
a) *Brown v. Board of Education*
b) The 1963 March on Washington

PART EIGHT

SHARING THE DREAM AND THE POWER

1972 - PRESENT

Los Angeles Mayor Tom Bradley.

LOOKING AHEAD - PART EIGHT - 1972 – THE PRESENT

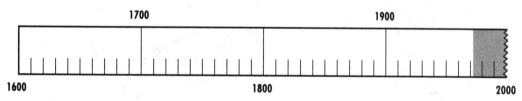

The Civil Rights Movement had a big effect on the lives of black Americans. It made many things in America more equal, but it opened up new issues. Most black Americans have been involved in the struggle for racial equality for a long time. Today, there are a number of other issues which interest them. Some of these are concerns from the past, but many are related to changes caused by recent events.

One issue which has always been important to black Americans is religion. Most black Americans who are religious are Christians. The church has been a major source of black strength. During slavery, it gave hope and comfort to blacks. Since slavery, the church has provided a means for black self-expression, recognition and leadership.

The black church has also been an important motivator for change. One recent example is the modern Civil Rights Movement. Its earliest and most prominent leaders were the black clergy. And many black leaders today have the church as their base of support.

Still, many ministers believe the church is not as strong in the black community as it once was. Due to changes in recent years, the church is not as necessary for survival and hope as in harder times. These ministers are concerned because problems such as drug abuse and teen pregnancy are harming so many young people. They think the church should be more active in solving these problems. And efforts are now being made to get more blacks involved regularly in the church. How successful they will be is yet to be seen. But it is certain that as new challenges arise, the black church will be there to meet them.

The success of the Civil Rights Movement has opened up other issues of concern for black Americans. One such topic is the role race plays in American society. Over the past two decades, many new opportunities have appeared for black Americans. And some have made the most of these opportunities. They now share in the dream and the power of American life. But a large number of blacks do not make a good living. They are still struggling for a place in the scheme of things.

This leads many people to argue over what effect racism and discrimination play in America today. Why have some blacks succeeded and others have not? William Julius Wilson claims that economic limitations are now more important than racism in preventing the black poor from getting ahead. Oth-

A white South African flees from anti-apartheid demonstrators.

Cardiss Collins, Member of Congress.

Author Maya Angelou.

ers, such as Bart Landry, argue that racism and discrimination continue to play a strong role.

Everyone agrees that the problems blacks still face have more than one cause. Some causes have to do with race, others do not. Solutions to these problems are important for African Americans today.

Many black Americans are concerned about continued oppression of blacks in other lands. In recent years, Americans have become especially active in the fight to free blacks in South Africa.

In 1977, the Reverend Leon Sullivan developed a code of conduct for American companies to provide a good example to South African business. Others, such as Randall Robinson of TransAfrica, lobbied Congress for national action against South Africa.

These groups have succeeded in bringing economic pressure against South Africa. Certain trade restrictions were passed. And more than one hundred American companies have quit doing business there.

The combination of the Civil Rights Movement and Women's Movement of the early 1970s forced black women to examine their own position in society. They found themselves **exploited**, (taken advantage of) from without and within. In society as a whole, they were exploited because of their race. In the black community, they were sexually exploited by men.

As they became aware of their situation, there was an explosion in the number of books written by black women. It began in the 1970s, and continues today. Because of their unique position, black women have been able to show how both racism and sexism have no place in a society based on equality.

One of the biggest gains obtained by black Americans in recent years has been in the area of elective politics. The Voting Rights Act of 1965 eliminated all restrictions on voting, and cleared the way for blacks to vote in large numbers. Their votes helped open the door for black politicians.

Today, there are over 6,000 African Americans in political office. Especially important are the number of blacks who now run some of the nation's largest cities. Blacks also serve as Members of Congress, and Jesse Jackson has run two strong campaigns for the presidency. Even in areas where blacks are not a majority, they often influence the outcome of an election.

Blacks have overcome many obstacles and hardships in their struggle for success. And one major source of strength has been their African past. When Africans were first forcibly brought to America, they drew upon their African background to survive. Many of these African customs were passed down for generations and have now become part of American culture. Music, art, language and religion are some of the many aspects of American life influenced by Africa.

One important development within the past two decades has been an increased interest in African American studies. Black history and African culture have become important areas of research. A new appreciation for the gains and accomplishments of black Americans has occurred. Also important has been the deepening understanding of the many contributions Africa has made to American culture. The legacies of its customs and its people have become great sources of pride.

Church-sponsored low-income apartments in New York in 1915.

CHAPTER 39

The Black Church Today

Abyssinian Baptist Church in New York City, 1923. Adam Clayton Powell, Jr., became pastor in 1937.

Religion has always been important to black Americans. But religion means different things to different people all over the world. This is especially true for blacks in America. They practice different faiths. And each faith can be seen in more than one way.

Most black Americans who are religious are Christians. The church has been a major source of black strength. During slavery, it gave hope and comfort to blacks. Because of the terrible conditions under which they lived, church was all that stood between

many blacks and despair. Since slavery, the church has provided a means for black self-expression, recognition and leadership.

But the church has caused some confusion as well. This is because Christianity can be seen as having two different messages. Some people think its message is to be content with what you have. For them, poverty and other misfortunes are God's will. They believe that faith and prayer will help them survive, and, in time, things will get better. Being content now will bring riches in heaven.

A Sunday service at Ebenezer Baptist Church in Atlanta where Martin Luther King, Jr. served with his father.

Others think Christianity has a different message. They believe that "faith without works is dead." For them, faith will bring only what they struggle for. Prosperity does not come from prayer alone. People must work for it. This faction of the church is more likely to believe that only struggle will bring about equality for black Americans.

The varying interpretations of Christianity have been one of its strengths. For some, Christianity has provided the strength necessary to survive the hardships of their lives. For others, it provided courage to struggle for change. At times, these different views have caused some conflict. Christians have argued over how active the church should become in the affairs of this world.

There has been conflict between the role of the spirit and the world since the early church was formed. The arrival of Africans in America added a new dimension to this conflict. Slaveowners debated over whether or not to Christianize their slaves. Some argued against it, since Christianity would make their slaves stronger. Others thought it was their Christian duty to spread the faith. Most slaveowners offered their slaves a partial version of Christianity. They emphasized the parts that stressed obedience. In this way, they hoped to keep their slaves "in line."

But it only half-worked. Some blacks found the new religion comforting and helpful. Others were strengthened and moved to action. Black church members were active in the Underground Railroad. The religious beliefs of Denmark Vesey and Nat Turner inspired them to lead slave revolts.

This activist, or "struggle," side of Christianity has been one of the most important influences in African American history. This is not to deny that the spirituality of Christianity has been helpful for many individuals. But from the beginning, the black church has been a motivator for change. Black ministers were usually the most educated members of the black community and served as both religious and political leaders. Many other blacks have used the Bible itself as a tool for liberation. It was through this book that they learned to read. These black Christians, whose faith gave them courage to enact change, have made things better.

As early as 1787, the prominent church leader Richard Allen founded the Free African Society. One of the first official black organizations, it was dedicated to black self-improvement and advancement. Since then the black church has been active in bringing about change.

One recent example is the modern Civil Rights Movement. Its earliest and most prominent leaders were the black clergy. The Reverend Martin Luther King, Jr. was the leading spokesperson for this movement. King drew enormous strength from his Christian roots. And his strength brought about crucial change for black people.

Blacks follow many forms of Christianity. There are Baptists, Methodists, Episcopalians, Lutherans, Catholics and other denominations. Of these, the greatest number of blacks are Baptists.

There are several possible explanations for this. One is that the Baptist services are less formal and involve a greater show of emotion. Also, the services have characteristics similar to African religious rituals which blacks adapted to Christianity. Both involve calls and exchanges between the minister and the congregation. Blacks never completely severed their ties to their African religious roots.

The Reverend Dr. Johnnie Colemon is founder and pastor of Christ Universal Temple on Chicago's South Side. The $6.7 million complex is spiritual home to more than 10,000 members.

There have also been smaller religious groups or sects. One example was Father Divine's Peace Mission Movement. Another was Daddy Grace's United House of Prayer for All People. In many of these sects, members worshiped the leaders as much or more than they worshiped God.

Also, as we saw in Chapter 37, a large number of blacks in the United States are Muslims. They practice Islam and believe in one God, Allah. The Nation of Islam has shown that hard work, efficiency and self-sacrifice can mean a better life. They have also established their own schools, and worked to increase black pride.

Religion Today and Tomorrow

As we have seen, religion and the struggle for black liberation have worked together. Leaders who sprang from the church have made great gains. One of the best-known examples of this group is the Reverend Jesse Jackson. He continues the tradition of drawing strength from Christianity to work for equality. This strength saw him through the Civil Rights Movement and through two presidential campaigns. Jackson is probably the leading spokesperson for black Americans today.

Other black leaders, including politicians, also have the church as their base of sup-

Congressman Walter Fauntroy, who represents Washington D.C., is an ordained minister.

port. Several black congressmen are ministers. There is Walter Fauntroy of Washington, D.C., New York's Floyd Flake, and Philadelphia's William Gray. John Lewis from Atlanta and Brooklyn representative Edolphus Towns are also ordained, but do not have churches. These congressmen continue in the tradition of Adam Clayton Powell, Jr. A minister, he served as congressman for Harlem from 1944 to 1970. Other prominent ministers are the NAACP's Benjamin Hooks, the SCLC's Joseph Lowery and activist Wyatt Tee Walker.

Religion plays a big part in politics for blacks. Still, many ministers believe the church is not as strong in the black community as it once was. They feel the church has lost its effect on the day-to-day lives of blacks.

There are several reasons for this. Since many blacks are somewhat better off now, the church is the center of fewer people's lives. It is not as necessary for survival and hope as in harder times. The black middle class pursues other interests, including business and the arts. Sex and drugs have taken many young people's minds away from religion. Ministers feel it is time for the church to get more involved in solving these problems. Family values and discipline must be taught by the church again. Problems like drug abuse have to be fought.

This is beginning to happen. At meetings like the 1988 Congress on Evangelizing Black Americans, plans are being made to fight drugs and teen pregnancy among blacks. The ministers also discussed how to get more blacks involved in the church on a regular basis.

Besides working on those issues, churches continue to provide other valuable community services. They serve as important centers for social activity. Also, many people are helped through hard times by the church. When families are hungry, the church pitches in. The church often comes to the rescue, for instance, if someone cannot meet a payment on a house. Bake sales and raffles are held, and collections are taken to provide for emergencies. Larger black churches run Alcoholics Anonymous pro-

grams and literacy workshops. They also operate schools and day-care centers, and provide affordable housing for blacks.

All these activities favor the "struggle" side of Christianity. This activism has made a world of difference. As we move into the 21st century, and blacks face new challenges, the church will be there to meet them.

CHAPTER CHECK

1. Give two ways of looking at Christianity's message.
2. Give at least three examples of black ministers who have had political careers.
3. What social services have religious groups performed in the black community? Name at least three.
4. Imagine . . . you are a minister. What would you say to blacks about the main duties of the church?

A young Jesse Jackson addresses a Chicago congregation. Martin Luther King, Jr. looks on.

Black Americans have risen to positions of political and economic power.

CHAPTER 40

Racism or Economics?

Black Americans have greater opportunities now than in the past. Many have made the most of those opportunities. Today there are blacks in positions that they could not have achieved a generation ago. Blacks have traditionally gained notice in sports and entertainment. Now there are many black business executives, college professors, politicians and other professionals.

Much progress has been made. Still, a large number of blacks do not make a good living. Does this mean that discrimination and racism remain a force in America? Are the blacks who live well still victims of racism? These questions get different answers from different people.

In his book, *The Declining Significance of Race*, William Julius Wilson makes an interesting argument. He says that the hard times blacks have faced have not been caused by racism alone. The problem has been a combination of racism and economic factors. The two have worked together to keep some blacks down.

Take slavery, for example. Slavery developed because planters were looking for the cheapest way to work their crops. To help justify the system, slaveowners claimed blacks were not intelligent, and were fit only for slavery. So, racism reinforced economic need.

These strong racist attitudes towards blacks did not end with slavery. Most whites refused to accept blacks as equals. Blacks were denied access to certain jobs. They were not paid the same wages as whites for the same work. And they were considered inferior.

This discrimination against blacks was based mainly on race. It is true their poor economic condition also made progress difficult. And it was more profitable for whites to pay blacks less. But racism, not economics, was the main reason that blacks were denied equal opportunities.

The Black Underclass

According to Wilson, something happened to this racist-economic relationship in the mid-twentieth century. It was the Civil Rights Movement. The movement killed segregation laws. It made discrimination punishable by law.

The Civil Rights Movement also did something even more important. By and large, it changed America's attitude. This does not mean there is no more racism. "It would be shortsighted to view the traditional forms of racial segregation and discrimination as having essentially disappeared," Wilson writes. But, segregation and discrimination are practiced much less. They no longer have the law to back them up. Also, **public opinion** is now against them. On the whole, people appear to see racism as unacceptable.

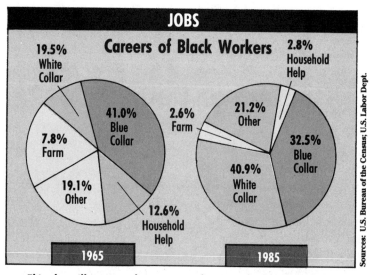

This chart illustrates the patterns of careers for black workers for 1965 and 1985.

So how has this affected blacks economically? Wilson writes: "Many talented and educated blacks are now entering positions of prestige and influence at a rate comparable to or, in some instances, exceeding that of whites with equivalent qualifications." In other words, educated blacks get important, well-paying jobs as much as whites, and sometimes more.

But many blacks are not better off economically. This is a group that Wilson calls the **black underclass**. In other words, there are poor people unable to reach the level of working class. According to Wilson, racism in the past, not the present, created this group. It made it impossible for some people to get work or an education. Now these individuals, and sometimes their children, cannot get ahead. Wilson argues that their problem today is economic, or class-based, not race-based. According to Wilson, "economic class is now a more important factor than race in determining job placement."

Landry Reacts

One person who disagrees with Wilson is Bart Landry, author of *The New Black Middle Class*. Landry disputes Wilson's claim that blacks are getting prestigious jobs as much as whites. There are more blacks in the lower middle class than the upper middle-class, he says. This is not true for whites.

Landry breaks it down into gender, as well. In the 1970s and early 1980s, white women moved into upper middle-class jobs more than black women. This is true even though black women had more work experience, generally speaking, than white women.

Landry agrees that in the last few years the number of black professionals has increased. Still, he has found that the income gap between black and white middle-class males has widened since the 1970s. To earn the same wages as white males, black males must have more education. When the economy is bad, and people lose jobs, whites get them back faster than blacks.

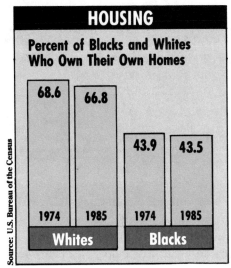

This chart shows home ownership by race for 1974 and 1985.

INCOME		
Living in Poverty	1966	1987
Blacks	41.8%	33.5%
Whites	11.3%	10.5%
Unemployment	1964	1988
Blacks	9.6%	11.8%
Whites	4.6%	4.7%
Median Income	1970	1987
Blacks	$6,279	$18,098
Whites	$10,236	$32,274

Sources: U.S. Bureau of the Census; U.S. Labor Dept.

This chart contrasts shifts in income for blacks and whites over several periods.

Roy Roberts, vice president and general manager of a $3 billion truck manufacturing division in Chicago.

Why is this so? Landry says it is evidence of "the continuing significance of race." In other words, discrimination still exists. Wilson admits that racism and discrimination are not dead. But Landry places more emphasis on them.

Racism ? ? ?

Indeed, blacks still have to deal every day with reactions to their color. Sometimes it is unconscious racism—the reactors do not realize what they are doing. Or, it can be purposeful. A *Time* magazine article gave examples of different kinds of reactions. In one, a black businessman hailed a cab in New York City and could not get one to stop.

Another black businessman, Roy Roberts, shopped for a house in a wealthy Chicago neighborhood. The real estate agent asked if he were a singer or a baseball player. Because the man was black, the real estate agent assumed, without thinking, that he was not a businessman. However, this is better than what some real estate agents have done. When blacks look for new houses, some agents purposely steer them away from white neighborhoods.

So, does racism of this kind explain the large number of disadvantaged blacks? If so, why do some blacks become successful while others do not? Wilson says that past discrimination is more important here than present discrimination. Those who are unable to overcome it through talent or education still feel its effects.

Wilson suggests other reasons for continued poverty in black areas. One is **middle-class flight**. As blacks become more successful, in large numbers they move out of poor, black neighborhoods. This takes financial support away from churches, schools and other places that give stability to poor people. It also takes away successful role models for black children in poor neighborhoods.

Another reason is the increase in technology. Now that machines and computers are able to do more, many unskilled and semi-skilled jobs are gone. Those without enough education to get middle- and upper-level jobs suddenly cannot get lower-level jobs, either.

This dilemma has caused Wilson to predict that there will be problems if nothing is done to stop the "vastly different mobility opportunities for different groups in the black population." While some blacks are doing extremely well, many others are becoming permanently stuck in the underclass. And Wilson sees "the black poor falling further and further behind the more privileged blacks." This widening economic gap among blacks could eventually cause tensions and conflicts in the black community.

Everyone can agree that there is more than one cause of the problems blacks still face. Some causes have to do with race, others do not. The solutions to these problems, then, must be as numerous as the problems themselves.

CHAPTER CHECK

1. What does William Julius Wilson mean by "the declining significance of race"? Do you agree?
2. What does Bart Landry say about the incomes of black and white middle-class males?
3. How has increased technology contributed to the problems of poor blacks?
4. Imagine . . . you are a wealthy black business owner. What effect, if any, would racism have on your life? How might your experience be different from that of blacks who are not members of the upper class?

CHAPTER 41

The Emergence of Black Women Writers

A scene from *For Colored Girls Who Have Considered Suicide When the Rainbow is Enuf*. The performers are (l. to r.) Rise Collins, Trazana Beverly, Paula Moss, Janet League, Aku Kadogo and Laurie Carlos.

The 1970s witnessed an explosion in the number of black women writers. Since then, women have come to dominate black literary expression. These women vary greatly in style. But all write about issues of racism, sexism and economic oppression. They explore racism at the hands of white men and women, sexism at the hands of black and white men and economic oppression as a result of both.

Black women writers not only write about sorrow and suffering. They also write about joy and strength. They especially describe the power of friendship among black women and write about romantic love and their ability to survive without it if necessary. They write about the commitment to family and the instinct for self-preservation. Most of all, they write about the survival and liberation of blacks and women.

The Roots and First Flowering of Black Women Writers

The growth of black women writers had roots in larger social changes. Two forces drove their emergence in the 1970s. First, the Civil Rights/Black Power movement generated an interest in black culture. Second, the Women's Movement sparked a greater interest in the female viewpoint. In the wake of these movements, society was open to the black woman's voice.

These larger movements gave black women an opportunity to examine their position in society. They found themselves exploited both from without and within. In society as a whole, they were exploited because of their race. And in the black community, they were sexually exploited by men. A kind of dual revolution took place, against both racism and sexism, initiated by black women. The most effective way for them to speak out was through the written word. And as the writer Calvin Hernton said, black women writers began to celebrate a "literary Fourth of July."

The publication of the anthology, *The Black Woman,* in 1970, signaled the beginning of the festivities. The book contained 33 essays, poems and short stories. Its 27 contributors included Nikki Giovanni, Audre Lorde, Paule Marshall and Alice Walker. The book was described as an "assembly of voices that demand to be heard." As a collection of writings by and about black women it was a pioneer event. Previously, when black women spoke out through literature, few listened. *The Black Woman* gave notice that this was about to change.

Toni Cade Bambara was the editor of *The Black Woman.* Bambara was born in 1939 in New York City. In addition to being an editor, Bambara is an important writer herself. Her prose echoes jazz and gospel music and sparkles with quirky comic twists. Her collections of short stories include *Gorilla, My Love* (1972) and *The Sea Birds Are Still Alive* (1977). In 1980, she published her first novel, *The Salt Eaters*, winner of an American Book Award. Reading Bambara is to relive slices of life during and after the civil rights movement.

Toni Morrison—Writer & Editor

One of the major novelists to emerge in the 1970s was Toni Morrison. Morrison was born in 1931, in Lorain, Ohio. By 1988, she would publish five highly successful novels, four set in the Midwest.

Her first novel, *The Bluest Eye*, was published in 1970. The novel explores the issues of identity and self-esteem. It is the story of a black girl pushed to the point of insanity because she does not fit the traditional standard of beauty. In short, she does not look like Shirley Temple.

Morrison's next two novels were *Sula* (1974), and the award-winning *Song of Solomon* (1977). In 1981, came *Tar Baby*, a story of class conflicts between two people in love. The 1987 Pulitzer Prize-winning *Beloved* was Morrison's fifth novel. Set in post-Civil War Ohio, *Beloved* is a tale of slavery's effect on motherhood.

Morrison's other important work was as an editor. She helped to advance other black women writers.

One such writer is Gayl Jones. Jones was born in Lexington, Kentucky, in 1949. She is best remembered for her graphic explorations of the psychological effects of emotional abuse. Jones published her first novel, *Corregidora*, in 1975, at the age of 26. Her

Author and editor, Toni Morrison, winner of the Pulitzer Prize for Literature.

second novel, *Eva's Man*, was published in 1976. Jones's other works include a collection of short stories entitled *White Rat* (1977).

The Color Purple and For Colored Girls

One of the most commercially successful novels by a black woman is *The Color Purple* (1982). This Pulitzer Prize-winning book was written by Alice Walker. In *The Color Purple*, Walker created the memorable character Celie. The novel offers a compelling account of Celie's ordeal with domestic abuse. But it is also the story of her triumph over circum-

stances and eventual evolution to wholeness. The novel's popularity was further increased when a Steven Spielberg movie based on it appeared in 1985.

By the end of the 1980s, Walker had an impressive body of work. It included several collections of essays, poetry, and short stories. She had also published three other novels.

Walker and other black women writers have often been accused of portraying black men in a negative light. Many black men think that only positive images of blacks should be presented. These charges were heightened by the tremendous success of *The Color Purple*. But Walker and other black women writers have not retreated in confronting racism and the equally harmful effects of sexism.

One black woman who has refused to silence her anger is the poet, playwright and novelist Ntozake Shange. Shange was born Paulette Williams in 1948 in Trenton, New Jersey. One of Shange's most famous works is *For Colored Girls Who Have Considered Suicide When the Rainbow is Enuf*. Shange calls *For Colored Girls* a choreopoem—an assemblage of dance, poetry and prose. It was first performed on Broadway in 1976. It captured the pain women experience in relationships with men.

Some saw it as a vicious attack on black men. Shange, however, saw it in terms of a larger issue. As she stated in *Black Women Writers At Work:*

> When I die, I will not be guilty of having left a generation of girls behind thinking that anyone can tend to their emotional health other than themselves. We see women who at

fifty look back at their lives; they are either very bitter or very childlike because their development was arrested. It is not incumbent upon us for this to happen as it was incumbent upon our mothers.

Caged Bird and Brewster Place

Another multi-talented woman who achieved fame in the 1970s was Maya Angelou. Her works included nonfiction, poetry, playwriting and performing. Angelou was born Marguerite Johnson in 1928 in St. Louis, Missouri. While Angelou is a highly acclaimed poet, she is best known for her numerous autobiographical books. Of these the best known is *I Know Why The Caged Bird Sings* (1970). *Caged Bird* recounts Angelou's childhood and adolescence. Her story is a sad reflection of the real and potential problems black girls encounter.

One rising star is New Yorker Gloria Naylor. Naylor's first book, *The Women of Brewster Place*, was published in 1982. It won the National Book Award for best first novel. Its interlocking stories describe the parallel lives of seven very different women. All struggle economically and emotionally. But they also struggle to maintain their dignity and humanity. In 1989, this novel was adapted for television and produced by talk-show host and actress Oprah Winfrey.

Naylor's second novel, *Linden Hills* (1985), offers a critical look at the lifestyle of the black middle class. *Mama Day* (1988), Naylor's third novel, is set on a mythical sea island. It is a love story within a larger tale of natural and supernatural forces.

Black women writers usually write about events close to home. While they speak of universal values and messages, the immedi-

Alice Walker, whose book, *The Color Purple,* won a Pulitzer Prize and was made into a movie.

ate story is usually the home, family and community. Their portraits of many different women have destroyed old stereotypes. Unlike the black female characters earlier created by whites and black men, rarely is there a trace of the happy mammy, mindless floozy, towering **matriarch** (a mother who rules her family), princess-queen or earth mother. Instead the black woman is a real human being, with all her flaws and glories. Black women writers create black heroines. Like real black women, these are ordinary women tackling extraordinary, everyday odds.

Foremothers

The black women writers of today are not the first black women to express their feelings in print or argue for both racial and sexual equality. As we saw in Chapter 6, Phillis Wheatley was one of the founders of black American literature. And in Chapter 17 we learned that Harriet Tubman and Sojourner Truth were early fighters for both abolitionism and women's rights.

But as is true for women in general, most of the work of black women in the past was considered unimportant. The recent attention to black women writers has fostered the rediscovery of their literary foremothers. Works of women long forgotten are back in print. A major tribute to the past is the *Schomburg Library of Nineteenth-Century Black Women Writers*. Published in 1988, this 30-volume collection contains 45 works of fiction and nonfiction.

There has also been new appreciation for the work of black women authors during the Harlem Renaissance of the early twentieth century. Some of these women include Jessie Fauset, Nella Larsen and Georgia Douglas Johnson. One woman of enormous impact was folklorist and anthropologist Zora Neale Hurston. Her novel, *Their Eyes Were Watching God* (1937), as well as Hurston's personal defiance of racism and sexism, has become a major source of inspiration for many black women today.

Another black woman who helped inspire the black women writers of today is Lorraine Hansberry. In 1959, her award-winning play, *A Raisin in the Sun*, first appeared on Broadway. It told the story of the housing problems and human needs of a black family in Chicago. It was later made into a successful movie starring Sidney Poitier, Claudia MacNeil and Ruby Dee.

The emergence and rediscovery of black women writers gave rise to more black women literary critics. Just as men had dominated black literature, so had they dominated literary criticism. Black women began to analyze and interpret themselves as well as others. Examples are found in *Black Women Writers (1950-1980): A Critical Evaluation* edited by Mari Evans. There was also Barbara Christian's *Black Women Novelists*:

Lorraine Hansberry, author of the prize-winning play *A Raisin in the Sun*. The title comes from a Langston Hughes poem, "Harlem."

Scene from the 1989 American Playhouse production of *A Raisin in the Sun*. Here Mama, played by Esther Rolle, thanks her grandson Travis, played by Kimble Joyner, for a new hat. The rest of the family, played by (l. to r.) Kim Yancey, Danny Glover and Starletta DuPois, look on.

The Development of a Tradition, 1892-1976. Among other noted critics are Eleanor Traylor, Mary Helen Washington and writer Sherley Anne Williams.

The growth of black women writers has broadened both black and women's studies. It has also helped expose contradictions in American society. Because of their unique position, black women can understand the oppression of both racism and sexism. They show us how both have no place in a society based on equality.

CHAPTER CHECK

1. What two forces fueled the emergence of black women writers in the 1970s?
2. What common themes can you find in the work of these writers?
3. Imagine . . . you are a young woman in the Civil Rights Movement. How would that effect your view of the role of women in American society?

Illinois Congressman William Dawson (left) and New York Congressman Adam Clayton Powell, Jr. in 1949 in back of the Capitol.

CHAPTER 42

Blacks in Public Office

When people think of politics, voting and elections usually come to mind. From this point of view, blacks play an important role in American politics. Many have been elected to office. But not all political activity occurs in elected offices. Pressure from outside groups often influences political decisions. We cannot consider black people's progress inside government without looking at the battle they have fought outside it. These two activities are, and always have been, crucial to each other.

Inside and Out

As we have seen, blacks held a number of elected offices in the mid-1800s. But when Reconstruction ended in 1877, the role of blacks in the formal political process declined sharply. When federal protection was withdrawn, blacks were denied their civil rights throughout the South. Most blacks lost the right to vote. The number of blacks in political office decreased. And by the end of the century, blacks no longer held national political positions.

For the most part, blacks were unable to take part directly in government. But this did not prevent them from organizing themselves. They could work for change from outside the government. Organizations like the National Association for the Advancement of Colored People and the National Urban League were often effective in fighting the oppression of blacks. Also, many black labor organizations were formed. One of the most important was the Brotherhood of Sleeping Car Porters, launched by A. Philip Randolph in 1925.

All this had an effect. The protests of Randolph's Brotherhood forced President Franklin D. Roosevelt to form the Fair Employment Practices Committee. Established in 1941, this committee strengthened the rights of blacks on the job. Roosevelt also appointed blacks to jobs in his administration. For the first time since Reconstruction, a large number of blacks had important posts in government.

But they were appointed positions, not elected. Blacks still had a hard time winning elections. This could only happen where there were many blacks, and their voting rights were guaranteed. This usually meant in Northern urban areas. A handful of black congressmen had achieved this. Oscar De-Priest, a Republican from Illinois, was elected in 1928. He was defeated in 1934 by a black Democrat, Arthur Mitchell.

Also from Illinois was Democrat William Dawson. He was elected to Congress in 1942. Dawson was the first black to head a congressional committee. Harlem sent the fiery Reverend Adam Clayton Powell, Jr., a Democrat, to Congress in 1944. And Charles Diggs, a Democrat from Michigan, was elected in 1954. For the most part, though, black elected officials were rare. Most black political participation remained outside the government.

The Voter Registration Movement

The most important political action for black Americans was the Civil Rights Movement. The bus boycott, student sit-ins, freedom rides and the March on Washington all took place outside the formal political process. But they were political, and the govern-

Barbara Jordan, former Member of Congress.

In 1967, the number of political victories was even greater. This proved especially true in mayoral races in Northern cities with large black populations. Richard G. Hatcher became the first black mayor of Gary, Indiana. And Cleveland elected its first black mayor, Carl Stokes.

The next year, Stokes' brother Louis won election to Congress. Louis Stokes was a founding member of the **Congressional Black Caucus**. This is an organization of black members of Congress dedicated to helping the cause of all minorities. Its highest ranking member is William Gray of Philadelphia, chairman of the House Budget Committee.

By the end of 1968, there were eight black members of Congress and seven black U.S. ambassadors. Over 1,700 blacks were in elected or appointive positions in state, county or local agencies. Some progress had also been made in the South. In 1967, Mississippi elected its first black representative in the twentieth century to the state legislature. And between 1965 and 1968, almost 400 blacks had been elected to public office in the South.

The progress made by blacks in the 1960s multiplied even further in the next two decades. Between 1970 and 1985, the number of black members of Congress doubled from 10 to 20. And between the same years, the total number of black elected officials went from just under 1,500 to over 6,000.

Among the many noticeable gains of this period were the election of many blacks as mayors of large American cities. Between 1970 and 1985, the number of black mayors jumped from 48 to 286. In 1973, Tom Bradley became the first black mayor of Los Angeles, the nation's second largest city. And in 1989,

ment took notice. And as we have seen in Chapter 36, one of the most important victories of the movement was the Voting Rights Act of 1965. This act eliminated all restrictions on voting. It cleared the way for blacks to vote in large numbers.

Their votes helped open the door for black politicians. At first, most blacks elected to office were still from the North. In 1966, Edward W. Brooke was elected U.S. Senator from Massachusetts. A Republican, he was the first black Senator since 1881, and served two six-year terms. Interestingly, he was elected in a state where only three percent of the population was black.

A 1983 meeting of the Congressional Black Caucus. From the left, George Crockett, Augustus Hawkins, Chairman Julian Dixon, Executive Director Harriet Pritchett (not a member), Charles Rangel and Walter Fauntroy.

Bradley was reelected to his unprecedented fifth four-year term. No one had been mayor of Los Angeles for so long.

Other blacks elected to run large American cities were Coleman Young in Detroit and Marion Barry in Washington, D.C. In 1983, Harold Washington was elected mayor of Chicago. He held that position until his death in 1987.

Black women also made progress in elective politics. By 1974, four black women had been elected to the U.S. Congress. Shirley Chisholm was the first, winning election from New York in 1968. Four years later, Chisholm became the first woman ever to actively run

for the U.S. presidency. Three times she was named on the Gallup Poll's list of Ten Most Admired Women in the World.

In 1972, Yvonne Burke was elected to Congress from California, and Barbara Jordan won election in Texas. That year, Jordan and Andrew Young from Georgia, were the first black representatives from Southern states elected to Congress since Reconstruction. In 1976, Jordan gave the keynote address at the Democratic National Convention. And in 1974, Cardiss Collins was elected as a representative from Illinois.

Blacks have also made gains in high level appointive offices. In 1966, Robert Weaver became the first black cabinet member. He served as the Secretary of Housing and Urban Development. And Andrew Young became the first black U.S. Ambassador to the United Nations in 1977. In 1982, Young was elected mayor of Atlanta.

Jesse Jackson Runs for President

Up until the 1980s, blacks had never supported one of their own for the presidency. Blacks had run for president before. Several had run in earlier years as candidates for small political parties. When, in 1972, Shirley Chisholm ran as a Democrat, she was the first black candidate in one of America's two major parties.

But none of these candidates were supported by the majority of black people. Most felt it better to vote for a white liberal who might win. This would be better than "wasting" a vote on a black candidate who had little chance for success. So, in presidential elections, most of the black vote went to the white Democrat.

This changed in 1984. The person who ran was Jesse Jackson. He began with a solid base of black support. But he knew he must expand from there. He formed what he called the **Rainbow Coalition** and reached out to all minority groups. He recognized the needs of Hispanics, American Indians and poor whites. And he worked for their support. Many of them voted for him.

In the end, he finished third out of the seven Democratic candidates. Only Gary Hart and Walter Mondale got more votes. Many blacks who had never voted before showed up to cast their ballots for Jackson.

The Reverend Jesse Jackson (center) with Mayor Richard Hatcher of Gary, Indiana, (left) and Washington, D.C. Mayor Marion Barry after Jackson announced his candidacy for the Democratic Presidential nomination.

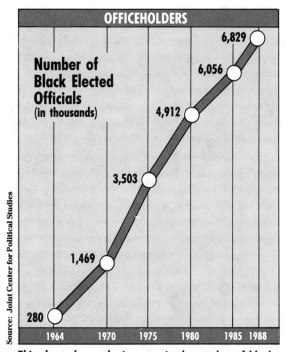

OFFICEHOLDERS

Number of
Black Elected
Officials
(in thousands)

6,829

6,056

4,912

3,503

1,469

280

| 1964 | 1970 | 1975 | 1980 | 1985 | 1988 |

This chart shows the increase in the number of black elected officials in the United States.

It was a good showing for him, and proof of what black voting power could do.

In 1988, Jackson ran again. Once more, he failed to get the Democratic nomination. But he came even closer than before, finishing second behind Michael Dukakis. He even carried the nation's largest city, New York.

At the Democratic National Convention, Jackson gave an electrifying speech. In it, he said how important it is for all disadvantaged groups to work together. He compared the groups to a patchwork quilt, and gave this inspiring message:

Blacks and Hispanics, when we fight for civil rights, we are right—but our patch isn't big enough. Gays and lesbians, when you fight against dis-

crimination and for a cure for AIDS, you are right—but your patch isn't big enough. Conservatives and progressives, when you fight for what you believe, you are right—but your patch isn't big enough.

But don't despair. When we bring the patches together, make a quilt, and turn to each other and not on each other, we the people always win.

Jackson's speech and his campaign, taught the value of unity, especially among blacks. And 1988 showed what unity can achieve. There were impressive gains by blacks at the local, state and federal levels. All 23 members of the Congressional Black Caucus were reelected. Donald Payne of New Jersey was elected to Congress, making the total now 24. And in 1989, Ronald Brown became the first black elected chairman of the Democratic National Committee.

One result of the Jackson campaign has been an increase in black registered voters. And most of them turn out to vote. Today there are over 6,000 black elected officials in the United States. Even in areas where blacks are not a majority, they often influence the outcome of an election. Black political might has reached the point where it cannot be turned back.

CHAPTER CHECK

1. Describe two effects of the Voting Rights Act of 1965.

2. Name two blacks who were elected mayor of a large city and two black women who were elected to Congress.

3. Imagine . . . you are a historian writing about the achievements of Jesse Jackson. What would you say?

The township of Soweto, outside Johannesburg, where more than 500,000 black South African workers and their families are housed.

CHAPTER 43

Understanding South Africa

In another land, blacks still suffer terrible indignities. The land is South Africa. It is located at Africa's southernmost point, and is about three times the size of California. About seven out of every 10 people in South Africa are black. But whites control everything.

South Africa has a system called apartheid, which means "apartness." Under the law, blacks live separate from whites. They have been forced into areas too small to contain them. These areas are overcrowded and poverty-stricken. As late as 1986, blacks could only go to white areas if they worked there. Even then, they had to have permits, or passbooks. If blacks got caught in a white area without a passbook, they could be arrested. In 1984, more than 238,000 blacks were taken to jail for "passbook offenses."

Schools in South Africa are segregated. Because many good schools will not accept blacks, their education suffers. It is almost impossible for black South Africans to become educated, prosper or move ahead at all. Apartheid takes away their rights, hopes and dreams.

Apartheid's Beginnings

Apartheid became law in 1948. But the events leading up to it took place earlier. Dutch settlers, or Boers, arrived in South Africa in the 1600s. In the early nineteenth century, the British also came to South Africa and claimed the Cape of Good Hope. Conflicts between the Boers and the British resulted in the Boer War of 1899-1902. When the British won, South Africa became part of the British Empire. But it was decided that South Africa would be governed by white people who lived there, many of whom were Boers.

The Boers, or **Afrikaners**, became determined to maintain their independence from Britain. They decided one way to do this was to protect and preserve their white heritage. In 1948, D.F. Malan, leader of the National Party, was elected prime minister. He instituted separation of the races, believing Afrikaners would be stronger if the white race remained pure. And so apartheid was born.

Timothy Mayisela, a black South African worker, displays his passbook.

Laws were made to uphold it. For starters, laws were passed against interracial marriages, and sex between whites and non-whites. Also the Group Areas Act was passed. This meant that blacks could not live in the same areas as whites.

In 1952, the Abolition of Passes and Coordination of Documents Act brought about the passbook system. Next was an act to force separate black and white areas in all public places. It became illegal for blacks to go to "white" movie houses, restaurants or other public accommodations.

The Resettlement of Natives Act was passed in 1954. This gave the government the power to move whole communities of blacks, Indians and **colored** (mixed race) people. Since this act, millions of blacks have been forcibly moved away from the cities to make way for whites. Other laws barred blacks from even limited participation in politics and labor organizations.

Black African Resistance

The situation was bad. But like blacks in the U.S., South African blacks fought back. In the 1950s, Nelson Mandela emerged as the leading figure in the South African liberation struggle. In 1944, Mandela had joined the **African National Congress (ANC)**, the oldest and most important anti-apartheid organization. The ANC was based on nonviolent resistance. But during the 1950s, with the growing apartheid legislation, the ANC became increasingly militant.

In 1960, following a riot in the black township of Sharpeville outside Johnnesburg, the government outlawed the ANC. By this time, Mandela no longer believed that nonviolence could stop a system as oppressive as apartheid. The next year, he formed a military arm of the ANC in exile. Its aim was to fight the government by sabotaging its buildings and property.

In 1962, Mandela was arrested. He was found guilty, and was sentenced to life imprisonment. He remains there today. His imprisonment is a symbol of what black South Africans have had to bear. His courage has inspired others to continue his fight.

In the mid-1980s, differences between various anti-apartheid groups in South Africa led to violence. People were killed, and homes were burned down. In the opinion of many, the organizations had lost sight of their real enemy.

One who tried to stop the violence was Bishop Desmond Tutu. Tutu became leader of the South African Council of Churches in 1978. He spoke out against apartheid. When differences broke out between the various anti-apartheid groups, he worked with each side and tried to resolve them. In 1984, he was awarded the Nobel Peace Prize in recognition for his nonviolent efforts at ending apartheid.

Nobel Prize winner Bishop Desmond Tutu.

Economic Sanctions

In recent years, there has been much action in the United States against apartheid. In 1977, the Reverend Leon Sullivan, a civil rights leader from Philadelphia, developed the **Sullivan Principles**. This is a code of conduct for American companies doing business in South Africa. It tries to make sure non-white workers are treated fairly. It requires companies to desegregate their work forces, educate blacks and improve community conditions in South Africa. More than 100 companies adopted this code.

One of the leading American organizations fighting apartheid is TransAfrica. Randall Robinson is the leader of this group. Robinson has led demonstrations in many U.S. cities and in front of South African consulates. He also lobbies Congress for legislation against South Africa.

Artists are another group active in the struggle against apartheid. In 1987, American film distributors helped close down whites-only movie theaters in South Africa, until they were opened to all races. Over 50 performers in pop music formed Artists United Against Apartheid. Among other actions, they produced the anti-apartheid song and video, *Sun City*. Also in 1987, Exhibition Art Against Apartheid appeared. This was a selection of 35 works from artists all over the world. It went on view in the main lobby of the United Nations building.

Artists from South Africa have also been

A 1985 student demonstration against apartheid in Johannesburg.

educating Americans about the evils of apartheid. Black South African musicians provided the harmonies and rhythms for Paul Simon's *Graceland* album. And various black South African theater groups have appeared on American stages. Among the more popular works were the drama series *Woza Africa!* and the musical *Sarafina!*

The most controversial action taken against South Africa has been the use of **economic sanctions**. This means refusing to do business with South Africa until the government agrees to stop apartheid. This action was originally requested by Bishop Tutu and other black South Africans.

Here in the United States, this request has met with much success. Students from all over the country have held demonstrations to protest their colleges' investments in

South Africa. Dozens of colleges have now withdrawn their money from companies doing business there.

At least 75 American cities have passed laws aimed at isolating South Africa. Most of these laws deal with **selective purchasing**. This means the city cannot buy goods from any business that still has connections to South Africa.

The biggest success came in 1985 when Congress forced President Ronald Reagan to agree to some national economic sanctions against South Africa. Prior to this, the Reagan administration had a policy called **constructive engagement**. This meant that the U.S. would quietly try to change apartheid with diplomatic pressure.

But this policy did not work. The South African government used the U.S. aid to help strengthen apartheid. TransAfrica and other American anti-apartheid groups pressured Congress. By 1985, Congress had determined that some type of economic sanctions were needed.

President Reagan realized that Congress had enough votes to override his opposition. As a compromise, he agreed to stop all sales of computers to South Africa. He approved use of the Sullivan Principles. And he banned most loans. Only those going to educational projects open to all races were allowed.

Johannesburg, South Africa.

Public pressure for economic sanctions has been effective. Most American companies that used to do business in South Africa now no longer do so. In 1985, about 250 American companies had operations in South Africa. Within a year and a half, 130 had decided to leave. And the number has increased since then. Among the many large American companies who have stopped doing business there are General Motors, Coca-Cola and IBM.

Even the Reverend Sullivan eventually agreed that American companies should leave South Africa. He originally thought the best way to change apartheid was by working from within the system. By using his code of conduct, American companies would provide a good example. And they would improve the quality of life for those blacks working in their companies. By mid-1987, he had changed his mind. He had concluded that apartheid was so entrenched that change by example would not work.

Economic sanctions and the pullout of American businesses have hurt South Africa. Inflation is high, and the price of gold has dropped. All this affects the political debate in white South Africa.

But this change has come at a price. Economic sanctions hurt both white and black South Africans. In fact, in many ways blacks are affected even more. During an economic crisis, the poor are always the ones who suffer most. Since most blacks are unskilled, they lose their jobs first. And there has been a decrease in black employment.

When the American businesses ended their operations, most sold to local or other foreign companies. Many of these new owners do not care about equal treatment for blacks. As a result, many of the gains that

An anti-apartheid demonstrator in the U.S.

change the system. And for now, it seems like most black South Africans are willing to make sacrifices.

All this has affected white South Africa. Under pressure from all over, the South African government made a few changes. Most movie theaters and some universities are now open to all. The passbook laws have been abolished. Laws against mixed marriages were dropped, but now, mixed couples have trouble finding a place to live.

There is still a long way to go. There has been violence in the streets of South Africa, as blacks become more and more impatient for change. And, as we have just seen, they are being asked to pay a big price to achieve it. No matter how the situation is resolved, one thing is certain. As long as apartheid remains in South Africa, black Americans will be active in the effort to destroy it.

CHAPTER CHECK

1. When did apartheid become law in South Africa, and what has been its effect?
2. Who is the leading symbol in the South African fight against apartheid? When was he jailed?
3. Discuss several tactics that have been used against apartheid in the United States.
4. Imagine . . . you are a young South African. What would you be willing to do to work for equality?

were made because of the Sullivan Principles have disappeared. Working conditions for many blacks have worsened. Also, the decreasing contact between the United States and South Africa has closed off the flow of anti-apartheid information. South Africans are becoming increasingly cut off from what the outside world thinks about them.

Many black South Africans are beginning to question the price they pay for sanctions. Even Bishop Tutu has admitted that it would be nice to destroy apartheid without them. But others say sacrifices are needed to

CHAPTER 44

African Legacies in America

As we have seen, the history of black Americans is full of accomplishment and creativity. Blacks have overcome hardship and met challenges with courage, grace and style. But all this did not emerge from a vacuum. American blacks owe much to Africa. It has been a major source of strength.

What makes the United States unique is its mix of people from all over the world. People from nearly every other country have come here to live. Most have kept alive some traditions from their old countries. For example, many Italian Americans speak Italian as well as English. The same is true with other ethnic groups.

These groups have had an advantage. For the most part, they were not forced to completely abandon their old ways. This was not true for Africans. To increase their power over captured Africans, slaveowners often kept them from speaking their old languages and practicing their customs. Slaveowners thought this would make their slaves easier to control. Thus, most African practices among slaves were punished. Only those skills which the slaveowners could use were allowed. When we think about this, the existence today of so many African legacies is astounding.

African legacies, or lasting African contributions to American life, have filled whole books. Africa has influenced American art, music, dance, religion, language and much more. How can this be, when many Africanisms were banned?

Useful Skills

Occasionally slaves were allowed to keep their African practices. Slaves were sometimes more knowledgeable in certain areas than their owners. In such cases, slaveowners used the African skills of their slaves to their advantage.

Fishing techniques and boating ability were skills that many Africans were encouraged to use in America. Slaves often worked along the waterways as fishermen and boatmen. They were especially skilled with nets. This was a widely used practice in West Africa. They also built boats based on African design. Today, many blacks still work on the waterways of the Eastern United States.

Even more important was the cultivation of rice. In the seventeenth century, most African slaves were more familiar with growing rice than their owners. And it is likely that Africans were responsible for the successful development of rice along the Carolina coast. The early techniques used for planting, hoeing, processing and cooking the rice were based on West African practices. Even the baskets used for "fanning" rice were patterned after an African design.

Until the end of the eighteenth century, many slaves kept their African names. Or sometimes they were given a close English version. Africans often named their children for the day of the week on which they were born. This practice continued among American slaves. African names became especially popular with free blacks, and many can be found among black Americans today.

Katherine Dunham, dancer and choreographer. Through her work, African and Caribbean rhythms and movements were seen on American stages.

Baptist church service in the South.

African Survivals

While some aspects of African culture were allowed by American slaveowners, most were not. As a result, some practices were modified, or changed slightly, in order to escape the slaveowner's notice. Others were too subtle for them to notice in the first place. But they were definitely African. And many have survived to this day.

One of the best examples is in religion. Most slaves adopted Christianity. But as we have seen, they brought something new to its practices. The shouting and call-and-response in black churches today originated in African religious practices.

When church members are "saved," they continue an old African tradition. In West Af-

rica, spirits were believed to possess worshippers. The worshippers would go into trances. This is similar to the experiences of many American Christians, particularly blacks.

Music was a large part of this African ritual. Pounding rhythms of drums accompanied the "possessions." The rhythms were thought to be spirits' voices, acting through the drummers. Music remains an important part of black church services in America.

American slaves practiced African funeral rites and burial practices. Funerals were elaborate affairs, often with much celebration. Great importance was placed on a proper burial, and objects were sometimes buried with the body to help it on its journey

Baptist church service in West Africa.

into the next world. Many of these practices continued after emancipation. Grave markings have been found in the South which are similar to those found in West Africa.

In general, American music, especially black American music, shows a strong African influence. The merging of African and American music began with spirituals. The words were English, but the sounds, rhythm and form were straight from Africa.

The **secular** (or non-religious) version of spirituals are the blues. In spirituals, slaves sang about God and salvation to comfort themselves. They emphasized that God would deliver them from their troubles. Blues songs do not mention religion. But they are about everyday troubles to make

them a little easier to bear.

Spirituals and the blues share a purpose: relief from sorrow. They share other similarities as well. Compare this slave spiritual:

> Poor man Laz'rus, poor as I, don't you see?
> Poor man Laz'rus, poor as I, don't you see?
> When he died he found home on high, he had
> a home in dat rock,
> Don't you see?

to singer Billie Holiday's "Fine and Mellow":

> My man don't love me, treats me oh so mean
> My man don't love me, treats me oh so mean
> He's the meanest man
> That you've ever seen

Cone-shaped structure found in West Africa (top).
Similar structures, like the one above, can be found
in the South.

The styles of spirituals and the blues are similar, and both show African influence. We saw earlier that drums played a major part in African music, especially in religious ceremonies. The same pounding rhythms can be found in contemporary black music.

Jazz, which has been called America's only original art form, actually has roots in Africa. Romeo B. Garrett writes, "The word *jazz* in African dialect means 'hurry up'. That is just about the tempo of jazz."

Blacks were brought here from Africa, but not allowed to be part of American society. Keeping to themselves, they continued many African musical traditions. This gave birth to spirituals, the blues and jazz. Even modern rap music can be traced to African influences.

There is also an oral tradition carried here from "the old country." Africans brought over folktales, animal stories and myths that survive today. The best known of these are probably the Uncle Remus tales. Some of the names were changed. For example, Shulo the Hare became Br'er Rabbit in America. But the stories are the same.

Proverbs are another powerful form of oral tradition. Proverbs served an important purpose in African society, and continued to do so for American slaves. They helped teach values and proper behavior. Now, many African proverbs have become part of American culture. Some of the more common ones include "The sun shines in every man's door once," and "If you can't stand the hot grease, get out of the kitchen."

Artwork produced by black Americans shows heavy African influence. Regenia Perry has written that "documentation attests to the fact that African slaves began to fashion artworks shortly after their arrival in this country." Many sophisticated, detailed carvings have been found in the South, and traced back to slave artists. And these pieces have African stylings that can be found in more modern works.

One example is Georgia folk artist and carver William Rogers. During the 1930s, he made a walking staff which has a man and an alligator carved on it. The choice of man and reptile, and the way they are carved, are purely African. As in African carvings, different points of view are used. The man is seen from the front, but the alligator is seen from above. The surface is decorated with beads, a tradition known in Nigeria and the Congo. Contemporary black American artists do similar work.

Other forms of American art which Africa has influenced include basket weaving, pottery, jewelry design, and woodworking. Similarities can also be found between African and American architecture. Circular buildings with cone-shaped roofs, common in West Africa, have also been located in the South. This building design has been used for churches, schools and homes.

Even the language we speak has traces of Africa in it. Most words have been lost, but some have survived. Words like *banana*, *chimpanzee* and *safari* are obviously African in origin. But so are *banjo*, *tote*, *okra*, *juke* (as in juke box), *yam*, *goober*, *canoe*, and of course, *jazz*.

We have seen how Africa has influenced American religion, music, art and even language. But perhaps the greatest legacy is simply our continued interest in Africa. Many Americans travel to African countries. Many more read works of African writers, like Nigeria's Chinua Achebe (CHIN-wa a-

Jazz musician Wynton Marsalis.

CHAY-ba), and Eddie Iroh (e-ROO), and Ghana's Kwesi (kwe-ZEE) Brew.

Major interest in Africa was sparked in 1976 with the publication of *Roots* by Alex Haley. This book traced Haley's heritage back six generations to Africa. It was made into a record-breaking TV mini-series. And it sent many blacks searching for their own "roots." This kind of fascination, and the numerous legacies already around us, keep Africa alive in America. Its presence here will never die.

CHAPTER CHECK

1. How has the cultural legacy of African Americans been treated differently from that of other immigrant groups?

2. How are spirituals and the blues alike? How are they different?

3. Imagine . . . you are a guide for tourists visiting the United States from another country. What African influences would you point out?

Main Events

1. The Brotherhood of Sleeping Car Porters is founded by A. Philip Randolph in 1925.

2. In 1937, Zora Neale Hurston publishes the novel *Their Eyes Were Watching God.* It will become a major influence on black women writers of the 1970s and 1980s.

3. Apartheid becomes law in South Africa in 1948.

4. In 1950, Nelson Mandela becomes a leading figure in the South African liberation movement.

5. By 1954, there are three blacks in Congress: William Dawson of Illinois, Adam Clayton Powell, Jr. of New York and Charles Diggs of Michigan.

6. Lorraine Hansberry's award-winning play, *A Raisin in the Sun,* appears on Broadway in 1959.

7. In 1970, *The Black Woman,* a collection of essays, poems and short stories is published. Contributors include Alice Walker, Paule Marshall and Nikki Giovanni.

8. *I Know Why the Caged Bird Sings,* Maya Angelou's first book, is published in 1970. It tells of the childhood and adolescence of a black girl.

9. In 1972, Barbara Jordan of Texas and Andrew Young of Georgia become the first black representatives from the South elected to the Congress since Reconstruction.

10. In 1978, William Julius Wilson publishes *The Declining Significance of Race.* In it, he says that economics has more to do with the conditions of blacks than race.

11. In 1985, the total number of elected black officials reaches 6,000.

12. In 1985, the film version of Alice Walker's *The Color Purple* is released. It gives the widest exposure to a work that shows black women as victims of sexism as well as of racism.

13. Bart Landry publishes *The New Black Middle Class* in 1987. In it, he says that racism is as strong as ever in America, and has an adverse effect on all blacks.

14. Toni Morrison receives the Pulitzer Prize for her fifth novel, *Beloved,* in 1988.

Words to Know

Match the following with their correct definitions. Number your paper from 1 to 12, and write the correct word beside each number.

African National Congress (ANC)	exploit
Afrikaners	jazz
black underclass	matriarch
Congressional Black Caucus	Rainbow Coalition
constructive engagement	secular
economic sanctions	Sullivan Principles

1. means "hurry up" in an African dialect
2. non-religious
3. black poor people who are unable to enter the working class
4. to take advantage of

An anti-apartheid demonstration in New York City.

5. Dutch settlers of South Africa also known as Boers
6. a mother who is the head of her family
7. organization of black members of Congress
8. a political organization founded by Jesse Jackson
9. Conduct code proposed for American companies doing business in South Africa.
10. the oldest anti-apartheid organization in South Africa
11. measures taken when governments or companies refuse to do business with South Africa until apartheid is abolished
12. attempting to change apartheid through diplomatic pressure

Thinking and Writing

A. Writing a Speech—Running for office
Imagine that you have decided to run for Congress in your district in the next election. Write a speech that tells why you are qualified to hold office and what you would do as a member of Congress. Review Chapter 42 and check with your library to find out who represents your district in Congress.

B. Writing a Character Sketch
Using the index of your textbook, locate all the references to Jesse Jackson. Write a short essay telling where he came from, what he has done, why you think he is or is not qualified to be U.S. President.

GLOSSARY

The numbers in parentheses indicate the chapter in which the term is defined. LA refers to the Looking Ahead sections.

abolition. the act of ending an existing situation, such as slavery. (14)

abolitionist. a person who stood for the legal end of slavery. (9)

acquitted. a person found not guilty. (18)

African National Congress (ANC). the major anti-apartheid organization in South Africa. (43)

Afrikaners. Dutch settlers in South Africa, also known as Boers. (43)

almanac. a publication, issued annually, that contains information about the weather and the stars. (13)

annexation. the process of adding territory to a nation. (9)

antebellum. a period before the Civil War. (LA5)

apartheid. a policy in South Africa establishing strict segregation of the races. (1)

arsenal. a place where weapons are stored. (19)

artisans. people engaged in the making of crafts, or skilled trades, such as carpentry, plumbing, tailoring. (5)

astronomy. the science applied to the study of the heavenly bodies. (13)

autocracy. a government in which one person has all the power. (30)

battalion. a company of soldiers. (12)

black underclass. poor black people unable to reach the working-class level. (40)

bondage. the state of being held in captivity. (12)

bondsmen. slaves hired out to others. (6)

boycott. an organized refusal by one group to do business with another. (9)

bulking stations. an African prison or holding camp for slaves. (3)

carpetbaggers. a term used to describe Northern newcomers to the South. (23)

cataracts. powerful river rapids. (2)

charter. the official document establishing an organization or college. (13)

claimant. a person who claims the right to a person or thing. (9)

click languages. an African language that uses clicking sounds. (1)

colonialism. the control of one nation by another. (31)

colored. a South African of mixed race. (43)

communes. settlements where people share their earnings and duties. (33)

Congressional Black Caucus. an organization of black members of Congress. (42)

conscientious objectors (COs). those opposed to fighting on moral or religious grounds. (38)

constructive engagement. a United States policy designed to affect changes in apartheid by diplomatic pressure. (43)

convict-lease system. the hiring out of convicts to private employers. (27)

deferment. a postponement, referring to a delay allowed in military service for college students. (38)

delta. a marshy triangle where a river enters the sea. (2)

demagogue. a speaker who plays to popular prejudices. (26)

discrimination. the act of treating people differently from others. (13)

disfranchised. denied the right to vote. (26)

draft. the required participation in military service. (30)

dynasties. a series of related rulers. (2)

economic sanctions. refusing to trade or do business with South Africa until apartheid is abolished. (43)

emigration. leaving one country to settle in another. (31)

exploited. taken advantage of. (LA8)

famine. severe food shortages that can lead to starvation. (1)

foragers. people who search for food. (20)

fraggings. grenade attacks on officers by their own men during the Vietnam War. (38)

franchise. the right to vote. (12)

Free African Society. a civic and religious organization founded in Philadelphia by Richard Allen in the 1790s. (11)

freedman. a newly freed slave. (LA5)

freedom rides. a series of actions by black groups to test segregation on trains and buses. (36)

Fugitive Slave Law. an act making it a crime to harbor escaped slaves. (LA4)

furlough. a leave, or time off, from military service. (34)

ginning. the process of separating cotton fiber from seeds. (6)

grandfather clause. an exemption from literacy and property tests of men whose grandfathers had voted prior to 1867. (26)

Harlem Renaissance. the celebration of black literature and arts that flourished in the 1920s. (LA6)

hieroglyphics. a form of early writing using picture forms. (2)

homo sapiens. the scientific term for human beings. (LA1)

immigration. the policy of residing in a country of which a person is not native. (12)

indentured worker. a person employed for a specific amount of time. (5)

injunction. a federal court order issued to enforce existing laws. (36)

interstate. between states. (36)

irrigation. a system that supplies water to crops through ditches or other means. (2)

isthmus. a narrow strip of land joining two larger bodies of land. (5)

Jim Crow. a term applied to the legal segregation of blacks from whites in everyday life. (8)

Liberty Party. the first anti-slavery political organization established in 1804. (14)

lingua franca. a common language. (1)

lynching. to put to death by hanging. (24)

maat. a code of laws applied in ancient Egypt. (2)

manumission. the state of freedom. (14)

Mason-Dixon. the line that divided the North from the South. (9)

matriarch. a mother who rules her family. (41)

Middle Passage. the sea lane slaveships followed from Africa to the New World. (5)

middle-class flight. when economically successful people move out of poor, black neighborhoods. (40)

mummification. the process of embalming a body for burial in ancient Egypt. (2)

mustered. officially enrolled a person in an army. (21)

mystic. a term describing a spiritual seer. (17)

Niagara Movement. a group opposing the policies of Booker T. Washington that formed the basis for the NAACP. (LA6)

nomes. early Egyptian villages in the Nile. (2)

nonviolent protest. an act of organized, peaceful disobedience. (37)

normal school. a training institute for teachers. (27)

oases. desert watering holes. (1)

overseer. the manager of a plantation for an absentee owner. (7)

Pan-Africanism. another term for black nationalism. (31)

papyrus. ancient form of paper made from water reeds. (2)

petition. a formal request from an organized group of people. (9)

plateaus. broad areas of elevated flatland. (1)

public accommodations. facilities such as restrooms and water fountains, that were often segregated before the 1960s. (29)

public opinion. the collective attitude of large groups of people in a community or nation. (40)

Rainbow Coalition. a political organization, formed by Jesse Jackson, that reaches out to all minority groups. (42)

Reconstruction. a period of reorganization in the South by the federal government after the Civil War. (22)

refugees. people who flee for safety or freedom. (17)

savanna. a grassland with scattered trees. (LA1)

scalawag. a term used by Southern Democrats to describe whites who helped Republicans. (23)

secede. to withdraw from a political organization. (20)

secessionist. a person who stood for withdrawal from the Union. (9)

secular. non-religious. (44)

segregated. to set apart. A custom in the South to separate blacks from whites in public places and on public transportation. (24)

selective purchasing. refusal to buy goods from companies that maintain connections in South Africa. (43)

sharecropping. where a worker produced a crop in return for housing, seed and credit at a company store. (LA5)

sickle-cell anemia. a blood disease genetically linked to blacks. (37)

sit-in. where blacks, and sometimes whites, peacefully integrated sections of a public facility. (36)

stevedore. a worker who loads and unloads ships. (30)

Sullivan Principles. a code of desegregation conduct used by American companies doing business in South Africa. (43)

triangular trade. a pattern of trade, usually of rum and molasses, linking Africa, the Caribbean and North America. (6)

Underground Railroad. a system of places and people organized to assist slaves to escape to the North. (LA4)

Union League. a political organization for Southern blacks following the Civil War. (23)

Vigilance Committee. an organization in several states to protect the rights of blacks. (17)

WACS. the Women's Army Corps. (34)

warrant. a written order giving its holder authority to take action. (9)

WAVES. women serving in the U.S. Navy. (34)

INDEX

311

PHOTO AND ART CREDITS